Creationism USA

Bridging the Impasse on Teaching Evolution

ADAM LAATS

OXFORD
UNIVERSITY PRESS

Oxford University Press is a department of the University of Oxford. It furthers the University's objective of excellence in research, scholarship, and education by publishing worldwide. Oxford is a registered trade mark of Oxford University Press in the UK and certain other countries.

Published in the United States of America by Oxford University Press
198 Madison Avenue, New York, NY 10016, United States of America.

Library of Congress Cataloging-in-Publication Data
Names: Laats, Adam, author.
Title: Creationism USA : bridging the impasse on teaching evolution / Adam Laats.
Description: New York, NY, United States of America : Oxford University Press, 2021. |
Includes bibliographical references and index.
Identifiers: LCCN 2020014319 (print) | LCCN 2020014320 (ebook) |
ISBN 9780197516607 (hardback) | ISBN 9780197516621 (epub)
Subjects: LCSH: Creationism—United States. | Creationism—Study and teaching. |
Evolution (Biology)—United States.
Classification: LCC BS651 .L33 2020 (print) | LCC BS651 (ebook) |
DDC 231.7/6520973—dc23
LC record available at https://lccn.loc.gov/2020014319
LC ebook record available at https://lccn.loc.gov/2020014320

1 3 5 7 9 8 6 4 2

Printed by Sheridan Books, Inc., United States of America

To Liz, who asked me about creationism on the porch

Contents

Acknowledgments

Many people helped with this book over the years. First, I need to thank Ron Numbers, who sparked my interest in creationism and its history at the University of Wisconsin. I also appreciate the help of my friend and collaborator Harvey Siegel for many talks about the relationships among science, religion, knowledge, and belief. David Long has also guided my thinking about the nature of creationism and evolution anxiety.

In addition, this book was improved by the suggestions of many readers, generous with their time. Glenn Branch read the entire manuscript and pointed out several errors and mischaracterizations. Conversations with Glenn helped me revise my approach to this subject, especially regarding the tricky subject of labels. Bill Trollinger also read the full manuscript and gave me invaluable guidance. I benefited as well from comments from L. Herbert Siewert and Brendan Pietsch.

Michael Lienesch contributed a crucial letter of support. I'm also grateful to Michael Lynch, the University of Connecticut Humanities Institute, and the John Templeton Foundation for fellowship funding. This book would not have come together if it were not for their assistance. The opinions expressed in this publication, however, are mine alone and do not reflect the views of those organizations.

Last but certainly not least, I want to thank Andy for inspirational housing as I wrote an early draft.

Introduction

We Don't Disagree about Evolution

Let's begin with a difficult proposition: Americans do not really disagree much about evolution. Not about the science itself that is, and not in ways that really matter for public life. Such a proposition might seem absurd to science teachers who have struggled to convince students that evolutionary theory is not an imminent threat. A friend and colleague of mine, for example, tried to introduce the topic of evolution in his middle-school science class only to have a sixth grader jump out of his seat and shout at the top of his lungs, "I didn't come from no stinkin' monkey!"[1]

And if we don't disagree about evolution, why do polls keep finding large majorities of Americans who doubt this central idea of modern science? We see Gallup polls going back to the 1980s in which about four of every ten Americans say they think our species was created by God in pretty much its present form at some point within the past 10,000 years.[2]

The idea that we don't disagree about evolution might also seem ridiculous to anyone who keeps up with the news. In the early years of the Trump administration, for example, the White House was full of creationist activists of one form or another: the vice president, the head of the Department of Housing and Urban Development, and the head of the Department of Education, to name a few.[3]

It seems the creationism culture war is rampant. In northern Kentucky, for example, a vast replica of Noah's ark rises from the fields. Its owners want to teach America that dinosaurs jostled comfortably inside the ark along with two of every other kind of animal, riding out a real global flood that killed off all life just as the Bible describes. And they claim over a million people trooped through its exhibits in 2018, although critics charge them of inflating that figure.[4]

It's not only Kentucky but also everywhere we look: Creationists seem to be teaching anti-scientific ideas about the origin of our species and the history of our universe. It might appear that they are not only fighting a creationist

Creationism USA. Adam Laats, Oxford University Press (2021). © Oxford University Press.
DOI: 10.1093/oso/9780197516607.001.0001.

culture war but also winning. It might seem that America is split between creationists who think humanity is about 6,000 years old and the rest of us who know better.

It's not.

As we'll see in these pages, America is full of creationists, but that assessment depends how one defines creationism. If we define creationism—as I do in this book—as a general sense that something divine must have played a role in the way our species came to exist, then almost all Americans qualify as creationists. Few of those creationists, however, feel a need to insist that dinosaurs must have ridden along on Noah's ark or that our species is only 6,000 years old or that a real global flood wiped out the entire planet. Few of those creationists, in fact, dispute the explanatory power of mainstream evolutionary theory.

Nevertheless, Americans do face bitter, long-lasting feuds about creationism and evolution. Some creationists—in this book we'll call them radical creationists[5]—refuse to accept mainstream science at all. But that fact is not as important as it might seem. After all, it is not creationists' private beliefs about science and religion that matter, it's their attempts to force those private beliefs into the public square. It might not be possible to convince radical creationists to accept mainstream evolutionary theory, but we don't need to do that. If creationists want to believe in a real, historic Noah's ark, that's just fine, as long as they don't expect to water down the science being taught in public schools or use public tax dollars to convince other people to share their beliefs.

And even these most intractable disagreements about evolution and creationism are not as durable as they seem at first. Creation-evolution battles, after all, are not fought between vast creationist armies on one side and evolution-loving scientists on the other. They could not possibly be, for two basic reasons. First, by any reasonable definition of creationism, almost all Americans are creationists of one sort or another. And second, even among the most radical American creationists, almost everyone wants their children to learn mainstream evolutionary theory.

This book will make the case for these notions, and if they are true, they lead us to some further questions. If America has not really been trapped for generations in a fight between creationism and evolutionary theory, why do we think it has? And once we understand the real battle lines concerning evolution and creationism, what can we do to move forward? Neither of these is an easy question and neither has an obvious solution. This book will attempt to tackle them, even if the conclusions seem uncomfortable.

A word of warning up front: This book will *not* do a couple of related things. It will not attempt to offer a thorough explanation of mainstream evolutionary science. We'll dip into the science here and there, but for readers looking for an evolution primer, there are better places to start.[6] This book will also not offer a refutation of creationist science or a defense. In the end, this book argues that creationist-fueled science does not deserve a seat in public school classrooms, but readers who want to read blistering attacks or defenses of various creationist ideas should look elsewhere.[7]

Unlike most of the writers that attack or defend creationism, I'm not a typical representative of either side. I'm no creationist, radical or otherwise. I certainly would never try to push more religion into public schools. In fact, as this book argues, the solution to our battles about creationism will come from more widespread agreement about the properly limited role of religion in public schools.

I'm also not an evolution educator. I do think mainstream evolutionary theory—and only mainstream evolutionary theory—deserves to be taught in every public school biology class, but that's not what motivates me to write this book. Unlike so many of my friends, colleagues, and mentors, I haven't had difficult experiences trying to convince kids and their parents that learning evolutionary theory won't steal their souls.

As a non-creationist, non-scientist, then, I'm not the usual suspect for a book about creationism. So why write one? I have spent twenty years researching the history of school battles about creationism and evolution. Time and time again, I have seen similar arguments tossed around by all sides, from the 1920s to the 2010s, arguments that sidestep the real issues to score points for short-term schemes.

In that sense, being an outside observer to the creation-evolution debates is a significant advantage. I don't have memories—good or bad—of long family debates about young-earth creationism versus evolution-friendly creationism. I haven't had bitter experiences trying to teach young people about real science, only to be stymied by angry parents or craven administrators. I have never converted from one idea about evolution to another; I have never had a long night of spiritual angst questioning my creationist commitments.

In that sense, an outsider might be the only person who could write a book like this. Instead of harping on the need to expunge creationist thinking from public school science classes or warning Christians of the dangers of evolutionary theory, I only hope to show how the unique history of American creationism has put us all in a miserable situation. Unnecessarily so.

Once we acknowledge this tangled history, it's easier to see a more productive way forward. To get there, we'll need to take some potentially awkward first steps. For one thing, we need to look in the mirror and realize that we might all be profoundly ignorant about both creationism and evolution. If we non-creationists think we are simply on the side of enlightenment and education, shining beams of knowledge into murky caves of antiquated ignorance, we are guilty of putting too much faith in our own press releases. The missionary faith of many of today's science pundits is more than just odd. It has kept our discussions of creationism and evolution in the same tired rut for a hundred years.

Second, we need to recognize a few things that creationism in America is not. It is not a holdover from an older, stupider America. Today's most prominent type of radical American creationism—young-earth creationism—is a profoundly modern thing, newer than space travel and rock 'n' roll. Creationism is not holed up in hillbilly hollers and other outposts of *Deliverance*-style Americana. Every big city, university, and government building is full of creationists of one sort or another. And, most important, creationism—even the radical kind—is not a result of simple ignorance about science. Creationists aren't people who just haven't yet heard the news about Darwin and his finches.

Finally, we have to come to terms with the difficult idea that we don't disagree about evolution as much as we might think. Yes, there are radicals on both sides who keep telling us that we do. But once we spend time getting to know our creationist neighbors, it's impossible to dispute the fact that we have a large and productive middle ground. At their heart, our disputes are not really about science or religion, but about something else. Once we recognize this, we'll be able to see a clear two-part prescription for a better way to talk about creationism and evolution education.

Road Map

The plan is pretty straightforward. First, in chapter 1, we will examine the real world of American creationism. Unlike what we might think if we only read the headlines, there is no single definition of creationism. Instead, we have Christian creationists, Jewish creationists, Muslim creationists, Native creationists, and even some non-religious creationists. On one hand, we have creationists who endorse peculiar scientific notions of a young earth and a recent, unevolved humanity. On the other, we see many, many more creationists who have no religious problem with mainstream evolutionary theory. The first step in seeing the real state of our creationist culture war is to recognize this dizzying diversity of American creationism.

In this book, we will focus not on the millions of distinctions possible between various versions of creationist belief but rather on a single, fundamental division among America's creationists: between the radicals and everyone else. The vast majority of American creationists—whatever their religious backgrounds—don't have any problem with mainstream evolutionary theory. And even among the creationists who do reject the mainstream science of evolution, only an even smaller subset tries to push public policy in creationism-friendly directions. As mentioned, this book will use the label "radical creationists" to describe this small group of creationists who object to the religious implications of mainstream evolutionary theory and try to influence public policy in creationism-friendly directions. (I will explain the term in more detail in the appendix.)

The second chapter tackles the surprising history of the most prominent form of radical creationism in today's America: young-earth Christian creationism. It's tempting to think of creationism as a holdover from medieval obtuseness, but it isn't. Instead, the radical type of young-earth creationism only became popular among large numbers of conservative evangelical Christians in the 1960s. And, most important, the birth of this sort of radical creationism was not merely a religious thing, but also a response to shifts in American culture overall, including changing ideas about sexuality, patriotism, and education.

In chapter 3 we dig into this powerful combination. In order to understand the creation/evolution culture war, it is vital to understand the way many creationists think of evolution. For many creationists, evolution means much more than a scientific theory. For generations now, radical creationists have blended together a slew of ideas into a potent and—to them—dangerous stew.

They haven't done it on their own. Throughout the twentieth century and into the twenty-first, radical creationists built a network of institutions dedicated to providing safe havens for those who want to loathe evolution. Young-earth science is certainly one of the things that is taught in some radical-creationist schools and colleges, but much more is mixed in.

Chapter 4 looks at the messages taught in these kinds of radical-creationist institutions; we will examine the ways they teach Christians to confuse evolution with every other social trend they despise and fear.

They don't need to. It is entirely possible and practical for creationists to separate their political and cultural feelings from the scientific implications of evolutionary theory. It only makes sense for them to do so, however, if non-creationists and non-radical creationists also recognize the ways we have misunderstood evolutionary theory. Radical creationists may often misunderstand and misrepresent evolution, but so do the rest of us. Chapter 5 evaluates the uncomfortable evidence that most Americans don't know much about evolution. What we say we think about evolution and creation tallies much more closely with whom we trust, not what we actually know.

In chapter 6 we'll confront one of the trickiest questions in our creationism culture war. If we don't really disagree about evolution, why do we think we do? In short, the problem comes from missionary attitudes on all sides. Radical young-earth creationists tell one another that they aren't as likely to go to heaven if they accept the premises of evolutionary science. Radical atheists encourage that sort of thinking, hoping deluded creationists will see the light and choose science instead of religion. The loudest voices on the fringes insist that the debate is between religion and science, creationism and evolution. Time after time, our public discussions focus squarely on this manufactured disagreement instead of our vast areas of agreement.

In chapter 7 we'll tackle perhaps the least obvious but most important fact of all. Namely, when it comes right down to it, almost all of us want our children to learn evolutionary science. Even the most ardent young-earth creationists do. The problem is not that Americans are divided about evolutionary science as such. Rather, the problem is that Americans are divided. Period. We distrust one another on every topic and evolution has been unnecessarily swept up into those deeper divisions.

Once we recognize the real meanings of creationism in America, a few ideas become clear. First of all, we need to get over our tradition of thinking about creationism and evolution in missionary terms. Evolution isn't a religion. People don't need to convert to understand it. Science teachers in public schools should have as little interest in deriding religion as they do in pushing religion. Veteran science teachers have been saying it for years, and they should continue to make it as clear as possible: Science teachers do not want to use evolution to drag people away from creationism.

Yet for a century now, creationist dissenters have had good reason to worry that evolution's promoters wanted to do just that. In spite of the fact that the vast majority of us—creationists and non-creationists, radicals and non-radicals alike—want our children to learn evolutionary theory, we have instead wasted our time shouting at one another about which science was better and which religion was true.

This book will argue that we don't need to agree on those things. Creationists can hold any religious beliefs they choose. They can insist that their preferred ideas about science are the best. And the rest of us can think they're wrong. In the end, those questions aren't really at the heart of our endless fights over evolution and creationism. The real difficulty, rather, is that like any divorce or family feud, our two sides have long since stopped trusting one another. It's not obvious or comfortable, but we can rebuild that trust if we understand the real issues. To move forward we need to agree on a simple two-part plan.

Simple, but not easy. As the following chapters will show, none of our typical assumptions about creationism are as obvious as they might seem. But once we know more about creationism as it really is, we'll be able to make progress together in how we talk about it in public.

1

After Their Kinds

When Walt Whitman "heard the learn'd astronomer," he didn't like it. You may remember the poem: The astronomer laid out "proofs" and "figures," "charts and diagrams." Presumably, the astronomer explained the best scientific understanding of the universe. He defined a star from a scientist's perspective. He explained how planets rotated around them and what made up the world beyond the heavens.

Whitman's narrator was unimpressed. The proofs didn't prove anything. The measurements didn't convince him. Instead, the astronomer's brand of confident scientific explanation only made Whitman's narrator "tired and sick." He wandered out of the lecture hall, into the "mystical moist night air." Only there did he find the truth about the universe. Out there, he saw the real truth, not a chopped and measured body on a sterile dissecting table. Only by looking up "in perfect silence at the stars" could the narrator free himself from the puffed-up pretensions of science and discover the way things really were.

I can't imagine that Whitman—with his proto-hippie facial hair and lusty homo-eroticism—would feel at home with the starchy Southern Baptists and bonneted Mennonites who troop through Kentucky's Ark Encounter and Creation Museum. But if we want to understand the entirety of American creationism, we need to make room for both buttoned-down evangelicals and the vague others who share Whitman's mystical, gut-wrenched skepticism about the goings-on in American science.

And if we want to wrap our heads around the fact that Americans don't really disagree about evolution, we need to come to grips with Whitman's vague unease at the presumption of science. We need to get a better handle on what it might mean in practice to be a creationist. We need to understand not only the ark-raising radical creationists but also all the varieties of creationist belief. We need to understand creationists who have devoted years of their lives to the study of creation and evolution, as well as those many more who simply feel, like Whitman, vaguely distressed by the claims of modern science. We need to understand creationists who feel their faith

Creationism USA. Adam Laats, Oxford University Press (2021). © Oxford University Press.
DOI: 10.1093/oso/9780197516607.001.0001.

requires creationism, as well as those who think of their creationism as a sort of idiosyncrasy, a quirk of their own choosing. In short, we need to understand that creationism as a whole isn't anything but rather a collection of things, of beliefs and habits, tenets and tendencies. The ideas that are labeled "creationist" on the front page are usually representative of only a small and shrinking sliver of America's real kaleidoscopic creationism.

We also need to understand how many Americans we can really call creationists. Every time the topic of American creationism is brought up, the same poll numbers get tossed around. Just under half of Americans, we're told over and over again, think our species was created fairly recently the way the Bible describes. How do we know? Because the folks at Gallup have been asking the same question since the 1980s, and in every decade, somewhere between 38% and 47% agree that "God created human beings pretty much in their present form at one time within the last 10,000 years or so."[1]

The truth, however, is not quite so simple. First of all, we need to recognize the many different varieties of creationists out there. This chapter will offer a quick sketch of those varieties, including young-earth creationism, old-earth creationism, evolutionary creationism, and intelligent design. We'll examine the many non-Christian creationists out there as well. In addition, we'll take a closer look at the poll numbers. Can it really be true that nearly half of Americans believe in a recent creation of our species? As always, the answers depend on the questions.

Field Guide to American Creationism

It was a powerful moment. In 2014, the radical creationists at Answers in Genesis ministries scored a major coup in the continuing creation-evolution battles. They convinced Bill Nye, "The Science Guy," to beard the creationists in their own lair. Hoping to register some points for evolution and "undeniable" mainstream science, Nye headed down to Kentucky for a debate with creationist champion Ken Ham.[2]

Both men were polished performers, and both gave confident presentations of their best cases. They were polite, cordial, and painfully relaxed. Ham started with a self-deprecating quip about his Australian accent. Nye opened with a joke about his trademark bow tie. Neither hero was stupid enough to yell or scream, to toss insults or to offer bare-knuckled attacks on science or religion.

Ham and Nye were so polite, the whole thing might have passed by without anything interesting going on at all if it weren't for the questions at the end. Someone asked, "How did consciousness come from matter?" Nye offered what he thought to be the best answer from the world of mainstream science. We don't know, Nye admitted. And that is not a problem. It is a mystery, and the essence of real science, Nye implied, was to refrain from too-simple explanations for the true mysteries of the universe. "We don't know where consciousness comes from," Nye spake to the creationist multitudes, "but we want to find out."

Actually, Ham retorted, we do know. Delivering a line that delighted Christian young-earth creationists (YECs) in the room and around the world, Ham explained, "there is a book out there that does document where consciousness came from." Where does consciousness come from? Simple, Ham explained: "God gave it to us." How does Ham know? Because it's all in the Bible.

To a lot of gawkers, the "Ham-on-Nye" debate epitomized the clash between creationism and evolution.[3] It joined a list of other epochal stand-offs, including most famously William Jennings Bryan versus Clarence Darrow in 1925 in Dayton, Tennessee, at the Scopes Trial.[4] Time and again, debates like this one have pitted creationism against mainstream science.

Or, to be more precise, they have claimed to pit creationism against mainstream science. The reality is more complicated.

Ken Ham doesn't represent American creationism any more than Bill Nye is typical of American scientists. If we want to understand creationism, we need to start by recognizing that the most flamboyant creationists—the Ken Hams of the world—tend to fight far more bitterly with other kinds of creationists than they do with bemused outsiders like Bill Nye. The real divisions in the world of America's creation-evolution battles don't occur between science guys and ark builders, but rather among various sorts of creationists.

Ken Ham and Bill Nye could afford to be affable. They represented starkly opposed visions of how we know things and what things we should know. Other fights about creation and evolution can get a lot uglier, especially fights between creationists who are trying to win support for their competing visions of creation.

Karl Giberson, for example, a university professor and non-radical creationist, has attacked Ken Ham as nothing but a "religious huckster."[5] Ham, Giberson warns, has only "the most limited of scientific credentials."[6] Ken

Ham and other fundamentalists might wrap their crusades in the mantle of science, but in reality they are fighting imaginary cosmic battles with Satan himself.[7]

For their part, YECs don't necessarily take the high road when it comes to these sorts of intra-creationist disputes. John MacArthur, for example, the YEC president of the Master's College in California and founder of Grace to You Ministries, called Giberson's sort of creationism nothing short of "open, flagrant, blatant sin." Creationists like Giberson who don't agree with Ken Ham's style of creationism, President MacArthur insisted, "follow the route that Satan wants them to follow."[8]

Ouch.

Our first step toward understanding the real culture-war battles about creationism is understanding its many varieties. Outsiders like me might assume that Ken Ham represents creationism as a whole, but Ham's sort of young-earth, global-flood creationism is only one small slice of a much larger pie. It is also a fairly new development on the creationist scene, though we'll save that story for the next chapter. In this chapter we'll examine the different sorts of creationism, including Ham's brand of young-earth creationism, Giberson's evolutionary creationism, old-earth creationism, Catholic creationism, Jewish and Islamic creationism, intelligent design, and a few odder ducks that quack around the outer boundaries of American creationism.[9] We'll also try to figure out just how many Americans really do embrace these sorts of creationist ideas and identities.

Seeing creationism as it really is reveals the obvious truth: Almost all Americans are creationists of one sort or another. Being a creationist, in the end, does not mean opposing evolution education.

If Ken Ham doesn't really represent American creationism, why does he get so much attention? For one thing, creationists like Ham make outrageous claims; they insist on eyebrow-raising departures from mainstream science. YECs insist that the earth is only a few thousand years old. They think that there really was a great worldwide flood that killed off everyone but Noah's lucky few. They think that God simply poofed everything into existence over the course of one tiring week. Dinosaurs on boats, real worldwide floods, a brash confidence that Bill Nye and all of his scientist friends are just fooling themselves . . . it is the YECs who are most successful in promulgating shocking ideas about science, history, and biology.

The message has been trumpeted in recent decades by a few prominent institutions. The Institute for Creation Research, founded and led by hydraulic-engineer-turned-creationist-preacher Henry Morris, has promoted the notion of a young earth and a real worldwide flood since its founding in the early 1970s. When Ken Ham first traveled to the United States from his home in Australia, he began his American career working at the Institute for Creation Research. By the mid-1990s, Ham formed his own radical-creationist group, Answers in Genesis.

It's easy to think of radical YECs as "anti-science," but it's also misleading. True, Henry Morris, Ken Ham, and all the many other YEC activists out there dispute the central principles of mainstream science, but they have always insisted that they are doing so in the name of science itself. YECs have always claimed that they have *better* science, "creation" science. We'll explore this notion in more depth in the last chapter, but it's important to note at the outset that creationists in general—even radical creationists—embrace science, as they understand it.

These days, for example, Ken Ham likes to say that science must properly be broken down into two sorts: "historical" science and "observational" science. To Ham, there is absolutely nothing wrong with "observational" science—the kind of science that relies on direct observation. The problem, in Ham's view, comes when scientists make false "historical" claims about the distant past. Ham's big guns in his debate with Bill Nye were the testimonials he trotted out from creationists who had made their mark in the world of science. Creationists, Ham argued, helped sequence the human genome. Creationists invented magnetic resonance imaging (MRI). Creationists, Ham claimed, are second to none when it comes to real science, "observational" science.

The problem, as Ham put it in his opening monologue, is that "the word 'science' has been hijacked by secularists." Instead of respecting the limits of observational science, Ham says, mainstream scientists have blundered into false claims about historical science. Too often, mainstream scientists make impossible assumptions about the past based on their own warped sense of how the universe works. They speculate that the way natural laws seem to work now must tell us something about the ways such laws have always worked.

Wrong, says Ham. And these sorts of unscientific, incorrect assumptions are more than just harmless errors. The terrible trends of mainstream science are not random mistakes, Ham thinks, but rather deceptions meant to snare the unwary. If we really want to understand the roots of our species, we need to look no further than the Bible. For all of our questions about humanity's origins, we can find the answers in Genesis.

It is possible, informed YECs will tell you, for someone to get to heaven if she doesn't believe that the earth and everything was created the way Genesis describes. Possible, but very difficult. The Bible, after all, is a loving God's instruction book for our troubled species. The truths of salvation are all there for anyone with eyes to see and ears to hear. If we doubt the explanations of humanity's origins as described in Genesis, what else will we doubt?

We'll explore the reasons why YECs find these ideas so important and so convincing in a later chapter, but before we move on to other common forms of religious creationism, it's worth pointing out one more thing about YECs. Outsiders like me often think that YECs take the Bible literally. That's close, but not exactly right. Most YECs will tell you that they don't take the Bible literally, but rather in the sense in which it was intended. In other words, if a passage is meant to be poetic, then that's how we should read it. Jesus didn't mean that his followers were actual salt of the earth, for example.

The danger comes, YECs think, when readers get too arrogant about their own knowledge and begin to pick and choose from Bible truths. The description of creation in Genesis, they will tell you, is meant to be a real description of a real creation. Unlike other sorts of Bible passages, like the Song of Solomon or the parables of Jesus, there is nothing to tell the savvy reader that the descriptions of creation in Genesis are meant to be taken as metaphors. As generations of Sunday-school teachers have told their students, when you read the Bible, "If the plain sense makes good sense seek no other sense lest it result in nonsense."

In other words, YECs start with a fairly simple assumption: The Bible is true, inerrant. Anything that conflicts with the Bible, therefore, must be wrong. And that's all that needs to be said.

Except, of course, there's a whole lot more to be said, even for those who agree that the Bible must be true. For plenty of creationists, the answers in Genesis are different.

There are creationists out there who agree with Ken Ham that evolutionary theory is mistaken, but they disagree about a lot of other things. For example, organizations such as Hugh Ross's Reasons to Believe (RTB) dusted off an old vision of creationism that allows for an ancient earth and universe. What if the "days" described in Genesis, they ask, actually represent long geologic "ages?" If we read Genesis that way, then it might be possible to reconcile the narrative of the first chapters of the Bible with the fossil record. The earth and the universe can be millions of years old, by this interpretation, even if we assume that the events described in Genesis are absolutely true and without error.

Like YECs, the old-earth creationists at RTB reject the notion of modern evolutionary science as the best explanation for the diversity of earth's species. But unlike YECs, Ross and RTB accept the notion of an ancient universe. They hope to convince religious creationists that they don't need to cower in the face of modern science. Rather, as the RTB folks put it, "sound reason and scientific research—including the very latest discoveries—consistently support, rather than erode, confidence in the truth of the Bible and faith in the personal, transcendent God revealed in both Scripture and nature."[10] As an astrophysicist, Ross finds it impossible to doubt the age of the universe. But as an evangelical Christian, Ross also insists that his "testable, falsifiable, and predictive" explanation of creation comes from biblical roots and supports evangelical Christian faith.[11]

Joining a long tradition of "day-age" and "progressive" creationists, Hugh Ross and RTB believe that God must have intervened directly and repeatedly to create new species. Over long geologic time, according to this view, evolutionary processes may have made some changes in animals, but only direct intervention by God can explain the big changes in the species that inhabited earth's shifting landscape.

Other creationists manage to be friendlier to evolutionary theory while insisting they are just as serious about their religion. For decades, devout Christian scientists have insisted loudly that they see no conflict between science and religion. Perhaps most famously, in 1973 Theodosius Dobzhansky, one of the leading scientists of his generation and a framer of modern thinking about evolution, insisted that he was both "a creationist and an evolutionist."[12]

Once we scratch the surface of the scientific evidence for evolution, many creationists argue, we see that it is simply overwhelming. We can't put our heads in the biblical sand, the way radical anti-evolution creationists do, and assume it will all somehow go away. For those who embrace various theistic notions about evolution, there is no need to. Yes, the Bible is true. And yes, evolution happened. The one doesn't have anything to do with the other.

One leader of this sort of evolution-friendly creationism is evangelical Protestant scientist Francis Collins. It's hard to dent Dr. Collins's scientific credentials. As the head of the National Institutes of Health and a leading mapper of the human genome, Dr. Collins has no worries about being called "anti-science." And, as Collins likes to explain, "The God of the Bible is also the God of the genome."[13]

This view has traditionally been known as "theistic evolution," or, as leaders of one of today's leading non-radical organizations BioLogos like to call it, "evolutionary creationism." By and large, Christian evolutionary creationists share YECs' reverence for the Bible.[14] But they also assume that mainstream science is on the right path. The main point, for most evolutionary creationists, is that evolution is nothing more than God's method of creation. There is no need for Christians or anyone else to pooh-pooh evolution. In fact, aggressive campaigns like those of Answers in Genesis drive people away from Christianity, evolutionary creationists often argue, because they force people into a false choice between science and religion.

But what if we take God out of the equation, at least officially? Lots of creationists in the twenty-first century have hoped to articulate a creationist vision that makes no claims about the Creator. Loosely clumped together under the name "intelligent design" (ID), today's ID theorists have revived and rejuvenated old ideas that life is simply too complex to have evolved without intelligent guidance. That guidance need not have come from God, though most of the leaders of the ID movement are religious in one way or another.

At the Discovery Institute in Seattle, for example, ID theorists and pundits hail from a variety of backgrounds. Some fit our definition of radical creationism—rejecting evolutionary theory and pushing public policy in creationism-friendly directions. Some fit our stereotype of Christian creationism. Others don't. Take David Klinghoffer. Klinghoffer embraced both the ideas of ID and orthodox Judaism. Other ID supporters don't claim to be motivated by any religion at all. Perhaps most famously, Lehigh University biochemist Michael Behe—though he comes from Catholic roots—argues that his embrace of ID is a primarily secular scientific commitment.

For Behe, and usually officially for more religious ID supporters as well, ID is simply the best scientific explanation for the mind-blowing complexity of organic life. As William Paley made the argument back in the early years of the nineteenth century, imagine walking in a grassy heath. If you suddenly came upon a watch lying in the middle of the heath, you would immediately assume that it had been designed by some conscious intelligence. There are simply too many moving parts—parts that need one another in order to have any function or purpose—for the watch to have simply come into being on its own.[15]

Professor Behe doesn't care about watches. Instead, he has argued that biological processes are internal evidence of what Behe calls the "irreducible complexity" of living systems. In humans, Behe argued in his 1996 book *Darwin's Black Box*, blood-clotting systems could not have evolved in bits and pieces. Only when the system as a whole is in place does it confer any benefit at all. No proto-humans, that is, received any sort of natural-selection benefit by mutating only one piece of the blood-clotting mechanism. Only if the whole thing popped into being at once would any species get any benefit. And the odds that such a complex mechanism could have somehow mutated into existence in one instant are so phenomenally remote that even the most ardent evolution supporter wouldn't suggest it. Evolution, in short, doesn't work as an explanation of real, complex, organic systems. The hand of some non-denominational intelligent designer had to be at work.[16]

By and large, mainstream scientists haven't been much kinder to Michael Behe's science-focused form of creationism than they have to Ken Ham's Bible-focused version. Yet there is a world of difference between them. We have to accept that only a sliver of American creationists would really ever agree with the creationist ideas that get the most public attention—like dinosaurs in cages on Noah's ark. There is no such thing as American creationism, but rather a vigorous and sometimes contentious marketplace of creationist visions and voices. Radicals, non-radicals, old earthers, young earthers, intelligent designers, evolutionary creationists . . . all compete to have their creationist vision embraced by religious people who might or might not look askance at evolutionary theory.

To make things even more confusing, we need to recognize some even more confounding truths about American creationists. Many creationists would never call themselves that. They wouldn't line up with any of the major creationist factions that we've just described. They don't subscribe to creationist newsletters, they don't read creationist blogs, and they don't send donations to creationist think tanks. Yet if we probe their beliefs about the origins of our species and our planet, by any reasonable definition we have to classify them as creationists.

Perhaps the most striking example of these sorts of unrecognized creationists are America's millions of Catholics. True, among the world's Catholics, Americans are famous for their "cafeteria" style approach to the Church's teachings. Many American Catholics, that is, like to pick and choose which doctrines they believe. For many American Catholics, the statements of the popes are interesting but not really personally binding.

In stark contrast to the actual teachings of their Church, lots of American Catholics take a typically American "that's his opinion and he's welcome to it" approach to papal pronouncements. All the same, those Catholics who sit in the back pews at Sunday mass have some relationship to official Catholic doctrine. And though that doctrine has never shared the fire-and-brimstone creationist certainty of many evangelical Protestants, Catholic leaders have never denied their fundamental creationist beliefs.

In 2014, for example, new Pope Francis doubled down on the Catholic Church's traditional vision of creation. God created everything first, most especially the human soul, but that doesn't mean that evolution isn't real. As Francis put it in 2014, Catholics are not supposed to think of God as a "magician, with such a magic wand as to be able to do everything." Those sorts of simplistic creationist beliefs only misled the faithful. Rather, God created everything and imbued it all with "internal laws that He gave each one." God creates, and evolution evolves. For Catholics—at least those who follow the teachings of their pope—evolutionary creationism is both science and faith.[17]

Among non-Christians, too, creation and evolution have a complicated relationship. Just as for American Christians, American Jews are most notable for their utter diversity. There is no single "Jewish" position on creation and evolution any more than there is a "Christian" one. Just as there are plenty of Christian creationists, so there are plenty of Jewish ones. Some of them reject evolutionary science; many more have no problem with it. No single statement of position could ever claim to speak for all American Jews, but a variety of Jewish leaders have articulated a few general non-radical principles. In 2005, for example, the Rabbinical Council of America, an umbrella organization for Orthodox Judaism, officially confirmed its belief that the "fact of creation" must remain undisputed. God is the Creator. Period. That fact, however, leaves plenty of room for evolution. The Council insisted that their "fundamental beliefs" in the creative power of God had nothing to do with "purported weaknesses of Evolutionary Theory." There was no way, the Council argued, for their steadfast belief in creation to be eroded by any advance in scientific knowledge of the origins of species.[18]

Like many Catholic creationists, Jewish creationists have historically tended to avoid public shouting matches over the teachings of America's public schools. They have tended to see those public fights as a Protestant affair. And some Jewish creationists have lamented that tradition. David Klinghoffer, for example, the ID pundit and a devout follower of Orthodox

Judaism, has complained that too many of his Orthodox coreligionists gave up the game too early. "Many Jews," Klinghoffer argued in 2009, "including many on the more liberal end of the Orthodox spectrum, see intelligent design as a purely Christian undertaking, with no support from Jewish tradition."[19] And such Jewish hands-off-edness is a shame, Klinghoffer thinks. In a 1999 memoir about his embrace of his faith, Klinghoffer hoped to push his coreligionists to a more radical vision of creationism. He insisted that his Jewish faith "has intellectual coherence on its side in ways that secularism does not." In the continuing fight between arrogant materialism and thoughtful religious skepticism, Klinghoffer believes too many Jewish thinkers have abandoned the field without any good reason.[20]

Even within Orthodox Judaism, though, the lines between creationism and evolution have never been clear. In the first years of this century, the case of the "Zoo Rabbi" Nosson Slifkin showed just how divided the Orthodox were. Slifkin had built a reputation as a leading teacher of a Jewish form of non-radical creationism. In his books and public talks, Slifkin taught children that God must have created, but that he created with an evolutionary process.

To Slifkin's surprise in 2004, he found his books and his ideas had been declared heretical by a group of influential Orthodox rabbis. Brooklyn-based Rabbi Yitzchok Scheiner, for instance, warned readers that Slifkin's books were "hair-raising. . . . He believes that the world is millions of years old—all nonsense!—and many other things that should not be heard and certainly not believed."[21]

Slifkin and other influential Orthodox voices protested. As Slifkin put it, all of his ideas were "fully 'kosher' views." There was nothing heterodox or even suspicious about Slifkin's teachings. In the end, as journalist Jennie Rothenberg concluded, the fight over Slifkinism was more about changing power dynamics within the world of Orthodox Judaism than it was about evolution or creation. No one disputed the basic fact of divine creation. Just as it has always been between various factions of Christian creationists, the fight over the Zoo Rabbi was more about religious authority than about scientific ideas.[22]

Among American Muslims, too, there is not and never has been a single simple Islamic answer to questions of creation and evolution. This point was driven home to thousands of American scientists and politicians in 2007 when a big surprise showed up in their mailboxes.[23] The *Atlas of Creation* they received was a gargantuan, coffee-table book, lavishly illustrated with full-color glossy pictures of birds, trilobites, and humans. The author, Adnan Oktar, writing under the name Harun Yahya, promised to prove that evolution was a lie. It was not only the religion of Islam that proved the falseness of evolution. If people would only open their eyes, Yahya explained, they would recognize that scientific proof had clearly "*refuted* the theory of evolution."[24] Just read the book, Yahya explained, and you will see why scientists say, "We never underwent evolution; we were created."[25]

It's difficult to think that many recipients of this odd and uninvited radical-creationist tome found themselves convinced by this purportedly scientific explosion of the myths of evolution by a Muslim creationist. Perhaps other Islamic creationist efforts will prove more influential. Unlike Harun Yahya's expensive splash, the work of Sheikh Hamza Yusuf might sink deeper roots among American Muslims.

In 2010, Yusuf opened Zaytuna College in Berkeley, California. Its mission is to provide an "academic home for Islam in the United States ... where ... the text of the Koran could meet the context of American culture."[26] The college promises to help Muslims wonder intelligently about creation and evolution, among other things. It offers support to Muslims who want their children to learn things not offered in their local public schools and to homeschoolers who do not want to learn things that are taught in those schools. The college encourages students and supporters to read the skeptical works of ID theorists such as Michael Behe.[27]

And, perhaps most important to Sheikh Yusuf, his new college could urge American Muslims to be more ferociously humble about what they think they know. As the Koran explains, Yusuf argued, the origins of life and of the universe are a total mystery. For anyone to think otherwise is nothing short of the "height of arrogance." We do know, Yusuf preached, that God said, "be and it is." It might be true that the latest scientific knowledge seems to support the creation story as told in the Koran, Yusuf pointed out. Whether it does or not, what we call science is not really knowledge, not in the way knowledge is defined by God. We know God created. Beyond that, we must carefully protect ourselves from our all-too-human tendency to crowd out God's word with our own puffed-up certainties.[28]

Sheikh Yusuf's brainy skepticism might not fit the stereotype of American creationism. At its heart, though, it is pretty similar to the intellectual creationism of Francis Collins and BioLogos. Both worry that human knowledge will get inflated beyond its God-given limitations. Both types assume that the truth is something beyond mere human striving. Both assume that mainstream science is something to be embraced, not demonized, but that real knowledge—ultimate knowledge—comes from God's holy book.

Those holy books, though, are not the only place to find creationist stories in the United States. It might not attract the same headlines, but among indigenous people, such as the Koyukon of Alaska, long traditions of storytelling have contributed to very different discussions of evolution and creation.

Among the Koyukon, tradition tells of the "Distant Time," in which Raven the creator caused a flood to cover the surface of the earth. Raven created a raft on which to save two of every species, humans excepted. After the flood, Raven recreated humanity in its current form.[29]

In recent decades, science educators have debated the proper classroom role of indigenous science, including creation stories like this one. Can public schools teach Koyukon students about mainstream evolutionary theory, while still respecting the cultural power and importance of Raven's creation? Some science-education scholars have said yes. Masakata Ogawa, for example, argued that "indigenous science," like the traditional knowledge of the Koyukon, can enrich a public school science curriculum.[30]

Ogawa's argument is far different from the Kentucky creationism of organizations such as Answers in Genesis—even if the stories sound remarkably similar—but the goal of incorporating non-Western contributions to science is surely another aspect of American creationism. And even these various versions of creationism, as diverse as they are, only scratch the surface of American creationism in all its true complexity. From Native Alaskan to Answers In Genesis, the litany can be exhausting, but it is not yet exhaustive.

Beyond these various sorts of creationists who put their religion first—in one way or another—we also need to consider intellectual leaders, such as Ken Miller, who refuse to put either their science before their religion or vice versa. Miller has long been one of the most fluent explainers of evolutionary science to regular Americans. Able to combine Ivy League science credentials with an engaging writing style, Professor Miller has become one of our leading champions of Bill-Nye-style science advocacy. Yet, by our definition, Miller remains a creationist. As a Roman Catholic, Miller insists that his opposition to young-earth creationism and ID do not rule out his ultimate belief in divine creation. When it comes right down to it, Miller believes, "absolute materialism . . . cannot fully explain the nature of reality."[31] Scientists do not need to water down their religious beliefs to wedge them into compliance with evolutionary truths, Miller argues. Rather, a

thorough knowledge of the way evolution works proves—to Miller at least—
that "God is every bit as creative in the present as He was in the past."[32]

Other leading scientists have had more idiosyncratic ideas about life's
origins. Maybe most famously, the late Fred Hoyle argued that our current scientific explanations of the origins of life just don't make sense. Like
Miller, Hoyle's scientific credentials are beyond impeccable. As a leading astronomer, Hoyle claimed credit for coining the term "big bang." But, as he
explained over and over, he meant it as a joke, not as a plausible idea. His
weak-minded fellow scientists, the irascible Hoyle explained, liked the big
bang idea because they were trapped in an archaic Genesis mindset. The
entire notion of complex species beginning from inert matter was too far-
fetched to be taken seriously. How far-fetched? As he put it:

> A junkyard contains all the bits and pieces of a Boeing 747. . . . What is the
> chance that after [a whirlwind's] passage a fully assembled 747, ready to fly,
> will be found standing there? So small as to be negligible, even if a tornado
> were to blow through enough junkyards to fill the whole Universe.[33]

A much more likely explanation, Hoyle said to anyone who would listen,
is that cosmic dust spread life to earth and throughout the universe.
"Panspermia" made sense, Hoyle argued, not Genesis or Darwin.

Outside of recognizable religious and scientific skepticism, too, we need
to be aware of America's vague unease with scientific explanations. Walt
Whitman's narrator didn't have a good counterargument to make against the
learn'd astronomer. He didn't think he needed one. It was enough for him
to know that he just didn't like it. Whitman's science nausea is a lot harder
to trace than Christian, Jewish, Muslim, or indigenous forms of resistance.
There are no organized groups, after all, no school-board petitions or charges
of heresy. Yet as far as we can tell, there are plenty of Americans who share
Whitman's parlor skepticism. And every once in a while one of them will
make her case.

A few years ago, for example, journalist Virginia Heffernan poked her
"postmodern" creationism in the faces of her liberal New York friends.
She wasn't raised in a religious creationist household, she explained. She
didn't think that her road to heaven was paved with skepticism about evolutionary theory. Nothing like that. No, Heffernan's creationism resulted
from the fact that creationists told better stories. It was more satisfying to
believe, Heffernan argued, that two humans wrestled with sin and obedience

in an idyllic garden than it was to believe that mutations led population change over millennia. Like Walt Whitman's narrator so many years earlier, Heffernan didn't know what to believe, but she knew she couldn't get excited about the sterile evolutionary theory offered by modern science.[34]

A thorough understanding of American creationism must include outliers like Heffernan as well as stereotype-busters such as Hoyle and Miller. It needs to recognize that creationism is not merely the province of sweaty TV evangelists, clutching Bibles in one hand and pairs of discarded crutches in the other. We can't even rest comfortably with the lengthy taxonomy of creationisms we've just described. To be thorough, we need to acknowledge that there is at least as much diversity within each sort of creationism as there is among the many varieties of it. That is, among YECs, for instance, beliefs may be as different from one another as Heffernan's postmodern creationism is from Alaska's native-mythological ones. Some of them may be just plain ignorant about modern science. But not all of them are.

Take Kurt Wise, for example. Dr. Wise is certainly a devoted young-earther, but he is far from typical and far from ignorant. Wise earned his PhD in the Harvard lab of the late Stephen Jay Gould, perhaps America's favorite anti-creationist. Yet Wise resolutely refused to give up his creationist beliefs even if he learned they weren't true. "I am a young age creationist," Wise famously explained, "because that is my understanding of the Scripture. . . . If all the evidence in the universe turned against creationism, I would be the first to admit it, but I would still be a creationist because that is what the Word of God seems to indicate."[35] There's absolutely no doubt that Dr. Wise knows his mainstream science. His career makes it impossible to assume that his creationism is simply due to ignorance, to a stubborn fundamentalist refusal to look modern life in the face. Dr. Wise chooses creationism for religious reasons, reasons safe from any possible scientific debunking.

There are likely plenty of educated, thoughtful Christian creationists out there who share Wise's educated, thoughtful embrace of scientifically outlandish ideas. Maybe some of them learned from Professor Wise himself at schools such as Bryan College, where Wise taught for many years. We must assume, however, that there are plenty of ignorant knee-jerk creationists out there, too. Plenty of American creationists must believe in a young earth because it's what they were told. Plenty of creationists must cling to the notion of a young earth because they haven't bothered to examine the science or because they never studied in any college, creationist or not. Radical creationism, just like so many other American ideas, thrives because plenty of Americans would rather fight enemies than collaborate toward truth.

And it seems there are lots of Americans who aren't sure why they are creationists. Recent polls have netted some strange fish. For example, in one 2009 poll, over one in ten of the most scientifically outrageous creationists say they have no religious affiliation, yet they agree that "humans and other living things have existed in their present form since the beginning of time." In other words, these are people who don't identify with any sort of conservative, creationist religion. They aren't Southern Baptists, or Orthodox Jews, or Seventh-day Adventists. Yet they don't think humans evolved. Why not? We just can't tell from the poll results. Similarly, a surprisingly large number of people who say they "seldom or never" go to religious services—17 percent— pick creationism when given a choice.[36]

Are these people creationists? If so, why? Do they simply not understand the questions? Have they never heard the scientific answers? Perhaps they are among the many fence-sitting Americans who call themselves "spiritual but not religious." Just as it was in Walt Whitman's day, American creationism is more than the headline-grabbing theatrics of Ken Ham and Harun Yahya. It is more than the ferocious wars of words between evolutionary creationists and YECs.

Most important for our purposes, creationism can mean a lot of different things to different people. If we define creationism as a vague assumption that human life came somehow from some sort of divine or superhuman spark, then nearly all Americans might qualify. If, on the other hand, we limit our definition of creationism to those loud-mouth radical types who actively dispute the ways evolutionary theory is taught in public schools, then we find a much, much smaller population. In every case, though, it pays to be humble about our assumptions. It's worth repeating: Creationism in America isn't any one thing; it is a jumbled and cross-referenced collection of things, some of which don't logically belong together.

Sometimes It Takes a Dipstick

Not surprisingly, this sort of complicated diversity drives pollsters crazy. The numbers we hear most often are shocking. Since the 1980s, according to Gallup polls, nearly half (38–47 percent) of Americans have agreed that "God created human beings in pretty much their present form at one time within the last 10,000 years or so." Nearly half! And another third or so of respondents (31–40 percent) think "human beings have developed over millions of years from less advanced forms of life, but God guided this process." Only a relatively small remainder, somewhere between 9 and 22 percent, have agreed with the nonreligious option: "Human beings have developed over millions of years from less advanced forms of life, but God had no part in this process."[37] Whenever pundits and policymakers talk about evolution and creation, someone is sure to trot out these eye-opening numbers.

If we poke the polls a little bit, though, we can see that people aren't really as consistent in their creationist beliefs as the Gallup polls seem to indicate. Political scientist George Bishop of the University of Cincinnati crunched the numbers of more sensitive and detailed poll questions. He came up with some confounding results. Of the people who chose the most extreme category of creationist belief in the Gallup polls, for example, over a third did not believe other common young-earth-creationist beliefs. So, in other words, of the 40-ish percent of people who thought that humans had been created in pretty much their present form within the past 10,000 years, only two-thirds believed that dinosaurs had lived at the same time as people. Ken Ham would be dismayed. And he should be. Of those purportedly YEC types, over half also believed that dinosaurs had gone extinct over 65 million years ago. And over half also believed that all animals share common ancestors. In other words, of the large number of people who think humans were created relatively recently, more than half also believe in an ancient earth and in the evolution of nonhuman animals. There's more: Over three-quarters (78 percent) of Americans think that fossils date back hundreds of millions of years.[38] So if 44 percent of Americans are really young-earth evolution deniers, then lots of them are also old-earth evolution believers.

For a lot of Americans, the tricky part seems to be focused on human evolution, not evolution in general. For example, a 2005 Harris poll found a big difference when pollsters asked people if "human beings" developed from earlier species or if "all plants and animals have evolved from other species." When it came to humans, only 38 percent of respondents agreed with evolution. For plants and nonhuman animals, though, just under half (49 percent) did.[39]

The wording of questions has an understandably enormous influence on the answers people give. In a 2009 Harris poll, for instance, only 29 percent of people agreed that "human beings evolved from earlier species." In the same poll, however, a much larger 53 percent of respondents indicated that they "believe Charles Darwin's theory which states that plants, animals and human beings have evolved over time."[40] When the Pew Research Center asked similarly God-free questions, they found that most people favored evolution. In their 2009 poll, the Pew survey offered two options: "Humans and other living creatures have evolved over time due to natural processes," or humans "existed in their present form since the beginning of time." Of those two options, six in ten chose evolution. But only just under a third (32 percent) thought that those "natural processes" did not include God. A large portion (22 percent) insisted that evolution was the way God or some other higher power used evolution to create.[41]

In the end, large majorities of Americans seem to believe that God created humanity, somehow. Evolution might be the method, or it might not. God might have done it the way the Bible says, or he might not have. Or maybe both at the same time. We can say with certainty that there are a lot of American creationists. If we want to get more specific than that, though, we need to watch out. The best answer seems to be that Americans believe a lot of things about creation and evolution, some of them contradictory. Often, the same people apparently believe a jumble of conflicting ideas that couldn't possibly all be true.

Just as in all things, there are plenty of Americans who define themselves neatly into logical categories. Lots of people are firm, consistent, convinced YECs, or evolutionary creationists, or intelligent designers, or any of our other categories of creationist thinking. Just as important, though, we need to recognize that lots more of us have strong opinions about creation and evolution, but we don't really care if our opinions are consistent, logical, or orthodox.

In the end, how many creationists are there in the United States? The unsatisfying but true answer is this: It depends. If we ask how many Americans believe that something besides evolution must be responsible for human life, or at least for the human soul, then the answer will be almost all of us. But if we ask how many Americans consistently reject the scientific consensus about humanity's origins and the origins of the planet in favor of a plain reading of the first books of the Bible, the answer will be a much smaller minority of us.

Maybe because of this muddle of beliefs, opinions, and knowledge, we can say one thing for certain: Americans don't want much evolution taught in their public schools. If we don't know something to be true beyond controversy, Americans tend to agree that it should not be part of a public school curriculum. And even if we acknowledge that it is true beyond controversy, we're often still not sure what to do. According to political scientists Michael Berkman and Eric Plutzer of Penn State University, even those Americans who acknowledge the scientific consensus about evolution don't often want schools to teach it. That's right: Of the 54 percent of poll respondents who recognize that mainstream scientists all agree on the fact of evolution, a large majority (74 percent) still want schools to teach both evolution and some form of creationism, or just creationism by itself.[42] Another poll found that plenty of Americans want evolution out of schools altogether. A 2009 Harris poll, for example, found that 10 percent of people want schools to leave out all mention of either creationism or evolution.[43]

This sort of attitude might be the best indicator of the true nature of the continuing battle over creation and evolution. It's tempting at times to see the whole thing as an extended fight between the Bill Nyes of the world and the Ken Hams. Science versus religion, skepticism versus biblical certainty, PBS versus Ark Parks. In reality, however, our creationist America is a free-for-all of contending and often confused ideas about science, religion, and education. There is no single "creationist" position out there, and no single "evolution" position. When a dog fight gets this chaotic and this turbulent, it's no surprise that nobody wants to stick his or her hand in the middle of the scrum to break it up.

As we'll see in the next chapter, these fights have a history of their own. If we want to make sense out of both American creationism and our creation-evolution culture wars, we should start by recognizing this sometimes-surprising history.

2

The Evolution of Radical Creationism

He didn't call himself a creationist. But no one did more during the 1920s to fight against the teaching of evolution in America's public schools than William Bell Riley. Riley was the tough-talking Minneapolis preacher who turned himself into the public face of a new kind of militant conservative Christian. He and his allies were the first generation of American fundamentalists; they hoped to save modern America from itself by purging its schools of evolution, its churches of compromise, and its streets of sin.

Even compared to the aggressive bluster of the rest of his class of first-generation fundamentalists, Riley stood out. He took a back seat to no one in his culture-war pugnacity. Though he didn't use the label "creationist," Riley—along with many of his allies in the 1920s—certainly fits our two-prong definition of radical creationism.[1] For one thing, he believed that his religious beliefs forced him to reject mainstream evolutionary theory. Second, he hoped to impose his religious beliefs on the public, fighting to have evolution banned outright from public schools. Yet unlike later generations of radical creationists, in the 1920s Riley didn't give a fig about a young earth. As he put it in 1927, there was not "an intelligent fundamentalist who claims that the earth was made six thousand years ago; and the Bible never taught any such thing."[2]

Fast forward fifty years. By the 1970s, leading anti-evolution activists—now generally calling themselves "creationists"—cared a lot about a young earth. The most prominent radical young-earth organization of that era, the Institute for Creation Research (ICR), provided the curricular hardware that encouraged activists to include ideas about a young earth and an instant creation in public school science classes. By the 1970s, the ICR creationists no longer dreamed of banning evolution. They only hoped to squeeze creationism into public schools alongside evolution.

The new attitude of radical young-earth creationists (YECs) was best articulated in 1978 by ICR pundit Wendell Bird in the pages of the *Yale Law Journal*. Bird didn't repeat the arguments of earlier radical creationists like William Bell Riley. Rather, like a lot of his 1970s radical-creationist allies, Bird

Creationism USA. Adam Laats, Oxford University Press (2021). © Oxford University Press.
DOI: 10.1093/oso/9780197516607.001.0001.

stole the lines of Riley's fiercest opponents. Back in the 1920s, Bird preached, it was evolution's *defenders* who had insisted it was "bigotry for public schools to teach only one theory of origins." Now the creationists fought against that same sort of bigotry, but from the other side.[3]

Bird's rhetorical shift helps illuminate the ways radical creationism—in its young-earth form, at least—went through radical changes in the twentieth century. Because even though it can seem as if the United States has been stuck in the same creation-evolution deadlock since the days of William Bell Riley and the Scopes Trial of 1925, by the time Wendell Bird tried to reframe his creationism as a beleaguered minority position, everything had changed.

This chapter will explain the ways radical young-earth creationism went through a dramatic double revolution in the twentieth century. First, the notion of a young earth and a literal six-day creation went from being a fringe belief—something that even the most ardent fundamentalists pooh-poohed—into an accepted, if extreme, mainstay of conservative Protestant thinking. Second, the goals of the radical-creationist movement dwindled. In the 1920s, activists like William Bell Riley sought nothing less than the ab-solute eradication of the teaching of evolution in public schools. By Wendell Bird's time, even the most ambitious radical creationists hoped only for a seat at the public school table.

These revolutions weren't just coincidental. As creationism found it-self rudely ejected from the institutions of mainstream science, creationists found it easier and easier to latch on to more eccentric ideas about science and salvation. William Bell Riley and his colleagues considered themselves—in the first few years of the 1920s at least—nothing less than the brains and conscience of the nation. They assumed that their role as America's pastors still gave them the sorts of Main Street clout that earlier generations of Protestant churchmen had enjoyed. As their ability to dictate policy to America's schools seeped away, their ability to indulge in their own peculiar brand of approved knowledge flourished.

The Price Is Right

Don't worry, George McCready Price told his fellow anti-evolution activists throughout the 1920s. Price reassured his allies that the dummies who thought evolution was better science just hadn't heard the latest. In popular funda-mentalist publications Price explained that cutting-edge "modern scientific discoveries" proved beyond a doubt that evolution would soon be discarded by all serious scientists, due to "recent discoveries in geology."[4] As his fellow anti-evolution campaigner William Jennings Bryan began the crusade against the teaching of evolution that would lead to his famous performance at the Scopes Trial, Price assured Bryan that any scientists who still supported evolutionary theory were sadly "out of date,—behind the times,—and don't know it."[5] Before he was heckled off the stage at a London debate in 1925, Price tried to prove this point to the skeptical London crowd. Those kooks who took evolutionary theory seriously, Price argued, were "living in a fool's paradise." Thanks to Price's monumental scientific discoveries, the foolish evolutionist would "wake up some fine morning and find that he needs an introduction to the modern scientific world."[6]

In the 1920s, fundamentalists ate it up. They loved Price's scientific-sounding assurances that evolution was a fantasy, a delusion of fools. Most of them, however, didn't dig deeper into the reasons why Price was so sure evolution was a fraud. If they had, they would have discovered some things about Price's sources that would make them decidedly uncomfortable.

George McCready Price was not only convinced that evolution was phony. He was also sure that the universe and everything in it had been created in literally six days, just as it was described in the book of Genesis. He was also sure that the earth had experienced a real worldwide flood, the one Noah and his family rode out on their gopher-wood boat.

Most of Price's allies in the 1920s didn't believe such things. Maybe more important, fundamentalists in the 1920s—though they fought against evolution as fiercely as anyone ever has—didn't think it was central to true Christian faith to believe such things. As we've seen, fundamentalist leader William Bell Riley thought it was absurd to think that opposition to evolution meant belief in a young earth. Instead, Riley assumed that the "days" referred to in Genesis referred to long stretches of geologic time.

Other leaders agreed. William Jennings Bryan became a household name—again—in the 1920s due to his high-profile efforts to ban evolution. He became the public face of the anti-evolution movement with his strenuous defense of Bible belief at the 1925 Scopes Trial. At that trial, Bryan set out to enforce a 1925 Tennessee law against the teaching of evolutionary theory. Bryan knew he faced strong opposition at the trial and around the nation, so he hoped to bring in a phalanx of expert scientists to back him up. Like most fundamentalists of his generation, Bryan was a big fan of George McCready Price and tried to convince Price to come to the trial to drop some science on foolish evolutionists.[7] Yet even Bryan didn't agree that his ferocious Christian faith required belief in a young earth. Yes, God created everything. Yes, evolution was a sinister pseudo-science. But no, a young earth didn't make any sense. The evidence clearly pointed to long geologic ages, Bryan believed.

Just like William Bell Riley, Bryan insisted that any foolish talk of literally six days of creation was nothing but a "straw man" foisted upon the faithful. No conservative Christians actually believed such things, Bryan huffed. Rather, their enemies accused them of such outlandish beliefs, just as they "accuse orthodox Christians of denying the roundness of the earth, and the law of gravitation."[8]

If none of the other leaders of the anti-evolution movement believed in a young earth in the 1920s, why was Price so convinced? Unlike the Presbyterian Bryan or the Baptist Riley, Price was a Seventh-day Adventist. Adventist faith had (and has) a very different history than those of most other conservative Protestant groups.

To make sense of it, we need to take a short trip back to the 1840s. In the great American tradition of apocalypse-watchers, back then a new prophet figured out that the world was about to end. William Miller explained his mathematical system of Bible prophecy with a crowd-pleasing array of light-up slides. Graphs and charts convinced many audiences at the time that Miller really had decoded the hidden messages in the Bible.

When Miller, reluctantly, put a specific date on Christ's return, thousands of people listened. Miller's followers—some of them, at least—did the sensible thing: They sold their worldly goods, donned white robes, and climbed up on the roofs of their houses and barns to greet Jesus when he returned in glory.[9]

Except, of course, he didn't. Not in the way most people had expected, anyway. Miller's predicted date came and went. Then Miller's new, corrected date came and went. His followers were flummoxed. Some of them went back to their day-to-day grind. Others, though, explained the seeming non-event in a variety of different ways. Some said Jesus really had returned but in a nonphysical sense. He had taken true believers to heaven with him and had shut the door behind him. Others concluded that they had been right about the date, but wrong about the event. Christ didn't return to earth the way some had expected, but he had revolutionized heaven.

Amid the chaos and hurt feelings, one of Miller's young followers came down with a bad case of prophecy. Ellen Harmon, soon to marry and become

Ellen G. White, leavened her disappointment with the beginnings of a series of luminous divine visions. The brilliant and charismatic girl saw heaven and earth; she saw creation and the end of days. And she wrote it all down for her followers in the new Seventh-day Adventist Church.

To those followers, White's prophecies explained a lot. For Seventh-day Adventists like George McCready Price, a literal six-day creation and a young earth were obviously true in ways that they were not for folks like William Bell Riley and William Jennings Bryan. Unlike Baptists and Presbyterians—and nearly everyone else—Seventh-day Adventists had a reliable eyewitness account of creation. Unlike other radical creationists of the 1920s, Price had a solid reason for insisting on a young earth. He had a solid reason for insisting that "days" meant "days." All the fundamentalists of the 1920s, along with lots of conservative Protestants who didn't call themselves fundamentalists, agreed that God had given them a book that explained everything, the Bible. But Seventh-day Adventists like Price believed that God had also given Ellen G. White a personal prophetic tour of the Bible. White hadn't simply *read* Genesis, she had *seen* it.

It makes sense, then, for smallish groups like the Seventh-day Adventists to believe in the scientifically outlandish idea of a young earth and a literal worldwide flood. But by the end of the twentieth century, Price's fringe beliefs—the odd progeny of a forced marriage between American prophecies—had spread far beyond the limits of Adventist thinking. They had come to seem normal and even orthodox to relatively large numbers of conservative Protestants. How did that happen?

As in so many things, the folks who care the most get to set the agenda. After George McCready Price was booed off the debate stage in London in 1925, he didn't quit. Price realized that public debates could only take his ideas so far. Too many people, Price thought, had had their heads foolishly turned by the damnable doctrines of evolutionary theory. In order to get the truth out, he needed to lay deeper foundations.

And that's exactly what he did. Along with a handful of dedicated Adventist young-earther allies, Price founded the Deluge Geology Society in Los Angeles in 1938. This group hoped to spread their belief in a young earth beyond the confines of Adventist belief, to all those who thought evolution was a menace to good Christians everywhere.[10]

Indirectly, at least, the Deluge Geology Society succeeded beyond its wildest dreams. One of its earnest early non-Adventist members was Henry Morris, at the time a civil engineer in Houston. Morris went on to a PhD in hydraulic engineering at the University of Minnesota and a successful career as a professor of engineering, working at such prestigious schools as Virginia Tech.

All the while, though, Morris's real life's work was to spread the word. He was no Adventist, but as a Baptist believer, Morris absorbed the notion that a young earth mattered. As did Price and his Adventist colleagues, Morris came to believe that taking the Bible seriously meant taking the face value of the book of Genesis seriously. If Christians put the Bible first—and no one could ever doubt that conservative Baptists had always put the Bible first—it was important to put Genesis first, as God had done.

Along with creationist theologian John Whitcomb Jr., in 1961 Henry Morris published a bombshell that thrust these young-earth ideas—which had long been debated and considered by creationists—into the mainstream of conservative evangelicalism. In *The Genesis Flood*, Morris and Whitcomb insisted that authentic Christian belief relied on the idea of recent creation and an even more recent catastrophic worldwide flood.

As we'll explore in more depth in our next chapter, Morris and Whitcomb established the parameters for modern young-earth creationism. They argued that young-earth creationism was better science than mainstream science, but not only that. They also insisted that evolution was more of a religion than a science, and that believing in either an ancient or a young earth was not a decision between better or worse science, but rather a matter of "one's own judgment and preferences."[11]

The most important point here is that Morris and Whitcomb didn't aim their book at only Seventh-day Adventists or Missouri Synod Lutherans—groups who already believed in a young earth. No, in *The Genesis Flood* these smart, educated, credentialed non-Adventists made the case that belief in a young earth was a central requirement of real Christian belief. As they put it, if Christians really had "full belief in the complete divine inspiration and perspicuity of Scripture," they should embrace the idea of a young earth. Whitcomb and Morris hoped to convince "those whose confidence, like ours, is centered in the revelation of God."[12] Their goal, they pronounced, was nothing less than "restoring His people everywhere to full reliance on the truth of the Biblical doctrine of origins."[13]

For conservative evangelical Protestants, Whitcomb and Morris hit them where it hurt: In their willingness to insist that the Bible was not just a collection of stories left over from an ancient Middle Eastern past. For generations, conservative Baptists, Methodists, Presbyterians, Lutherans, and all sorts of Protestants had insisted that real Christianity meant reliance on the trustworthiness of Scripture. For that sort of Christian, Whitcomb and Morris weren't just laying out another possible interpretation of Genesis. They weren't simply arguing that their young-earth ideas were another, possibly better way to understand the Bible. No, the reason *The Genesis Flood* released such a flood of young-earth creationist belief, far beyond the limited boundaries of Seventh-day Adventism, was because it linked its vision of true creationism so tightly and so convincingly to its vision of true Christianity. And, as we'll see in our next chapter, they did it at precisely the time when American evangelicals were looking for answers.

Who Rules the Schools?

The Scopes Trial was exciting, but it wasn't really the most important episode in the creation-evolution debates of the 1920s. More important in the big picture, the laws and bills that state legislatures considered in that decade tell us what evolution meant to schools at the time.

Nevertheless, the Scopes Trial still looms large in people's memory, even if we don't usually remember it correctly. Some of us think of *Inherit the Wind*, the McCarthy era reinterpretation of the trial. In that dramatic but historically misleading vision, heroic defenders of science deflated the ignorant, closed-minded pretensions of creationist curmudgeons.[14]

In real life, there certainly were some people who hoped the trial would do just that. Clarence Darrow, for example, came to the trial in order to prove to America and the world that evolution's day had come. Darrow put radical-creationist hero William Jennings Bryan on the witness stand and tried his best to poke holes in Bryan's anti-evolution logic. If the Bible is a trustworthy source of facts, Darrow asked, then where did Cain find his wife? There shouldn't have been other people around. And was it really possible for Jonah to be swallowed up by a giant fish? . . . Did Joshua really command the sun to stand still?

Most important, Darrow tried to prove that thinking people couldn't possibly believe such outlandish stories. Did any real scientist endorse them? When Bryan cited his expert George McCready Price, Darrow pounced. Price, Darrow announced gleefully, was a "mountebank and a pretender and not a geologist at all."[15]

These interchanges made great copy. Newsmen at the trial reported the conflict breathlessly. What fewer people noticed—at the time or since—was that the clash between Bryan and Darrow was not really the most important or consequential back-and-forth of the era. With the benefit of historical hindsight, we can get a better view of the real issues.

The Scopes Trial only happened, after all, because of a new anti-evolution law in Tennessee. As did four other states, Tennessee had passed a law or resolution denouncing or restricting the teaching of evolution in public schools. The political power of those laws—and all the bills that almost became laws—can tell us more about the state of creationism and evolution in the 1920s than the Scopes Trial can.[16]

The best example is probably the first one. In 1922, Kentucky considered a new law to ban the teaching of evolution in public schools. It didn't pass, but it only missed by one vote. In fact, lawmakers had corralled the votes to push the bill through, but at the last minute a few supporters switched sides and voted against the law. Why? Because they were assured in a backroom deal that Kentucky's schools would quietly ban evolution anyway. If conservative lawmakers could be confident that no public school in Kentucky would teach evolution, then they agreed the bill wouldn't be necessary.[17]

For anyone with the time to slog through the records of Kentucky's state legislature, the really dramatic story of creationism in the 1920s leaps out from the dusty pages. In Kentucky, the bill that almost passed would have done much more than simply allow Kentucky's teachers to teach creationism. It would have done more than protect the academic freedom of teachers to tell students about the scientific weaknesses of evolutionary theory. The bill that just barely didn't become a law would have banned the teaching of evolution entirely. And not just that. In addition to evolution, the bill would have banned atheism or agnosticism from Kentucky's public schools. Even more remarkable, a Senate amendment would have prohibited any public library in the state from owning any books that could "directly or indirectly attack or assail or seek to undermine or weaken or destroy the religious beliefs and convictions of the children of Kentucky."[18]

It's worth pausing for a moment to consider the implications of such a bill. What would it mean to ban every book from a public library that might "indirectly" challenge the religious beliefs of children? Would every book that included information about different religious traditions be banned? After all, a young evangelical student might start to wonder why so many humans did not share her religion. Would all writings of prominent religious skeptics like Thomas Paine be pulled from the shelves? Or even the religious musings of Thomas Jefferson?

In retrospect, the theocratic ambition of a bill like this one from Kentucky seems breathtaking. Lawmakers did not hesitate to ask public institutions to embody their religious beliefs. There wasn't much talk of a wall of separation yet between church and state. It seemed appropriate—to some legislators at least—to denude library shelves of any books that children might find religiously challenging.

In the end, though, the bill didn't pass. And because it didn't become law, it might be tempting to dismiss its language as the overinflated fantasy of 1920s radical creationists. Tempting, but wrong. Remember, this bill was defeated by only one vote, and some supporters voted against it at the last minute. They did so only after receiving reassurance that the state would go ahead and do everything the bill promised.

For our purposes, the lesson here is that radical creationists back then had every right to feel confident that public schools would do more than merely *respect* their religious beliefs. Back then, radical creationists expected public schools to *reflect* their religious beliefs.

In other words, in Kentucky in 1922, radical creationists weren't satisfied merely to wedge creationism into science classes through a back door. No, back then radical creationist leaders wanted much more. They hoped to install—frankly and unapologetically—theocratic rule on their state's schools and libraries. No schoolteacher could have taught evolution, not legally at least. No schoolteacher could have even taught children that smart people might wonder about the existence of God. And the state's public libraries would have had to purge their shelves of any book that might challenge a student's religious beliefs. It's hard to imagine what books might be left after getting rid of everything that might possibly "indirectly" challenge traditional, conservative Protestant beliefs.

The World Broke in Two

It's easy to imagine that those Kentucky lawmakers felt nervous about the ways America was changing. From their vantage point in 1922, the cultural tectonic plates seemed to be shifting beneath their feet in dramatic and unpredictable fashion. And conservative Christians in Kentucky weren't the only ones to notice it. As novelist Willa Cather later quipped, "The world broke in two in 1922 or thereabouts."[19] The modern world promised—or threatened—to transform everything. From the perspective of the twenty-first century, it certainly seems as if theocrats back then had every reason to be concerned as they peered into their society's future.

For one thing, in the years between 1922 and 1961, the ideas of Kentucky's lawmakers about the proper role of religion in schools and society received a thorough drubbing. New ideas about the proper relationship between religion, science, education, and government had begun to sink deep roots in the hearts and minds of all Americans, even conservative religious Americans. By the time Whitcomb's and Morris's *Genesis Flood* hit the bookshelves of religious bookstores around the nation in 1961, everything had changed.

As philosopher Charles Taylor argues, the kind of secularism that came to dominate twentieth-century America obviously can't be thought of as the absence of religion. There were plenty of religious people doing religious things in prominent ways. Nor can it even be thought of as the dwindling influence of religious people and religious ideas. If you doubt it, try running for political office as an atheist.[20] Rather, the secular society that exerted new and ever-growing influence in twentieth-century America comes closest to what Taylor calls "secularity 3," in which both religious and nonreligious people are forced to live together, in Taylor's words, all "very aware of the options favored by others."[21]

In other words, by the 1960s the rigid theocratic anti-evolution rules pushed in Kentucky and so many other states came to seem outdated, a relic of an earlier time. Over the course of the twentieth century, a different sort of attitude came to dominate. More and more Americans—even religious Americans—came to agree that American government ought to be somehow secular, somehow free of ties to any religion. Of course, plenty of other Americans disagreed.

The give and take between these differing visions of America fueled endless rounds of culture wars. There were a few spectacular battles during these decades-long culture wars, such as the Scopes Trial itself. But more generally, the big changes happened in more subtle ways, without big headlines or dramatic confrontations. While everyone was watching show trials from Tennessee, America's secular ideas about itself grew increasingly more powerful and more common, in fits and starts over decades. To track these subtle but enormously powerful long-term changes, snapshots from the Scopes Trial don't tell us as much as a few time-lapse looks at key types of institutions.

For example, if we take a longer view, the changes in America's elite universities become startlingly clear. In the old way of doing things, universities were generally considered places for young people to imbibe the wisdom of the ages, to see how God's goodness permeated all aspects of life and thought.

At the end of the 1800s, scholars at elite colleges saw their jobs this way. As one young hothead at the time remembered of his time at Amherst College in Massachusetts, "the older minds of the faculty" didn't put much truck in research. After all, the truth had "already been found . . . in the Bible." These older scholars, during the late decades of the nineteenth century, "regarded research as more or less heretical."[22] By the 1960s, that kind of thinking would be considered old-fashioned even by the most rigid of radical creationists.

And many of the scholars who worked at the new kinds of research universities changed the face of science itself. Back when William Jennings Bryan took the stand in Dayton, Tennessee, to fight against the pretensions of evolutionary science, Bryan could legitimately claim that mainstream scientists did not agree on the mechanism of evolution. Darwin, of course, had proposed the idea of natural selection as a principal way that species came to look different from one another. Up through Bryan's time, however, the ability of natural selection to account for the diversity of species seemed unconvincing, even to many non-creationist scientists.

Beginning in the 1930s, however, scientists closed the gap. A new generation of scientists argued that an old idea about genetics could solve the apparent problems with Darwin's theory. By combining a few intellectual ingredients—including Gregor Mendel's ideas about inheritance and a wider population-level perspective—with Darwin's ideas about species change, scientists no longer disagreed about the basic premises of evolutionary theory. There was still plenty of room for scientific disagreement, of course, lots of it bitter and heated. By the late 1940s, however, the neo-Darwinian or modern evolutionary synthesis had come to be taken as a fundamental truth of biology.[23]

Science was changing. Universities were changing. And, as part and parcel of this widespread, amorphous change in Americans' attitudes toward the proper relationship between God and government, judges and courts ended up settling age-old questions in new, secular ways.

Perhaps most important, in 1947 US Supreme Court Justice Hugo Black dusted off an old phrase from America's rich religious history. The case came from religious schools in New Jersey. Though the Court ruled narrowly that New Jersey could indeed use tax money to pay for buses to Catholic schools,

Justice Black based his reasoning on a relatively obscure letter written by Thomas Jefferson to a nervous group of Baptists. Rest assured, Jefferson had written in 1802, the US government would never impose taxes and rules on religious groups the way the British did. No, instead the United States of America would build a "wall of separation between Church & State."

Jefferson wanted to reassure his Baptist friends. Their conservative great-great-great grandchildren, however, wouldn't feel reassured. Yes, the 1947 *Everson v. Board of Education* decision came down in favor of religious schools, but the principle of a wall of separation between church and state was soon used to drive a wedge between traditional Protestant religious practices and America's public schools. In 1962, for example, the Supreme Court ruled in *Engel v. Vitale* that public school students could not be led in a bland ecumenical prayer. The next year, in *School District of Abington Township v. Schempp,* the high court decided that public school teachers could not lead their students in the Lord's Prayer or in reading devotionally from the Bible, even if dissenting families could opt out.

The conservatives who howled that these court decisions had kicked God out of the public schools missed the point. Their world didn't break apart in 1963. Willa Cather had been right. The kind of theocratic rule favored by so many of Kentucky's lawmakers in 1922 had been kicked out of public schools long before. The Supreme Court decisions of the 1960s only recognized the fact that the wall of separation had been moved in those earlier decades. It now ran on the far side of the schoolhouse.

Creating New Science

By the 1960s, when Whitcomb and Morris scored enormous successes with their ideas about a young earth and a real worldwide flood, they couldn't build their scientific credibility high enough to push creationism over this new wall.

In this new era, the first big defeat for radical creationism came in 1968. Arkansas science teacher Susan Epperson didn't like hiding her evolutionary light under a bushel. In Arkansas, it had been illegal since 1928 for teachers to teach evolutionary theory in public schools. Lots of them did it anyway, and the textbooks that many Arkansas schools used assumed that evolution would play as central a role in science education as it did in science itself.

By the time the case wended its way to the US Supreme Court, evolution educators had new language to make their case. The National Science

Teachers Association offered a statement signed by 179 leading biologists. The modern scientists assured the judges that "scientists and other reasonable persons" no longer wondered if evolutionary theory was the best scientific explanation of the origin of species. It was.[24]

The Court agreed, and the language of Justice Abe Fortas reveals how drastically things had changed for radical creationists since they had passed the Arkansas law. The idea of banning a scientific idea, Fortas wrote, was decidedly against the grain of "the modern mind."[25]

Thoughtful radical creationists had minds as modern as anyone. Yet the rejection of laws banning evolution presented them with a new dilemma. If evolution could no longer be banned, how could public schools be saved from the damning doctrine of evolution?

In 1978, as we've seen, creationist law student Wendell Bird made his case for a new radical-creationist strategy in the pages of the *Yale Law Journal*.[26] True, Bird noted, creationism had been kicked out of its dominant position as the de facto origin story of America's public schools. But science had never been kicked out. If creationists could scrub their religious beliefs out of their ideas about the origins of species, Bird reasoned, then public schools would have to teach them. If creationists could offer better science, not just better religion, there would be no constitutional problem. "Biblical creationism" might be out, Bird argued, but "creation science" could be in.

Activists in organizations such as the ICR offered ways to make this happen. Henry Morris teamed up with science teacher Richard Bliss to craft a new model curriculum, one that gave equal time to evolution and creationism. According to them, anything less would be scientifically unacceptable. As Bliss explained in the two-model curriculum, "the creation model, in its modern sense, has been developed scientifically by scientists who interpret present scientific data about life as the result of *original design*."[27]

Bliss's emphatic repetition of the word "science" was no accident. When states such as Louisiana and Arkansas passed two-model laws, creationists hoped that courts would agree that teaching all sorts of science—even creation science—was a reasonable approach for public schools.

Judges didn't agree. When the Louisiana law found its way to the US Supreme Court in 1987, it was rejected roundly on the same grounds as earlier creationist attempts. Despite the protestations of Bird and his radical-creationist allies, the Court ruled in *Edwards v. Aguillard* that the law had a religious intent, not a secular scientific one.[28]

The lesson, for radical creationists, was clear. In the mid-1980s, another group of creationist intellectuals dusted off another ancient idea and tried to cleanse it of blatant religious language. Calling their new approach "intelligent design," (ID) these activists cranked out books and textbooks that argued against evolutionary theory based on the sheer complexity of life. How was it possible, they asked, for complex biological systems to pop into existence if gradual changes wouldn't confer any evolutionary benefits?[29]

As had earlier visions of creationist science, ID had its day in court. And, just as earlier creationist sciences had done, ID lost. In *Kitzmiller v. Dover* (2005), federal district Judge John E. Jones III ruled that the idea was religious, not scientific. It shouldn't be taught as science in public schools.

By the beginning of the twenty-first century, the legal situation seemed clear and clearly gloomy to ambitious radical creationists. Merely offering alternative science wasn't enough. Radical creationists faced a much more difficult task: They had to prove, somehow, that they didn't want creation science or ID taught for religious reasons. And of course that was an impossible task for religious thinkers who had always decried the dangers evolutionary theory posed to religion.[30]

More and more frequently, then, radical creationists made a different sort of argument. Unlike the strident creationists of the 1920s who banned evolution outright, by the end of the twentieth century some creationists began to insist on their rights as beleaguered minorities. Though courts— including the court of public opinion—have largely disagreed, Wendell Bird argued in 1978, "Exclusive public school instruction in the general theory of evolution abridges free exercise of religion."[31] Creationism should be taught to protect vulnerable students, Bird reasoned, as well as to have better science classes.

A new generation of radical-creationist lawmakers followed suit. When Louisiana passed its two-model law in 1981—the law rejected by the US Supreme Court in 1987—Louisiana lawmakers insisted that their main purpose was "protecting academic freedom." It was vital, the short-lived law insisted, that both creationist students and teachers not be "discriminated against" due to their scientific and religious dissent.[32]

Duane Gish, too, eagerly embraced the language of minority empowerment. As one of the leading, "galloping" creationist debaters of his generation, Gish shouted throughout the 1980s that it was bigotry to teach only one idea about the origins of species. At a meeting hosted by his scientific archenemies, the American Association for the Advancement of Science, Gish pointedly complained that he had been fooled into thinking it would be a meeting of equal parts creation scientists and mainstream scientists. When he noticed that there was only one other radical creationist at the table, he loudly protested that he would "proceed to take one of the two seats on the back of the bus reserved for the creationists in this meeting."[33]

Gish wanted to be the Rosa Parks of American creationism. More common these days, creationist activists hope to make themselves into latter-day John Scopeses. Since the early 2000s, lawmakers in states from Maryland to Michigan have pushed "academic freedom" laws to change public schools. Teachers and students, creationist lawmakers argue, must be allowed to include non-mainstream ideas about evolution and creation.[34]

These bills have taken a variety of forms. Some of them promise to teach students "the full range of scientific views" about evolution. Other bills claim to teach students vital "critical thinking" skills about controversial issues such as evolution. Just like the earlier creation-science and intelligent-design laws, these radical-creationist efforts hope to keep public school safe for creationist kids. They hope to preserve some intellectual space in science classrooms for the religious ideas—not scientific ideas—that have always been the real heart of American creationism.

The World Broke Apart Even More

Doubtless, evolution educators find the lingering political strength of radical creationism frustrating and lamentable. But anyone even vaguely familiar with the real history of creationist activism will see that everything really has changed.

Politically, radical creationists don't even bother anymore to dream about banning evolution. Over the decades, the public school ambitions of radical creationists have dwindled to today's disingenuous whimpers about protecting academic freedom and promoting critical thinking.

Radical creationists needn't blame themselves. The underlying reasons for this change are far broader than any creationist strategy. The United States has undergone a profound revolution in its general attitudes about the proper relationship between God and government. The theocratic rules that made sense to so many lawmakers in 1922 would now be politically impossible. Over the course of the twentieth century, in spite of the culture-war efforts of generations of conservative religious people, public life in the United States has become divorced from religion in ways that would have seemed shocking in the 1920s.

And that's not the only dramatic historic change in the world of American creationism. Theologically, creationists today must deal with a powerful young-earth sentiment within their midst. Among the first generation of anti-evolution activists in the 1920s, the idea of a relatively recent creation, in literally six days, was embraced only by a small minority of conservative Christian thinkers. Conservative Baptists and Presbyterians considered such an idea outlandish and intellectually indefensible.

Yet these days, large numbers of conservative Protestants assume that real faith in the Bible requires real faith in a recent, six-day creation. Being a faithful Bible believer means being faithful to the plain message of the book of Genesis. At least, that's something that many more American creationists believe today than they did in the 1920s.

Radical creationism, we might say, has become more radically creationist just as public schools have become more radically secular. These two historical transfigurations in American creationism are tightly bound together. Only because creationist ideas were booted from mainstream scientific and intellectual thinking could they flourish in the extravagant hot-house form of young-earth creationism.

As long as radical creationists felt they represented mainstream American thinking, they had to insist on mainstream respectability for their creationist ideas. Back in the 1920s, William Bell Riley and William Jennings Bryan ridiculed the idea of a young earth because no legitimate mainstream scientists supported such an idea.

Later generations of radical-creationist activists lost any possibility of intellectual respectability among mainstream scientists. That rejection felt harsh and unfair to creationists, but it also freed them to accept ideas that seemed scientifically outlandish.

By 1961, when Henry Morris and John Whitcomb penned their young-earth magnum opus, they simply assumed that mainstream science had gone to the dogs. Like other radical creationists, they never gave up their love of science. They never abandoned their fondest hope of swinging mainstream science back their way, but in the meantime they did not try to frame their arguments in ways mainstream scientists would agree to. Whitcomb and Morris assumed that "uniformitarian" scientists were so bound by their "dogmatic" evolutionary thinking that no creationist argument could sway them.[35] Whitcomb and Morris no longer tried to accommodate mainstream views into their scientific theology; they knew the attempt would be hopeless. As a result, they were open to ideas that made religious sense, even if they made absolutely no scientific sense.

In other words, the fact that radical American creationism grew more and more radically different from mainstream science just as American public schools grew more and more insistently secular was not a mere coincidence. As creationism was excluded from mainstream institutions, it grew in wild new varieties that could only flourish outside the mainstream.

For those of us trying to figure out why we keep fighting about creationism, this history of creationism's creeping exclusion from public schools and mainstream intellectual life sets the stage. In the 1920s, radical creationists still hoped to put their religious stamp on public institutions, even if they often failed. Since the 1960s, though, it has become harder and harder not to notice that all of that broke apart back in the 1920s. These days, any radical creationist who yearns to make science great again might come to a tragically mistaken conclusion: Evolutionary theory didn't simply accompany sweeping changes in American life, evolutionary theory caused them.

If we pause for half a moment we will see without a doubt—even radical creationists will—that the actual science of evolutionary theory couldn't possibly have caused the social changes that drove prayer and the Bible out of many public schools. Yet too often that obvious fact has been obscured by the efforts of radical creationists to make it seem as if it did. All too often, the loudest voices in our creationist culture wars have talked about everything except actual evolutionary science. As we'll explore in the next chapter, the anger and heat that emanate from our debates about creationism result from how evolutionary theory has been framed to seem like something it's not.

3

Evolution and All That

Now that we have a better handle on the vast diversity of American creationism and on the history of the radical strain, we can finally turn to the
toughest questions of all: If Americans don't really disagree about evolution,
why does it always seem as if we do? Or, to use the words of one observer,
how have our fights about evolution evolved from a "mere debate" into a "social institution?"[1]

We need to throw out the most obvious answer right at the gate: It's not
that creationists hate science. We saw glimmers of this notion in our discussion of the Ham-on-Nye debate, and we'll talk about it more in chapter 7, but,
by and large, creationists love science.

After all, as we've seen, some of the most articulate defenders of evolution education are creationists themselves. Ivy League scientists, like Ken
Miller, are part of the vast majority of Americans who are both creationists
and lovers of evolutionary theory. Even the radical young-earth crowd—
surprising though it may seem—loves science as a whole. In their own way,
many radical creationists even want their kids to learn evolutionary theory,
as we'll see in coming chapters.

What is it, then? If creationists—even radical creationists—love science,
and if they want to teach evolution to their children, why do we continue to
fight about creationism and evolution?

Like the bumper sticker says, the first and most obvious answer is Jesus.
For most of America's radical creationists—at least the ones who think about
it—the main problem with evolutionary theory comes from theology. It
may make no sense to nonreligious or non-Christian people, but for a lot of
Christian creationists, it's not evolution they hate, but rather the theological
implications that they associate with it.

I'm no theologian, but we'll try to tease out those perceived spiritual
dangers in this chapter.

But theology alone can't do it. The reasons radical creationists give for
their often visceral disgust and distrust of evolutionary theory go deeper
than reasoned theological arguments. Yes, some creationist activists think

Creationism USA. Adam Laats, Oxford University Press (2021). © Oxford University Press.
DOI: 10.1093/oso/9780197516607.001.0001.

of themselves as religious protesters against the implications of evolutionary thinking. But there is a broader reason for their protest, too, a vaguer feeling that evolution is somehow responsible for—and tangled up with—a whole range of social problems that have only the most tenuous connection to formal religion and theology.

Behind the religious arguments, behind the scientific hair-splitting, there lurks a deeper truth about radical creationism. Creationists often love science, but they don't trust how science has been used. They embrace modern thinking, but they fret that ill-informed activists will misuse evolutionary theory to attack their faith. Evolution, for many Americans, has come to symbolize and embody the untrustworthy directions of modern culture. As we'll see in more depth in chapter 7, radical creationists don't fear science, but rather they mistrust the motives of certain people who have claimed to speak in the name of science.

Distrust of evolutionary theory among some creationists can be seen as one particular manifestation of a more general breakdown of social trust and cohesion. In order for members of any society to trust one another, as political scientist Francis Fukuyama has argued, they need to feel confident in a set of "commonly shared norms."[2] People need to sense a "shared 'language of good and evil.'"[3]

Over the course of the twentieth century, some radical creationists have come to the conclusion that their vision of good and evil is not shared by the mainstream scientific establishment. It's not science itself that radical creationists are mad at. Rather, it is the notion that some prominent members of that scientific establishment—along with other elites in fields such as education, journalism, and academia—have abandoned the traditional moral code that bound together American society. Even worse, some creationists feel, is that some of those elites haven't only abandoned America's moral code, they have also actively attacked it.

This broad tendency is hard to analyze but easy to notice. In every dispute over evolution, in every decade, radical-creationist protesters make the same sorts of arguments. To cite just one example, in the mid-1970s an explosive school controversy rocked Charleston, West Virginia. Literally explosive in this case, with school buildings firebombed and dynamited. Why? The state had selected a new set of language-arts textbooks. Conservatives and concerned parents blew up when they heard about the contents of the new books. And, not surprisingly, one of the most common charges was that the textbooks taught evolutionary theory.[4]

But . . . they didn't. Not really. The most contentious titles were literature textbooks, not science books. Yet time and time again, protesters accused all the books of teaching evolution.

What was wrong with the new books? One of the protest leaders, Avis Hill, explained his beef. Rev. Hill patiently warned one interviewer that it was not just one selection, not just one bad part. Rather, the whole book series had been tainted with the "philosophy of . . . secularism." The new textbooks, he explained, were contaminated by "attitudes of evolution and all that."[5]

What did he mean? For Rev. Hill, apparently, as for generations of anti-evolution activists throughout the twentieth century, evolution was more than a scientific idea. It was a vague and disgusting "attitude." Worse, it was the lead suspect for the decline of Western civilization. Why had society gone to hell in a handbasket? You could spend hours and days explaining all the reasons, but it was simpler and just as accurate to blame "evolution and all that."

The blame lay not with the science of evolution, but rather the "attitude" with which evolution was preached. It wasn't even science alone, but an array of ideas about morality, culture, and politics that radical creationists found objectionable. In addition to their possible religious objections, and fueling their ferocious political campaigns, the Rev. Hill and other creationist protesters felt a deep and abiding distrust. They distrusted a vague but powerful group of distant educational experts who had dictated a new approach to education. In the end, this kind of distrust has fueled our endless back and forth about evolution and creationism, rather than the specifics of any single scientific or religious idea.

In other words, for Hill and other creationist protesters, evolution didn't just represent a scientific idea. It didn't even only represent a religious danger. Rather, evolution bubbled out of the same witches' cauldron that produced so many other terrifying trends of modern life. At one and the same time, for many creationists, evolution came to symbolize and cause everything that was wrong with America—from communism to abortion, from drug use to sexual perversion—for many creationist protesters, evolutionary theory was a canary in the Devil's coalmine, warning unwary Christians about the dangers all around.

Radical creationists may believe that the scientific idea of evolution itself may not be the problem, just like a loaded gun by itself might not be dangerous. In the wrong hands, however—as it always seemed to be—evolutionary theory could lead to both social collapse and eternal damnation.

If we hope to move forward in the debates about creationism and evolution, we need to do a better job of separating concrete evolutionary theory from these culture-war threads that are so tightly wound into the fabric of our creation-evolution discussions.

Evolution at a Crossroad

Before we try to unpick the twisted knot of creationism, science, morality, sexuality, politics, and "all that," we need to start with the more obvious problem. For many religious people, evolutionary theory is primarily objectionable because it represents to them an anti-theistic way of thinking.

Of course, if you ask a hundred religious people, you'll get a hundred different theologies. And if you ask a hundred self-described creationists, you'll get plenty of evolution-friendly responses. Nevertheless, we need to try to understand the theological charges against evolutionary theory, at least in broad outline.

Historically, as we saw in earlier chapters, radical creationism in the USA has been tied most prominently to conservative evangelical Protestantism, including Main Street churches such as Baptists, Methodists, and Presbyterians as well as the vast kaleidoscope of independent enthusiasts who pray fervently in tents and storefronts. And since even before the publication of Darwin's *Origin of Species* in 1859, evangelical Christians have been intensely anxious about the religious implications of evolutionary thinking. Could a good Christian also accept modern evolutionary science? If so, how?

There hasn't been a steady stream of nervousness. Rather, the anxiety among American Protestants has spiked at specific historic moments. At certain times, creationists have been confronted with tough decisions about evolution and faith. Not surprisingly at those times, creationists have latched onto certain scholars who offered compelling answers.

The first moment came somewhat later than we might think. As mentioned, Charles Darwin published *Origin of Species* in 1859, and the book caused an immediate firestorm of debate and controversy. But not among conservative American Protestants. Why not? First of all, the looming threat of civil war consumed much of America's capacity for worry.

There is a more important and subtle reason, however. After all, the Civil War did not stop America's naturalists from fighting ferociously about

Darwin's argument. Rather, as the careful archival research of Jon H. Roberts has shown, theologians in the 1860s tended to assume that Darwin's controversial thesis wouldn't last. They assumed that the apparently absurd idea would soon be shuffled off into intellectual oblivion along with the rantings of so many other cranks and false prophets.[6]

Darwin's novelty didn't come from the idea of evolution. Thoughtful people had noticed the similarities between different kinds of plants and animals for thousands of years. It was no revelation to note that different breeds of dogs or roses could be cultivated over time. In Darwin's era, plenty of naturalists offered a variety of explanations of the ways one species had evolved into another. And, as historian Ronald Numbers has pointed out, Darwin's generation of zoologists and naturalists mashed together creation and evolution in a dizzying array of combinations.[7]

It was not the idea of evolution itself that proved so devilish, but rather the apparent lack of design allowed by Darwin's specific explanation of evolution. In *Origin of Species*, Darwin offered a one-two-three combination to explain the variety of plants and animals. In a nutshell, Darwin suggested that the first element was variability. Apples didn't fall far from trees, but every apple tree had some differences from its progenitors. Second, life was competition. There were always going to be more consumers than resources. The third idea was the most controversial: If one apple fell a little farther from the tree, so to speak, it might find that distance beneficial. If it did, it would be able to secure more resources; it would be able to thrive and survive and pass along its seeds to new generations of apples. If it didn't, it would shrivel and peter away, with fewer new generations of apples sharing its quirks. There was a "natural selection" process at work, and, given time, it could develop some traits just as distinctly as did the artificial selection process that dog and rose breeders had used for centuries.

Darwin's reliance on a process instead of a plan was the core of his hypothesis. And it proved so profoundly controversial that many religious thinkers in the 1860s simply sat back to wait for its seemingly inevitable dismissal.

But it never came. By the middle of the 1870s, it was becoming clear to intelligent people of every religious background that Darwin's argument was not going away. And that made America's serious Christians very nervous. As always, at times of high religious anxiety, the religious public latched onto writers and theologians who offered sensible explanations.

Christians looked to thinkers at elite institutions for solutions to their Darwinian dilemma. Was Darwin a devil? Or was his headline-grabbing thesis just a better way for good Christians to understand nature?

From Harvard College, botanist Asa Gray became well known as Darwin's friendly American defender. And from Princeton Seminary, theologian Charles Hodge attacked. However, the two men's explanations were not as far apart as people tended to assume. By dipping into their writings from the 1860s and 1870s, we can get a sense of the theological objections so many people associated with Darwin's ideas.

Professor Gray was a close personal and professional friend of Darwin. Long before the publication of *Origin of Species*, Gray had been in touch with his English colleague. Gray hoped to explain to America's Christian public that Darwin's ideas were not guilty of the atheistic implications so many critics charged them with. As Gray put it, the "first aspect" of Darwin's ideas "is suspicious, and high authorities pronounce the whole thing to be positively mischievous."[8] Upon closer inspection, however, Americans would agree that Darwin left "the argument for design, and therefore for a designer, as valid as it ever was."[9]

Like a nervous young person bringing their betrothed to meet the family for the first time, Gray warned Americans not to believe all the terrible rumors they might have heard about Darwinism. True, Professor Gray explained in an article in the *Atlantic Monthly* in 1860, Darwin's notions might seem uncomfortable. But that was only because they were new. Like new clothes, they might rub a little in awkward ways, but soon they would feel natural.[10]

Critics had charged that Darwin's purported process was tantamount to atheism, but Gray insisted the charge was simply untrue. Granted, Darwin's idea was certainly compatible with atheism, but so too was the theory of gravity. Any "physical theories," Gray wrote, could support an atheistic view of the universe. But, Gray hurried to add, they go just as well with a belief in God.[11] For Gray, a theistic vision of evolution combined the best modern science with the most enlightened religion.

Darwin himself, Gray assured American Christians, believed in a "supernatural beginning of life on earth."[12] There was absolutely no reason to think of the process Darwin described as anything other than an intimation of God's creative process. Consider, Gray offered, the analogy of a weaver who had been somehow transported from the medieval era to the modern. Show her a bolt of cloth and ask her how it was made. She will likely explain the process as she knew it, with handlooms and spinning wheels, and hour after hour of blistering labor.

If we tell her that this bolt of cloth was created by machines, Gray asked, would she therefore be justified in thinking that the cloth was a mere accident? That design played no role in its creation? Not at all. Though she had had no inkling of the existence of a machine-driven factory, of "carding-machines, spinning-jennies, and power-looms," she would quickly understand that these things are merely more wondrous versions of the processes with which she was already familiar. If our time traveler thought a moment, Gray explained,

> It is certain that she would believe in design as firmly as before, and that this belief would be attended by a higher conception and reverent admiration of a wisdom, skill, and power greatly beyond anything she had previously conceived possible.[13]

Christians could do the same, Gray reasoned. Understanding the process by which species came to be differentiated was only a better way to worship God. Beware, Gray warned, of the loud-mouthed rabble-rousers who will tell you that Darwinism is atheistic. The naysayers were nothing more than "intellectually short-sighted people" who leaped too quickly to condemn without bothering to understand.[14]

Darwin's emphasis on natural selection was nothing but a better understanding of God's great creation, Gray assured anxious American Christians. In spite of all the fuss and bother, it was a science that brought believers closer to God, not one that pushed them away from him.

Balderdash, Charles Hodge huffed. Among the crusty, rock-ribbed conservative scholars at Princeton Seminary, Hodge was among the crustiest. Though he wasn't quite as hostile to the idea of evolution as later generations of creationists have assumed, Hodge was not willing to welcome Darwinism with open arms.

In the 1870s, Princeton Seminary was an odd duck and proud of it. It stood apart from most elite seminaries in its relentless opposition to theological modernism and other cutting-edge trends in Christian thinking. It also stood steadfastly apart from the obvious trend in American higher education. At the time, most universities were moving in fits and starts toward our modern understanding of higher education. They were fighting with one another to attract top researchers in all fields, assuring them that their research would be unfettered. They were trying to shake their past as stuffy church colleges and become modern research universities.[15]

The Seminary, meanwhile, was not. As Princeton's most insightful historians have pointed out, the Seminary did not want to be merely a modern school, but rather a traditional school of thought.[16] It nurtured and guarded its signature Princeton Theology, a distinct way of understanding Christianity and the Bible. For Princeton theologians, authentic Christianity meant a devotion to the Bible. The Bible, Princetonians insisted, was not merely a book of moral lessons, or a collection of anthropologically interesting myths. Rather, the Bible was God's very Word, a revelation for humanity, a guidebook for salvation. Real Christians, the Princetonians assumed, would not be popular. Or comfortable. Rather, as heirs of John Calvin, the Princetonians took for granted that some of God's truths would not go down well with the modern Pharisees and the Philistines of the world. Ignominy and calumny, however, did not make those truths any less true. Real Christianity, the Princetonians taught, meant putting Christ and his Word above all worldly concerns, no matter how awkward they might feel about it.

For obvious reasons, Princeton theologians became the revered godfathers of creationists and conservative evangelicals throughout the twentieth century. Thoughtful armchair theologians reverently cited eminences like Charles Hodge and his fellow Princetonian B. B. Warfield as the intellectual heavyweights who conclusively proved the continuing need for fidelity to Bible truths in modern America.[17]

In spite of what so many twentieth-century creationists have assumed, however, Princeton's theologians did not dislike the idea of evolution. Rather, though they would never have changed their thinking merely to keep up with changing times, leading thinkers such as Charles Hodge embraced evolutionary thinking as part and parcel of God's eternal plan.[18]

It makes some sense for today's radical creationists to assume Hodge was on their side. After all, the often-quoted conclusion from his 1874 book seems to spell it out. "What is Darwinism?" Hodge asked. The answer was clear: "It is Atheism."[19]

But Hodge didn't mean that the idea of evolution was atheistic. The idea of evolution itself was obvious and Christian. God had a plan. Things did not simply stay the same but changed as God's plan unfolded. Darwinism, however, was not the same as evolution. Darwin sought to rob evolution of design, to strip God's plan of both plan and God.

The sticking point, for Hodge, was Darwin's idea of natural selection as the driving force behind evolution. If you believed that changes piled up over time based on their accidental successes, you couldn't also believe that species and individuals were designed by an eternal and loving God.

If we understand the basic truths of authentic Christianity, Hodge reasoned, then we will see this truth plainly and clearly. Those basic truths included the notion that God was first. God was "infinite, eternal, and unchangeable in his being, wisdom, power, holiness, goodness, and truth."[20] God explained himself and his truths to us as clearly as he could. He gave us the Bible, an "infallible authority."[21] More than that, he came to live among us as Jesus Christ. If we follow Christ, and hearken to the Bible, we follow God. If we do anything else, we spurn him.

Though Darwin didn't admit it, Hodge insisted, Darwin spurned. When Darwin hypothesized a process that shut out God's grand design, he inadvertently called Christ a liar and the Bible a lie. After all, Hodge wrote, Christ told his disciples that God was a loving, personal God, a nearby presence, not an interminable process. God cared about every lily, every sparrow, every blade of grass. As Hodge put it, "Christ brings God constantly near to us."[22]

At best, Darwin's notion of an indifferent process as the mechanism of evolution did the opposite; it drove God ever farther away. If you were a true Christian, you believed the testimony of the Bible. If you were a true Christian, you believed the words of Christ. Both give us a universe infinitely better than the hardscrabble Darwinian system.

And with his customary piercing acumen, Hodge ruthlessly punctured the usual intellectual refuges of those who wanted to keep their religion while accepting Darwin's popular idea. In his day, Hodge warned, lots of self-identified Christians hoped vainly that Darwinism and Christianity could go hand in hand. To Hodge, such optimists were deluded at best.[23] Some theistic evolutionists hoped that God might have created, then left evolutionary processes at play to do the rest. Inconceivable, Hodge thundered. One could not assume that "since the first creation of matter and life, God has left the universe to the control of unintelligent physical causes." At least, one could not do so and still "retain his faith in Christ." If God had created and retreated, Hodge reasoned, "there have been no supernatural revelation, no miracles; Christ is not risen, and we are yet in our sins."[24]

Nor could naive modern Christians hope to segregate science from faith and leave each to their separate, non-overlapping magisteria, as some argued in Hodge's day and have argued ever since.[25] Religion was not merely a "state of feeling," Hodge argued, and could never be banished from the "domain of science." All truths were the same, Hodge insisted, and restricting God's truths meant a blasphemous attempt to restrict God himself.[26]

As American Christians wondered in the 1870s what they should do about the Darwinian revolution, Hodge gave them a clear answer, even if many missed the subtlety. The idea of evolution—in the broadest sense—was fine, Hodge assured them. Darwin's version of life that changed via its own processes, however, was not. Without faith in God's plan, Darwinists were not Christian, whatever they might call themselves. Real Christianity meant faith in Christ and the Bible. Both testified to God's close, personal involvement with every living thing. To endorse Darwin's mechanism of natural selection was to reject their testimony. It was the same as rejecting Christianity as a whole.

And yet for all his rock-ribbedness, Charles Hodge leavened his vitriol with a curious dose of conditionality. "Are we to give up the Bible and all our hopes," Hodge asked plaintively, for a mere hypothesis? When even Darwin's most fervent supporters agree "that it has not been proved that any one species has thus originated?" Are we supposed to abandon our religion, our dreams of salvation, our faith in a universe lovingly designed by a God who lived among us and lives within us for Darwin's impersonal process? The obvious answer for Hodge was a ringing no; yet in that ringing answer linger curious tones of conditionality, of what-if. We can't give up our religion, Hodge writes, *if* Darwin's alternative has not been proven.[27]

The implication is both strange and unavoidable. If Professor Hodge were to see satisfying proof of Darwin's hypothesis, would he then give up his religion after all?

A Hundred Years Without Darwin Are Not Enough

Luckily for Hodge, he never had to. When he died in 1878, just a few years after he published *What Is Darwinism?*, the scientific questions about Darwin's hypothesis remained just as troubling as ever. Indeed, it was not until much later that the significant problems of Darwin's hypothesis were figured out.

As mentioned in the last chapter, Darwin's ideas gained their true explanatory power in the light of modern genetics. Darwin couldn't figure out how some helpful variations would be passed along. If one group of frogs, for example, expressed a helpful mutation, it would disappear as soon as they interbred with regular frogs. At least, that's what Darwin assumed would happen.

The once obscure genetic theories of Gregor Mendel, however, showed that some genetic traits can survive latently, even if they are not expressed. Moreover, offspring do not evenly mix the traits of their two parents. Rather, genetic traits are passed down in a more complicated manner. Our mutant frogs would maintain the helpful variation in their DNA, even if some of their tadpoles didn't show it. If the mutation helped in a given environment, the population of frogs that did express it would tend to survive in greater numbers, passing along the tendency. The once mutant frogs would become a population of a new species of frog, for the time being better suited to their environment.

In Hodge's time, Darwin and other leading scientists hadn't made those connections. By the middle of the twentieth century, however, they had. As historian Edward Larson explained, by the 1950s the "modern evolutionary synthesis" had become "dogma" among mainstream scientists.[28] Not that it was seen as a religious idea, but it was taken to be a central truth of modern science, what leading paleontologist George Gaylord Simpson called "one of the basic facts and characteristics of the objective world."[29]

Evangelical Christians in the 1950s were confronted, then, with a very different objective world than the one Charles Hodge saw outside his Princeton windows. By the 1950s, Christians had to wrestle with the notion that mainstream science was evolutionary science, along the lines that Darwin had laid out and that Hodge had condemned as atheistic. Evangelical Christians were again on the defensive, coping with newly strident evolutionary science. Mainstream science had become intensely confident in its neo-Darwinian ideas. Mainstream scientists, like Professor Simpson, began to clamor angrily that "One Hundred Years Without Darwin Are Enough."[30]

What were evangelicals to do? Just as in the 1870s, when they turned to scientists and theologians such as Asa Gray and Charles Hodge, in the 1950s and 1960s Christians embraced a variety of creationist answers.

Some evangelical scholars agreed with Simpson. Most famously, Bernard Ramm blasted his fellow evangelicals' tendency to put their scientific heads in the biblical sand. Ramm never wanted to talk anyone out of creationism. But as an evangelical theologian, he was intensely frustrated with the untenable intellectual position he had been forced into.

The "modern mind," Ramm complained, pooh-poohed the need for theology. In his 1954 book *The Christian View of Science and Scripture*, Ramm wanted to turn that century-old tendency on its head. He wanted to re-sacralize science and re-scientize theology.[31] As Ramm put it, evangelicals had been squeezed into only two ridiculous choices: either "fiat, instantaneous creationism" or "atheistic developmentalism." It was a "gross over-simplification" of the real dilemma of creation and evolution, Ramm insisted.[32]

On the one hand, Ramm minced no words in his critique of hard-nosed radical creationism. Such folks, whom Ramm called the "hyperorthodox," had abandoned all pretense to thought and reason; they had retreated from "logic and experimentation"; they "lacked the measured control of cultured men."[33]

Authentic Christians, Ramm argued, needed to have more confidence in God. They needed to have faith that God's revelation could never be disproven by mere scientific exploration. Evangelicals, Ramm insisted, must overcome the traditional "narrow hyper-dogmatic attitude toward science" that had come to define radical-creationist thinking.[34]

Good theology would never require Christians to hold their intellectual noses and swallow bad science. With God as the source of all truth, there was no way that good research of any sort could prove him wrong.

Anyone who teaches that humanity first appeared on earth only 6,000 years ago, or who insisted on a real, literal worldwide flood, Ramm wrote, wasn't just peddling bad science. Such ideas were bad theology as well. They were needless misinterpretations of Scripture. They were needlessly introducing conflict between good science and good religion.[35]

But Professor Ramm did not suggest evangelicals surrender to science. Too many theologians, Ramm believed, had foolishly abandoned the scientific field. The doctrine of creation was a central part of real Christianity. Whatever else Christians might find out through theological thought and scientific research, they must never abandon their creationism. God created. And the universe God created had a divine purpose. In other words, life was not a collection of accidents, but a story with both an author and a plot.

This fundamental truth of creation allowed Christians to do more than merely accept scientific ideas. Christians—creationists—could take the lead. Creationists could reject the artifices of radical creationism and claim an intellectual vitality that many secular scientists could not. While too many modern scientists fumbled around the edges of truth, Christians could explain the true meaning of every discovery. If Christians had real faith, they would never need to retreat from modern science, but rather they could insist with confidence that their truths would soon be approached by scientific discovery.

For example, Ramm pointed to "recent studies in astrophysics" that suggested a single moment of creation from nothingness. Godless astrophysicists could not explain it, but Christians could.[36] Similarly, atomic weapons had left secular scientists agog with their own destructive power. Scientists lacked the ability to think clearly about the morality of such discoveries. Secular science—an intellectual adolescent that had foolishly cast away its religious foundations—"now realizes it has need of moral safeguards which it is not able to produce of itself."[37] As science matured, it would realize the value of its own religious roots.

Creationism was the answer. A certain kind of creationism, at least. The radical answer of the young-earth crowd was no good. There was absolutely no need to cower from modern discoveries about the age of the earth and of the human species. Plus, it was both bad religion and bad science to insist on truths that made no sense. A sun that went around the earth, a humanity born in 4004 B.C.E., a worldwide flood that deposited all the fossils at once . . . such ideas had been decisively disproven by scientific inquiry. To insist upon them was not only scientifically outlandish. It was also theologically ridiculous. A true understanding of the Scriptures never led to such anti-scientific conclusions.

It couldn't. Ramm argued that true Christianity meant having faith that all truths came from the same divine source. Scientists and theologians could make mistakes, for sure, but real science and real theology could never fall out of harmony.

However, Christians did not need to assume that today's science was the right answer. Mainstream science had taken the wrong course when it pushed aside the eternal lessons of Scripture. And too many liberal theologians had rushed foolishly to help push. Those liberal Christians erred grievously in assuming that the Bible's truths could be explained away as mere myth or poem.

There was another way, a better way. Real Christians were creationists. They knew that God had created. They did not need to insist, however, that he had done so in the past 10,000 years only. They did not need to insist that the flood covered the entire earth during Noah's time. They did not need to insist that evolutionary science was an absolute lie meant to fool the unwary.

But neither did they have to assume that mainstream science provided all the answers.

Christians could take the lead in both science and theology. They could accept the contributions of mainstream science, knowing that their Christian truth would always prevail. Evangelical intellectuals could rest easy in their faith, but they could never rest. They must learn the latest discoveries in science, hoping to discover more details of God's creation.

In short, in the face of the new confidence of mainstream evolutionary science, Bernard Ramm offered evangelicals a better way to be creationists. They did not need to insist that mainstream science was satanic. They did not need to abandon their faith. They did not need to assert outlandish scientific ideas of their own as "creation science." Instead, they could embrace an old idea that Ramm resuscitated: "progressive creationism."[38] Instead of walling themselves off from the modern intellectual world, creationists could reclaim their rightful place as its leaders.

Ramm's message resonated with a new generation of evangelical intellectuals. Like Ramm, many American creationists struggled to understand how they should come to terms with evolutionary science. Many of them had studied at secular universities and had been duly impressed by the arguments in favor of the modern evolutionary synthesis. The only reason so many Christians rebelled against it, they felt, was due to an unhealthy defensive attitude.

One biologist at Wheaton College—a school historians have called "the Fundamentalist Harvard"[39]—pulled together his fellow evangelical scientists to explore and extend Ramm's argument. It was possible, Russell Mixter insisted, to embrace both science and Scripture; to remain a fervent creationist while acknowledging the incontrovertible evidence for evolution. Indeed, to do anything else seemed like a very anti-Christian abandonment of faith in God's goodness and power. Would a loving God create false evidence of an ancient earth and an evolutionary process just to fool twentieth-century scientists? Would God really want his followers to close their eyes to obvious scientific advances?

In 1959, to mark the centenary of Darwin's *Origin of Species*, Professor Mixter gathered the thoughts of this creationist movement into a new book: *Evolution and Christian Thought Today*.[40] Its authors did not push for a single way to be a creationist. As one author wrote, thoughtful creationists could and did disagree. There was more than one way to understand God's creative process. Modern science hadn't and couldn't disprove that. Rather, modern science had pushed creationists to think of new and better ways to understand God's creative process. Intelligent creationists did not abandon their religion when they learned about scientific advances; they improved it.[41]

As James O. Buswell III of Wheaton's anthropology department argued, Ramm was right. Too many evangelical Christians had been fooled by the false promises of hyper-orthodoxy, of fundamentalism and radical young-earth creationism. They didn't know enough about either real science or real Christianity to see the obvious truth. Ideas such as a young earth or an instantaneous fiat creation of every kind of plant and animal didn't make sense. They weren't in the scientific record, and they weren't in the scriptural record. Rather, such notions were radical fundamentalist add-ons to authentic religion. In the words of Professor Buswell, they were "peripheral, relative, and changeable interpretations" that too many well-meaning Christians had seen as real scriptural absolutes.[42]

For the intellectuals gathered around Professor Mixter at the "Fundamentalist Harvard," a new creationist day had dawned. Some of the advances of mainstream science were indeed indisputable. Species really had changed. The earth really was ancient. Accepting those truths, these new evangelicals argued, did not mean abandoning creationism. Rather, it only meant an improvement, a maturation.

Real creationism, whether it remained progressive creationism or a more evolution-friendly theistic evolution, meant maintaining faith in the intellectual supremacy of God's revelation. The Bible never lied. If there seemed to be disharmony between science and Scripture about the age of the earth, the problem might be in the science. By the mid-1950s, Professor Ramm and his fans had decided that it wasn't. Mainstream science seemed correct. Even if the Godless descriptions of some mainstream scientists missed the point, progressive creationists argued, mainstream science had answered the big questions correctly. Progressive creationists did not agree with mainstream scientists about how species changed, but they agreed on the basic fact that species changed.

The problem, then, wasn't in the science, and it wasn't in Scripture. Instead, it must be in foolish fundamentalist interpretations of Scripture.

Not surprisingly, many fundamentalists disagreed.

This disagreement was the second crucial moment in the history of American creationism. If nineteenth-century American evangelical Christians wondered whether to listen to Asa Gray or Charles Hodge, in the twentieth century and ever since they have been torn between evolution-friendly ideas about creation or a radical young-earth alternative.

In order to understand America's true dilemmas about creationism and evolutionary theory, we must make sense of the reasons why the radical choice seems attractive to so many conservative evangelical Protestants. Crucially, we need to see that radicals do not really hate evolutionary theory as such. Instead, for most radical creationists, the "attitudes of evolution and all that" are the problem.

Time and again, radical creationists have bundled evolution together with other trends in American culture, such as secularization, loosening moral traditions, and a generally diversifying population. And they have loathed specifically the "attitudes" with which all that has been foisted on them and on their society.

We need to ask: If radical creationists can agree with Bernard Ramm on the importance of Scripture and the necessity of God's creation, what do they disagree about?

Our first evidence will be the work of Henry Morris and John Whitcomb Jr. Henry Morris might not have held a faculty post at the "Fundamentalist Harvard," but he had a respectable PhD from the University of Minnesota. And his degree might not have been in pure science, but it was in the scientific field of hydraulic engineering. And John Whitcomb Jr. didn't teach at Princeton or Harvard, but he had respectable evangelical credentials, teaching at Grace Theological Seminary in Winona Lake, Indiana.

Like many fundamentalists, Whitcomb and Morris seethed at Ramm's charges of sloppy faith and anti-intellectualism. In their 1961 book *The Genesis Flood*, they hoped to set the record straight.

As we saw in the last chapter, Whitcomb and Morris didn't give any ground to the premise that mainstream evolutionary science had won the scientific day. *The Genesis Flood* refuted point by point the apparent superiority of such supposed science. Was it true that a worldwide flood was geologically and hydrologically impossible? Not at all! Was it true that new techniques had demonstrated the ancient age of the earth? No, not if we keep our minds open to the evidence before us.

Whitcomb and Morris reassured evangelical readers that real scientists had given up their evolutionary hypothesis; real scientists could see "there is no evidence of present-day biological change, except within small limits."[43] Whitcomb and Morris admitted that there was "widespread acceptance" of mainstream evolutionary ideas, but there was in fact only "a small amount of actual scientific evidence in favor of it!"[44]

If that was the case, Christians might wonder, why did everyone from Russell Mixter to George Gaylord Simpson seem so confident that evolutionary science was the heart and soul of real science? According to Whitcomb and Morris, most mainstream scientists suffered from a curious kind of anti-Christian myopia. They had been blinded by their "evolutionary basis and bias."[45] By assuming that geological processes now were the same as they had always been, mainstream scientists made the fundamental intellectual error of basing their conclusions on their assumptions rather than on the evidence.

If, instead, Christians did what they should have been doing all along, if they simply took the Bible seriously, they could see a much better way of understanding the history of life on earth. Instead of a "uniformitarian" view of the distant past, Whitcomb and Morris suggested a catastrophic vision. The earth's history did not unfold in long ages, with layers of geologic evidence piling up over millions of years. Rather, sudden cataclysms and catastrophes chopped history into very different sorts of epochs.

If different physical rules applied at different times in the past, then the assumptions of mainstream scientists would lead them to wildly incorrect conclusions. And that, in fact, was what had happened. According to Whitcomb and Morris, scientists who assumed that the earth's crust formed as slowly in the past as it did in the present could certainly conclude that the earth must be millions of years old. But better scientists—creation scientists—could see the truth. Creation scientists understood that time was not uniform, but rather staggered by periodic catastrophes that shook up and speeded up geologic processes. How could they know? Because they had proof from the most reliable witness in the universe, the Bible. The Bible revealed these scientific truths as plainly as it could. Only scientists stubbornly committed to ignoring the Bible's obvious lessons would miss them.

There was a real, literal Eden, for example, where later rules of life and time simply did not apply. Not just Adam and Eve, but also all creation sang with Edenic glory. Plants grew without thorns and thistles; vegetarian tigers cavorted without blemish or corruption.[46] The Fall and expulsion from the garden served as a dramatic divide in the history of the planet. Things before Eve ate the apple were simply not the same as things afterward. A literal worldwide flood, too, punctuated the earth's history and left traces that some mistaken scientists had interpreted in erroneous ways. By opening our minds to the evidence in the Bible—the only trustworthy evidence about the earth's ancient history[47]—could we hope to make sense of our geological and biological past.

At least as important as their argument that real science always sided with real revelation, however, were Whitcomb's and Morris's theological claims. For authentic Christians, they argued, evolutionary theory simply couldn't be true. Though some good Christians might accept evolution by mistake, once they learned the truth every Christian should hasten to adopt a young-earth position.

Like Charles Hodge in the 1800s, Whitcomb and Morris insisted that they were only stating the obvious: True Christianity required faith in Christ and the Bible. For Christians, the Bible was the source of all truth. Some parts were certainly meant to be taken figuratively, as when Christ told his listeners they were the salt of the earth. But parts that were clearly intended as the literal truth must be understood that way.

If readers picked and chose what parts they wanted to take literally, they were putting themselves ahead of God. Nothing in Genesis suggested that it be taken as anything other than its obvious meaning. It was obviously a story of how life and everything came to be created by God. Any other interpretation stretched the truth in order to make the Bible say what the reader wanted it to say, instead of the other way around.

If there were any doubt, Christians must always accept the words of Jesus himself. As Whitcomb and Morris argued, it seemed striking that "our Lord made a special point of choosing His illustrations and warnings from those portions of the Old Testament that would become objects of unbelieving scorn and ridicule throughout the coming centuries."[48] God knew that scientists in 1859 or 1959 would offer tempting explanations to turn people away from their faith. God knew that his people would wonder over and over if they should accept the seemingly obvious notions of the non-Christians all around them. And so God endorsed the words of the whole Bible; God even underlined those sections that the false prophets of modern pseudo-science would find most outrageous.

The false prophets gave fair warning, according to Whitcomb and Morris. Mainstream scientists, unlike some wayward evangelical theologians, made no pretense that their ideas could accord with Christian belief. "All the prominent founders of the modern theory of evolution" Whitcomb and Morris explained, "were firm opponents of the entire Biblical view of the world and of man." In their day, leading scientists, such as George Gaylord Simpson, trumpeted the essentially anti-Christian nature of evolutionary theory. Evolution, Simpson wrote, meant that humanity could free itself from the "superstition" of religious belief. Evolution, Simpson wrote, meant that humanity was an organism like any other, definitely "not the darling of the gods."[49]

At its heart, *The Genesis Flood* offered American evangelicals a sharp choice. No matter what Bernard Ramm might say, there were really only "two basic philosophies or religions among mankind."[50] The first was Christianity. The second was based on the idea of evolution. Evolution was at heart an anti-God philosophy, a way of thinking about the universe that cut God loose from its foundation and center.

Evolution put human knowledge first; Christianity relied on God's wisdom. The two were fundamentally opposed. And *The Genesis Flood* left Christian readers in no doubt which side was which. Evolution, Whitcomb and Morris wrote, "must have its source in the pride and selfishness of man and ultimately in the pride and deception of the great adversary, Satan himself."[51]

If mainstream scientists wanted to shout that a hundred years without Darwin were enough, let them. If some foolish Christians hoped to incorporate those Darwinian ideas into their pseudo-religion, so be it. But for Whitcomb and Morris and many of the young-earth creationists inspired by *The Genesis Flood*, real religion meant something much clearer and much grander. Evolution was not new, not modern. Evolution was as old as the serpent in the garden. Like Eve, modern Christians faced a stark choice: sin or fidelity; pride in false knowledge or humble acceptance of God's eternal Truth.

Attitudes of Evolution

Faced with such a theological quandary, it becomes a little easier to see why evolution represents such a difficult idea for so many religious people. For me and people like me, it's not. For me, evolutionary theory seems like a straightforward bit of scientific thinking. Evolutionary theory isn't capital-T True, necessarily, but it is our best current understanding of the ways species came to be different from one another. If new evidence comes along to change that idea, fine.

For some folks, however, that kind of thought process represents an intense religious dilemma. Accepting the status of evolutionary theory as the best understanding of the emergence of species would mean repudiating the theology they have always held to be true.

If we really want to get a handle on the nature of American creationism, though, we can't stop there. Yes, creationism of one kind or another is taken to be a theological necessity by many Americans. But creationism is more than just a theological idea; creationism is more than just an intellectual choice made by creationists. Like all of us, creationists believe what they believe for an inextricably tangled combination of reasons.

Creationism, as Dan Kahan of Yale Law School puts it, is not only about what people know. It is more precisely an expression of who they are.[52] This notion helps explain the strange poll numbers we saw in chapter 1. For many creationists, that is, their identity as creationists is clear, but the details of what that means are not. It is easy to line up on the side of creationism or evolution, but it is far more difficult to suss out the details of either system of thinking.

And, as educational anthropologist David Long argues, we'll never understand radical creationism if we think of it as simply as a decision or a religious idea. We need to get deeper, Long writes, to see why and how some creationists view evolution as something "troublesome or even dangerous."[53] As Long suggests, "For Creationists, evolution . . . is simply a straw man or placeholder for a larger and much deeper conflict of ideologies or worldviews."[54]

Yes, most radical creationists, like West Virginia's Rev. Avis Hill, think of evolution as theologically damnable. And that matters. But it is not the whole story. For many radical creationists, evolution is part and parcel of everything bad in society. Somehow, evolutionary thinking is connected to everything foul, everything mysterious, and everything devilish. Evolution is seen not merely as a scientific idea that may or may not be true but also as the tool used by scheming secularists to disrupt Christian faith and wholesome social norms. As Rev. Hill explained, it is not only evolution that is the problem but also the "attitudes" and "all that" go with evolutionary thinking.

Radical creationists have always insisted that the problem with evolution was more than theological. In every decade, in every culture-war battle, radical creationists have simply assumed that they were fighting for everything good and decent. They were not only engaging in a theological dispute, they were also battling for the very soul of America.

The most prominent radical creationist of the 1920s, William Jennings Bryan, certainly disapproved of the religious implications of Darwin's theory.

But he insisted that his "chief concern" was different. The real problem of Darwin's "groundless hypothesis," the real reason it caused "incalculable harm" was due to the "demoralization" involved.[55] In a world in which Darwin's idea were accepted as true, young people would have no way to be moral, no way to distinguish right from wrong. Yes, Darwinism was theologically wrong, but of more immediate danger was the social chaos that it would lead to.

Radical-creationist preachers and pundits have always tied evolutionary thinking to every moral hazard of American life. In 1964, for example, Bob Jones Jr., president of fundamentalist Bob Jones University in South Carolina, warned that evolutionary theory must be understood as more than just a scientific idea. Evolution, Jones warned, was as "equally satanic and equally dangerous" as other dangers, including Catholicism and communism. All of them spewed forth as part of Satan's "attack upon the citadel of faith."[56]

Other fundamentalist leaders agreed. In 1980, Jerry Falwell implored America to *Listen!* to his plea. Evolutionary teaching was obviously at the heart of everything terrible in modern society. It just made sense. If you teach kids that they are just a "biological machine," the Rev. Falwell reasoned, they will predictably chuck everything good and decent out the window. They will wallow in their "sexual immorality." They will fight against "basic values such as morality, individualism, respect for our nation's heritage, and the benefits of the free-enterprise system."[57]

From the 1920s to the 1980s, radical-creationism's culture warriors fought about much more than science and religion. In fact, because so few people had clear understandings of either the science or theology involved, most of the debate about creationism has been on other grounds. Radical creationists all agreed that evolution was both the cause and the primary symptom of America's social blight. They all agreed with Rev. Hill that the real problem was not evolutionary theory alone, but "all that" came along with it. And today's radical-creationist leaders make similar sorts of all-encompassing moral arguments. In the late twentieth and early twenty-first centuries, no one has made this case more clearly or more powerfully than leading creationist pundits such as Henry Morris and Ken Ham.

Morris didn't pull any punches. Evolutionary thinking and teaching, Morris explained, didn't just rob Christians of salvation. It had also wrecked American society. Take your pick of social ills, Morris wrote, and you'll find evolution at their root. In modern times, America had more evolution than ever in its schools. The result? Skyrocketing rates of "premarital sex, adultery, divorce, and homosexuality." That's not all. America was suffering from "unrestrained pornography. . . . Prostitution, both male and female, is at an all-time high, as is its attendant criminal activity."[58]

Want to know how "abortionism" moved from "criminality to respectability"?[59] All you need to understand is the sinister influence of evolutionary thinking. Such thinking, Morris argued, degrades respect for life itself. It was no stretch to see why euthanasia was on the rise. Indeed, it was no stretch to connect Darwin's devilish evolutionary thinking to the Nazi Holocaust, an event Morris called "the fruit of two generations of evolutionary racism."[60]

No taboo is too sacred for evolution to smash, Morris argued. For instance, there is no reason not to expect evolutionary thinking to lead to cannibalism. If people are just accidents, after all, why not? The truly disgusting ideas were not cannibalism or gas chambers, Morris repeated. Such things were only symptoms, reasonable conclusions to draw from the pernicious logic of evolutionary thinking.[61]

Everywhere you look, Morris warned, you can expect to see more of the same. Everything bad, from abortion, to Nazis, to homosexuality—all resulted predictably from evolutionary thinking. Everything, including a seemingly haphazard Devil's grab bag of "the modern drug crisis (rock music, peer pressure, organized crime, etc.)" could be laid at the feet of "the evolutionary philosophy."[62]

It's easy enough for people like me to poke fun at this sort of scattershot get-off-my-lawn polemic, but Morris's warnings demonstrate more than just one man's cranky idiosyncratic vision. For Morris and his radical-creationist fellows, evolution means more than just a scientific idea, more than even a specific theological hazard. For some creationists, listening to evolutionary ideas was tantamount to considering the possible benefits of cannibalism, Nazism, and, yes, even sex, drugs, and rock and roll. Plus organized crime.

Nor is Morris alone in his broad-brush condemnation of the vast social implications of evolutionary thinking. Morris's former protégé, Ken Ham, agrees that evolution had led America into a terrifying "moral decay."[63] Ham lines up some of the usual suspects. The sinister influence of evolution could be blamed for the legalization of abortion; for the growing acceptance of same-sex marriage; for the diminishing respect for Christian ideas in public schools; and even for the widespread efforts to turn Christmas into merely a "Happy Holiday."[64]

The only effective way to fight against these things, Ham explains, is to fight them at their evolutionary root. Without insisting on a real, historic, recent Adam and Eve, for example, there is no logical way for Christians to dispute same-sex marriage. In every case, creationism is the "foundation of this battle" for a moral society.[65] It was foolish and pointless to fight against social problems one by one, Ham reasons. They all came from the same source, and the battle against them must be a battle against evolutionary theory itself.

For many creationists, Ham's and Morris's warnings make sense. For the Rev. Hill, for example, the "attitudes of evolution and all that" went far beyond science and religion. Evolutionary thinking connoted a bundle of terrible social trends. For Hill and people like him, the connections didn't need to be spelled out; they were simply common sense. When textbooks and schools were based on a rotten moral foundation, it would be surprising if anything happened other than widespread moral decline.

When interviewers asked Hill why he didn't like Charleston's new textbooks, Hill could point them to a few specifics. In one section, for example, the new language-arts series suggested that teachers help their students "act out a street riot."[66] A street riot! For Hill, one didn't need to explain why that sort of thing was bad. Teachers were not meant to do such things, and young people were not meant to be encouraged to riot.

The whole book series, Hill explained, was full of "that garbage, that trash, that four-letter words."[67] But it was more than just the specific contents of the book series. When Hill condemned the books as reeking with the "attitudes of evolution and all that," he also meant that such evolutionary ideas had led to a total breakdown in society. These days, Hill explained, he "drive[s] by the schools and I see quart wine bottles and I see beer bottles and I see students drinking and I see them smoking their dope."[68]

Back when he was in school, "You didn't see students leaning against the wall with their feet on the wall dirtying and defacing the school with initials and names all over it."[69] What was to blame? The new morality, or better yet the new immorality, a cowardly abrogation of moral teaching that had resulted predictably from the teaching of the attitudes of evolution and all that.

It was not only the schools, Hill explained, but every moral issue. Those false Christians who had accepted evolutionary thinking also tended to be friendly to the "gays and homosexuals . . . and being proabortion." Only false Christians, Hill thought, could smile at such sins. And those false Christians wouldn't stop there. Without a moral rudder, they would embrace everything dangerous, even communism.[70]

It is hard to miss, too, in Hill's explanation of his reasons for opposing Charleston's new textbooks, an even more complicated aspect of the radical-creationist view of the world. For some creationists, like Morris and Ham, evolution was not only a damnable heresy. It was not only the cause of legalized abortion, communist-friendly policies, cannibalism, and Nazi genocide. For some creationists, evolution represented an imposition, a mind-bogglingly arrogant assumption by elite secular intellectuals that they have the truth on their side.

Unlike Charles Hodge and Asa Gray, after all, later generations of radical-creationist intellectuals weren't often hired by Harvard and Princeton. They had to open their own universities, such as Bob Jones and Liberty. They had to fund and found their own think tanks, such as the Institute for Creation Research and Answers in Genesis. And they had to deal, time and time again, with mainstream assumptions that creationism could only come from ignorance.

As Avis Hill explained, he was tired of being seen as a "backwoods fundamentalist Bible-toting, foot-stomping, Bible-thumping preacher."[71] When his fifth-grade daughter came home and told him that she had to write a book report about evolution, he told her she didn't have to. But the teacher disagreed. When the teacher insisted that the young Miss Hill give her report, she stood up instead and read from her Bible.

Did the teacher respect her wishes? No. Did the teacher understand or even listen to her objections? No. Did the teacher call Avis Hill and talk with him about his family's views on evolution? Not once. Instead, the teacher simply gave the girl an F. For Avis Hill and his daughter, standing for what they viewed as both true and right pushed them to fight against arrogant authority figures who never even pretended to listen to their side.

Hearing, as creationists so often did, that every scientific authority had accepted evolutionary theory wouldn't matter. Nor would it even be a surprise. Evolution was a lie, the root of every social malady. It came from the Devil himself, and puffed up the heads of those who chose to take his seductive bait. As had Charles Hodge and so many Christians before and since, creationists like Henry Morris, Ken Ham, Avis Hill, and his daughter would never truckle to any idea simply because of its popularity.

Choosing Sides

Understanding our real culture-war battles about creationism will require understanding this complicated mix of sources and reasons; we need to see radical young-earth creationism as it really is. We can't assume that it is only a religious idea, although it is. We can't assume that it is mainly a political position, although it is that too. We can't assume that creationism primarily comes from a lack of exposure to our modern ways of thinking, although, in some cases, it certainly does.

Like Avis Hill's vague but powerful protest against his town's new textbooks, radical creationism is an attitude. It is a protest against something besides a specific scientific idea. It is a protest against a certain way of seeing the world, as well as a protest against a host of social trends.

For many radical creationists, the problem is not really evolutionary theory, but the changes in society that have accompanied the widespread acceptance of evolutionary theory. When radical creationists look askance at evolution, it is primarily because they mistrust the uses to which evolutionary theory will be put. As we'll see in more detail in chapter 7, even the most radical young-earth creationists often teach their children evolutionary science, but they do so without the "all that" that bedeviled Rev. Hill and his allies.

Creationism is better understood as a way of being American. It is just as complicated and just as simple as every other sort of social identity, and it means things for creationists that might not make sense to the rest of us.

For example, for Avis Hill's daughter, creationism meant defending her father against her teacher. For followers of Ken Ham, it can mean saying "Merry Christmas" instead of "Happy Holidays." For those who agree with Henry Morris, it can mean a resolute stand against drug use, rock music, and organized crime.

For people like me, accepting new advances in evolutionary science is a relatively straightforward affair. I think of them as improvements in a never-perfect way of understanding the world.

For some creationists, however, the same ideas might represent something far different. If evolution represents everything bad, it makes some sense to fight against it, no matter how many people disagree. If evolution is a re-pudiation of my family, my friends, my school, and my church, it certainly makes some sense that I wouldn't want to accept it. More important, if evo-lution represents a sinister social experiment, no amount of explanation is likely to persuade its opponents. If evolution is seen as a conspiracy foisted by scheming leftists—by everyone from Abbie Hoffman to Al Gore—it is not difficult to see why it generates such ferocious, durable resistance and resentment.[72]

It is vital to keep in mind that the most heated culture-war battles about creationism are not really about evolutionary science itself. Yes, evolutionary theory is swept up in every disagreement. In the end, though, the many Americans who embrace radical-creationist thinking are embracing something more than just a specific evangelical theology or scientific theory. Instead, they hope to make America great again, to fight against the grasping arrogance of generations of "experts" who have cast them heedlessly aside as nothing but a "basket of deplorables."[73]

4

What Not to Know and How Not
to Know It

They were totally wrong, but they had a good excuse. Back in 1922, when the
editors of the Louisville *Courier-Journal* made a big goof about creationism,
the public fight about creationism was just getting started. The Louisville
editors couldn't know yet what the relationship would be between education
and creationism, and it's not fair to blame them for not predicting the future.
We've got no such excuse. With almost a full extra century of hindsight, the
connections between creationism and schools are much clearer. Pundits who
dismiss creationism as merely an absence of knowledge—or only a wacky
commitment to a ludicrous idea—have only their own stubborn ignorance
to blame.

Back then, Kentucky's lawmakers were seriously considering the nation's
first proposed law to ban evolution from the state's public schools. The
editors of the Louisville newspaper felt obliged to take a stand against it. It
was a courageous move at the time—the bill had enormous political support.
Opponents were often tarred as both anti-Christian and anti-American.

So when the Louisville editors implored readers to "stop and think," they
should be given credit for their bravery. But their reasons were almost entirely wrongheaded. If evolution were banned, the editors warned, there
"would be little left for [schools] to teach."[1]

From the twenty-first century perspective, it's easy to see that the editors
were dead wrong. Not for their stand against radical-creationist rule in public
schools. Then and now, we all need to fight to keep our public schools free of
religious imposition. It's something radical creationists should want just as
much as secular folks, but that's an argument for chapter 7. In this chapter,
we'll talk about the future the Louisville editors couldn't have foreseen.

If the twentieth century has shown us anything, it's that the editors' argument was almost the exact opposite of true. Schools don't wither without evolution. Rather, creationist schools have even more to do. As this chapter will
explore, the young-earth strain of radical creationism—the kind that puts

Creationism USA. Adam Laats, Oxford University Press (2021). © Oxford University Press.
DOI: 10.1093/oso/9780197516607.001.0001.

dinosaurs on Noah's ark and assumes the Grand Canyon was created in a few turbulent weeks—can only thrive *because of* formal education and schooling, not in spite of it.

Before we can understand the real reasons for our continuing battles about creationism, we need to understand how these radical-creationists schools work. As we'll see in this chapter, the distinguishing feature of radical-creationist institutions is not that they teach specific creationist ideas, but rather that they relentlessly preach a sweeping distrust of mainstream thinking.

The distrust of mainstream scientists at the heart of radical creationism has always extended to a distrust of mainstream institutions as well. Beginning in the early 1900s, creationists worried that colleges and universities had begun attacking the faith of their children. In response, creationists established and nurtured a trustworthy creationist network of institutions. As we'll see, those institutions don't ignore evolution. In fact, they often promise to teach students a lot about evolution. But they promise to do so in a safely creationist environment, that is, an environment creationists can trust not to undermine the faith of young people.

The most important of these institutions are schools: From pre-kindergarten through graduate school, creationists have their own flourishing network of day schools, vacation Bible schools, colleges, and graduate programs. And if creationist parents want to yank their kids from school and teach them at home, there is no shortage of support. There are creationist textbook publishers and curriculum designers to supply everything schools and homeschoolers might need, including creationist science textbooks and everything else, from history books and chemistry labs to creationism-friendly yearbooks and class rings.[2]

Outside of school, too, creationists can rely on a bustling network of institutions, from conventions and church speakers to summer camps and sports leagues.[3] As we'll see in this chapter, one of the best known and most eye-opening of these institutions is the Creation Museum in Kentucky, a sprawling complex that offers a nearby life-size replica of Noah's ark.

It's hard not to wonder: What would Louisville's 1922 editors make of all this?

As we'll see, radical creationism is a big part of the message of these institutions. We'll get only a partial and skewed understanding of them, though, if we only look at the ways they talk about evolution and creation. Rather, we need to understand young-earth creationist schools and institutions as what they really are: Not just mainstream schools with creationism added in, but rather a fully coherent alternative world in which young-earth creationism seems obvious, informed, intellectually satisfying, and overwhelmingly morally superior.

Yes, radical-creationist schools teach creationism, but they do much more than that. They create a social and intellectual world in which students can be creationists without giving up their sense of being educated. In creationist schools, students learn that radical creationism is part of a superior intellectual and religious system. Even if one doesn't grasp all the nuances, one can be confident that the system itself is far better than the deluded notions on offer at mainstream schools. Most important, radical creationist schools teach students not to trust anyone outside of this charmed circle of righteousness. If any mainstream evidence seems convincing or appealing, students are encouraged to remember the flawed source.

The best way to understand creationist schools is to look beyond their creationist curricula and to try to comprehend the context in which those curricula makes sense. The big-picture goal of radical creationist education, as we'll see in this chapter, is not only to pass along creationist ideas but also to inculcate students in a way of thinking that will protect them from the dangerous ideas in mainstream society.

Evolution is one danger, of course, but it is not actual evolutionary science that presents the real problem. For many radical-creationist institutions, evolutionary thinking is only the most obvious expression of a damnable witches' brew of ideas and attitudes that threaten to lead the unwary into perdition. Creationist schools strive to equip students with an intellectual suit of armor that will protect them. The protection, though, is not really from evolutionary science itself but from the many supposed dangers that an atheistic way of thinking will lead.

In other words, radical-creationist institutions do not avoid the topic of evolutionary science. They do not merely teach and preach a different vision of the origin of species and the age of the universe, leaving evolutionary ideas out. Rather, students at radical-creationist schools and visitors to creation museums will hear a lot about evolution and mainstream scientific thinking. At each turn, however, they will be told about the dangers and supposed flaws of mainstream science. They will be told about the implications of evolutionary thinking, over and over, in often gruesome fashion.

After all, radical-creationist schools and museums are not meant to serve as permanent refuges from mainstream society. Students are not meant to live in Amish-style seclusion from an evolution-laden mainstream culture.

They do not have to choose between their American values and their crea-tionist ones. Rather, the radical-creationist school system hopes to prepare students to engage aggressively with warped mainstream values, to fight against liberalism and secularism, and to move the entirety of American society in a more creationism-friendly direction. It tries to imbue students with a thorough distrust of outside ideas, so that even the most convincing arguments will be recognized as merely more of Satan's lures.

Instead of thinking of the creationist institutional network as a retreat, then, we're better off considering it as a set of hothouses. Not refuges or asylums to protect children forever, but rather training grounds for young creationists, safe spaces where the young can prepare to venture safely into the wider culture without ever losing their radical creationist convictions.

Creationist U

In the twenty-first century, it is easy to see that the dreams of creationist school founders have largely been realized. In the 1920s, for instance, evan-gelist Bob Jones Sr. promised that his new college would be absolutely safe for creationist families. Jones emphasized first and foremost that parents could trust his new school to nurture their students' faiths, not attack them. As Jones put it in 1928, "fathers and mothers who place their sons and daugh-ters in our institution can go to sleep at night with no haunting fear that some skeptical teacher will steal the faith of their precious children."[4]

Back then, Bob Jones College (now Bob Jones University, or BJU) had to swim against the tide, in one sense. Sure, in the 1920s the Bob Jones style of radical creationism had a lot more public support. Institutionally, how-ever, the notion of a dedicated network of creationist schools was still new. Back then, most Bob Jones College students came from public schools. No longer. In 2010, for instance, only 10 percent of the incoming class at BJU came from public high schools. More than half had attended private, evan-gelical schools. An additional third had been homeschooled.[5]

The century-long dream of radical creationists had been fulfilled. They could send their children to securely creationist schools, from elementary all the way through graduate school. They didn't have to give up the traditional perks of American education, including sports, clubs, yearbooks, and stan-dardized tests. They could earn professional licenses and certifications, be-come lawyers, teachers, doctors, engineers, and more, without ever stepping out of the charmed circle of creationist institutions. The creationist school network was secure and satisfying.

How did this network come into being? It didn't start with kindergarten and work its way up. Rather, the school network began with schools like Bob Jones College: colleges and universities that sprouted in the 1920s and promised to keep young people safe from troubling modern ideas and immorality. Then and now, colleges and universities were the most important institutions in the creationist network. It was creationist colleges, after all, that trained creationist K–12 teachers. It was usually creationist colleges that printed textbooks for younger grades as well. And it was the network of creationist colleges that hosted conferences and professional development opportunities for creationist teachers at all levels.

Yes, these schools preach a very different sort of science, but creationist science is only a small part of the appeal of creationist colleges. The biggest allure for creationist families is the idea that creationist colleges will keep their children *safe*. Safe from mainstream science, for sure, but more importantly, safe from all the trends and tendencies that bedevil mainstream America.

In the 1800s, there was no need for a separate, dedicated creationist higher education system. Mainstream intellectual life had plenty of room for ardent creationism. By the 1910s, however, it was clear to many conservative evangelical intellectuals that things had changed in mainstream colleges and universities. Instead of inculcating students with Christian faith, leading schools had adopted a new attitude toward knowledge and the role of higher education. Schools that had been founded by evangelical Protestants—especially leading schools such as the University of Chicago, Duke, Northwestern, Yale, and many others—sought to teach students to be skeptical inquirers, delving into knowledge with an open mind.

At many schools, evolutionary theory served as both a symbol and a symptom of this academic revolution. As opposed to old-school colleges and universities, modern ones enthused about the potential of modern science. Modern research universities rushed to show their disdain for catechisms and orthodox religious assumptions. They competed vigorously with one another for top professors. They wanted desperately to join sophisticated European universities in their attitude toward knowledge and modernity.

For many, evolutionary theory seemed to capture the mood and the method of the new approach to knowledge and university life. As historian Jon H. Roberts put it so well, Darwin's ideas about evolution "effectively cut the Gordian knot between science and supernaturalism" at leading universities. It was no longer kosher, in other words, to explain nature by invoking God.[6] Or, to put it more exactly, most elite universities no longer wanted to remain kosher at all. They wanted to be known as modern kinds of schools, ones in which faculty experts chased down knowledge wherever it might lead, even if that were in heretical directions.

Evangelical intellectuals were aghast. Conservatives were terrified that young people would be taught to think that science and supernaturalism must now only gaze at one another from a respectable distance.

What to do?

Creationists fought back. They tried to evict evolution and evolution's intellectual allies from colleges as well as elementary schools. At public state colleges and private liberal ones, however, they almost always lost.[7]

What creationists really needed, some concluded, were new schools of their own. In 1923, Lowell Coate of Marion College in Marion, Indiana, called for the aggressive pursuit of a "new scholarship." Coate wanted a whole new network of colleges and universities, one that would "ignore the whole worldly system." The new schools would attract the best kind of "conservative scholarship." They could toss out "the present unchristian philosophy" that ruled most colleges. If they did so, they would soon be joined by a torrent of new schools, schools "rally[ing] to the new standard."[8]

It was a breathtakingly ambitious idea. Instead of giving up the field of higher education to the modern secular ideal, conservative evangelical intellectuals called for an entirely new network of schools. And the easiest way to weed out unsafe schools was with a new sort of creationist litmus test. After all, it wasn't immediately clear how a college could call itself "Christian" yet still dive headlong into the modern academic mindset.

As Charles Blanchard of Wheaton College in Illinois had insisted a few years earlier, evangelical parents and students had every right to be profoundly alarmed. Many modern colleges—including schools that called themselves "Christian"—seemed blissfully content to promote "infidelity, atheism, [and] anti-Christianity" as the hallmarks of a modern education. Real Christians, Blanchard argued, needed to investigate schools to see which ones had abandoned real religion. One easy way to tell, he advised, was to inquire about evolution. If a school taught "that man has descended or ascended from brute beast," there was no way it could remain truly Christian.[9]

The danger was not really evolutionary theory itself but rather the attitudes of universities in which evolution had been elevated to a new false idol. Mainstream colleges didn't only teach evolution as if it were true; they also taught a bundle of misleadingly seductive ideas that pooh-poohed traditional evangelical ideas about God and humanity. The real issue, as always, was trust. Fundamentalist intellectuals in the 1920s had lost their trust in mainstream higher education.

Blanchard boldly swung his school into the radical-creationist camp. He pledged to hire only faculty who taught resolute creationism; he committed to maintaining a campus in which only creationism would be taught. Like Dean Coate, he hoped to create a new sort of school, one that resolutely refused to go along with the evolution-friendly parts of the academic revolution. Like Coate, Blanchard hoped that his beloved Wheaton College would be joined by other authentically Christian schools, enough to create a viable dissenting network of creationist institutions.

And though the idea of evolution served as a useful symbol and rallying cry for these schools, it was only part of the whole package. Creationist college leaders in the 1920s wanted safe, trustworthy schools above all, schools that would protect students from what one leader called "the grave danger of sending them into a skeptical atmosphere."[10]

It didn't always work. One of the most ambitious attempts to set up a new creationist college crashed and burned.

In 1927, Des Moines University was struggling financially. Creationist leader T. T. Shields of Toronto offered to take over the school and purge it of any liberal, modern, or evolutionary thinking. He fired all the faculty, forcing them to reapply. He hoped to weed out anyone with suspicious scientific or religious views.

The new creationist school faced an uphill struggle. All the science faculty quit. The fundamentalist football team was taunted by chants of "Darwin! Darwin!" from its opponents' bleachers. Worst of all, inept creationist administrators caused a student riot in 1929. Fearing that their academic credits would not be honored, outraged students pelted administrators with rocks and garbage, demanding either their diplomas or their tuition money back. In the end, T. T. Shields was kicked out, and the school reverted to its roots as a blandly Baptist school.[11]

At most creationist colleges, however, things went much better. At Blanchard's Wheaton College in Illinois, for example, planting a flag for creationism—and all that went along with it—meant big boosts in student enrollment. While many schools expanded in the era, few could match Wheaton's explosion in students, charting 400 percent growth between 1916 and 1928.[12]

Down South, too, the upstart creationist Bob Jones College also grew in leaps and bounds. When it opened in 1926, it only offered a two-year associate's degree for a mere eighty-eight students. By the time it moved to its current campus in Greenville, South Carolina, in 1947, the newly designated Bob Jones University hosted 1,585 students and offered multiple degree programs in five colleges.[13]

Dean Coate's prediction wasn't entirely off base. In the 1920s and for decades to come, parents and students really did rush to reliably creationist schools. Parents wanted their children to be safe from evolutionary ideas. Or, to be more precise, they wanted to save their children from the desperate soul-crushing attitudes that they thought would inevitably accompany evolutionary thinking. They wanted schools they could trust to inculcate their children with traditional Christian ideas and morals.

Safety Schools

Whether or not evolutionary ideas would really threaten Christian faith, the fear was real and intense. In his wildly popular evangelistic tours throughout the 1920s, Bob Jones liked to tell a story of the dangers of modern higher education. He related one harrowing tale of an ordinary evangelical family. They had scrimped and saved to send their daughter to the best college they could find. After her first year of school, though, their daughter came home a stranger. Jones told his crowds:

> At the end of nine months she came home with her faith shattered. She laughed at God and the old time religion. She broke the hearts of her father and mother. They wept over her. They prayed over her. It availed nothing. At last they chided her. She rushed upstairs, stood in front of a mirror, took a gun and blew out her brains.[14]

It doesn't really matter if the story is true. For our purposes, the important point is that some creationist families saw the trends in modern higher education as a literal life-or-death dilemma. Their distrust of mainstream higher education had reached such an alarming crescendo that they worried for the very survival of their children. And suicide wouldn't even be the worst outcome. Another apocryphal tale that 1920s conservatives liked to pass around took the form of a letter home from a college-going "mother's son." About his modern education the student wrote:

> My soul is a starving skeleton; my heart a petrified rock; my mind is poisoned and fickle as the wind, and my faith is as unstable as water. . . . I wish that I had never seen a college.[15]

Going to a regular college, in other words, might send students straight to hell.

What could parents do? For starters, they could send their students to reliably creationist colleges. Creationism at those colleges meant much more than just teaching non-mainstream ideas about evolutionary theory. Leading colleges in the creationist camp during the first half of the twentieth century—schools such as Wheaton, Bob Jones, Moody Bible Institute in Chicago, Biola University in Los Angeles, Bryan College in Tennessee, Gordon College near Boston, and many more—promised to wrap students in a culture-war cocoon, to protect students from modern dangers that included improperly understood science but also included a whole lot more.

Most obviously, students at creationist colleges did not have much freedom to experiment with dangerous ideas and behavior. If you sent your kid to a creationist college, you were supposed to feel confident that she would not come home transformed by modern ideas, not least because she would not have learned to smoke, drink, dance, and attend worldly cinema and plays.

At Chicago's Moody Bible Institute, for example, control of students ranged far beyond the dangers of mainstream science. One student was kicked out for sneaking out to "pool halls etc." He had been cashing the checks his parents sent him for tuition and spending the money in Chicago's bustling nightclub scene. Moody Bible Institute's administrators sent a sad and stern letter home in 1932, informing the family of the son's delinquencies. The reply from the father is heartbreaking, even for those of us who aren't creationists. "I have did every thing in my power," the father wrote to the school administrators, "to bring him up a Christian boy but now I only see failure."[16]

At Moody Bible Institute, the school's administration kicked out students for an array of seemingly minor offenses. One student, for instance, skipped a mandatory chapel service, then lied about it. Another was caught smoking. Another cheated on exams. One expelled student drank alcohol and kept an "untidy room." And one was charged with the agonizingly unspecific crime of "moral delinquency."[17]

All colleges at the time had much stricter rules than colleges do today. However, creationist schools like the Moody Bible Institute went to extraordinary lengths to keep their students on the straight and narrow. The strict discipline wasn't accidental, nor can it be separated from the school's ardent creationism. Rather, the promise of such schools, today as much as back in the 1930s, was to keep creationist students safe from any threat: physical, moral, intellectual, or scientific.

Indeed, these stories of harsh creationist discipline give us a sense of what our creationism culture wars are really about. Yes, creationist colleges taught creationism. But more than that, they went to extraordinary lengths to shield students from the manifold spiritual dangers of modern American life. Evolutionary theory itself was only a danger if it was in the wrong hands. Just as a glass of wine by itself, or a popular vaudeville show, or an "untidy room" did not by themselves threaten creationist religion, so too evolutionary theory was more of a danger by implication.

Students allowed to drink a little, or see a show, or strew their clothes about their bedrooms might be showing signs of dangerous spiritual decline. What if the wine became a habit? If the saucy repartee became habitual? If sloppy rooms became sloppy prayers?

If we hope to understand creationism in America, we need to understand the way these educational institutions saw their role. Yes, they sought to protect their students from unchaperoned exposure to mainstream science, but only because of where that exposure might lead. The ultimate goal was not creationism itself, per se, but rather safety. Students were warned not to trust mainstream scientists, just as they were warned not to trust bartenders, dancing girls, or slobs.

Chicago's Moody Bible Institute was not alone in its single-minded focus on protecting students. On the West Coast, leaders of Biola University kicked out a student in 1966.[18] His crime? The student had "admitted to at least twenty-five homosexual acts." In the world of creationist schooling, the sex itself was bad enough. Even more important, the reasoning given by Biola's leader gives us a glimpse into the administration's mindset.

President Samuel Sutherland explained, "honestly now, would you want a son or daughter of yours to come to a school where any known aggressive homosexual is allowed freely to pursue his activities?" In the mind of Sutherland one homosexual student put every other student at risk.

According to him and the other denizens of the world of creationist higher education, even asking the question that way gave its own answer. If families were to trust Sutherland's school, they had to trust that he would purge homosexuality as well as evolution, and immoral behavior as well as mainstream scientific thinking.

Of course, there is no scientific connection between sexual behavior and creationism. For that matter, there is no reason why someone couldn't believe in a literal worldwide flood, or a literal Adam and Eve, even if he visited a cabaret from time to time or kept an untidy bedroom. If we hope to understand the world of creationism, though, we need to understand that creationism itself is only one aspect of a powerful drive to keep young people safe. It was not actually evolutionary science that creationist colleges preached against. Physically, intellectually, and spiritually, the creationist college network made its first priority the creation of a trustworthy campus where young creationists could live and learn without endangering their eternal souls.

Engineering Creationist Knowledge

The atmosphere at creationist colleges was not merely negative, however. Creationism doesn't mean only keeping threatening ideas and attitudes at bay. Creationist schools have offered a rich and—to some of us—surprisingly intellectually complicated package of ideas as well.

For example, as the surprising results of the 2016 presidential election reminded us, conservative evangelical creationist schools have always trumpeted a certain sort of patriotic vigor, a dream of making America great again, a conservative embrace of "love-it-or-leave-it" nationalism. If we try to understand this college network only in terms of creationism and evolution, we won't be able to understand why President Jerry Falwell Jr. of the creationist Liberty University likes to call President Donald Trump his "dream president."[19] After all, President Trump has never pretended to embody evangelical values. With several divorces and several casinos under his belt, we might think morality-obsessed creationists might be horrified.

They're not. Creationist colleges have always encouraged the evangelical public to think of their schools as patriotic "America-first" colleges. Back in 1935, for example, the president of Wheaton College celebrated the notion that Wheaton was "one college where parents can send their children without any fear of their being inoculated with any 'isms but Americanism and Christianism."[20] Down the road at Chicago's Moody Bible Institute, in 1947 President William Culbertson offered a similar guarantee. His fervently creationist school, Culbertson proclaimed, would always be "glad to take our stand for the old-fashioned kind of Americanism."[21]

At Bob Jones University, President Bob Jones Jr.—he inherited the title from his father and would eventually pass it along to his son—agreed that there was no sensible distinction between creationist religion and conservative love-it-or-leave-it politics. As he put it in 1962, "A good, Bible-believing Christian is by nature a good, patriotic American."[22]

For these creation-college administrators, patriotic Americanism—buffed to a conservative shine—was an important part of their schools' appeal. Yes, their colleges would teach creationism. And, yes, their colleges would obsessively enforce strict rules on their students. And of course, their schools would teach and preach a certain fundamentalist vision of evangelical Protestantism.

But if we really want to understand American creationism, we have to make sense of its broader meanings and the ways creationist institutions have nurtured those multiple meanings. The impetus for founding and maintaining separate creationist colleges is not only to teach a different creationist science. Rather, creationist schools are about many other things, including conservative, patriotic politics. Evangelical support for President Trump in 2016 was no exception.[23] For decades, from Reagan to Romney, conservative creationist colleges have actively supported conservative politicians and conservative political thinking.

It's not just politics, either. Many creationist colleges and universities have offered students more than just rules against movies and smoking. Students have learned more than just a negative attitude toward mainstream science. Perhaps the most successful aspect of intellectual life in creationist America—maybe the most vital and yet the most difficult for outsiders to understand—is that creationist institutions have provided students with a different way of thinking about the ultimate relationship between Scripture and science. Students initiated into the mysteries of creationist hermeneutics don't just reject the immorality supposedly implied by evolutionary theory. Rather, they understand the world in such a way that radical creationism seems both true and obvious.

In order to suss out this alternative creationist intellectual culture, we need to toss out a few of our likely assumptions. It is tempting to assume that creationist colleges are, intellectually speaking, medieval fortresses, clinging to an outmoded idea of the relationship between God and science. We might think that creationism is primarily a rejection—of science, certainly, but more profoundly an utter rejection of our modern way of thinking about both science and religion.

They're not. Rather, today's young-earth form of radical creationism is a decidedly modern American enterprise. As we'll talk about in more detail in chapter 7, creationists hardly ever say a disparaging word about science itself—as long as they can stipulate the kind of science they mean. And one of the most important religious ideas that creationist colleges teach is similarly profoundly modern. When students attend creationist colleges, they often learn this sort of dissenting modern vision of proper religion, a religious idea that doesn't say anything directly about creationism or evolution but creates an intellectual world in which radical creationism is the obvious conclusion.

Not every creationist college teaches this way of thinking, and, indeed, some of its fiercest critics have been scholars at other creationist colleges, but as historian Brendan Pietsch argued brilliantly in his 2015 book *Dispensational Modernism,* the dispensational approach to the Bible has been a dominant intellectual presence at many leading schools.[24]

Adepts in dispensational thinking hope to initiate students into a way of reading the Bible that puts all human and supernatural history into one intimate conversation. To make sense of it, we need to go back in time to the mid-1800s, when scholars offered new interpretations of the Bible. To many modern readers, the inconsistencies and contradictions in the Bible seem jarring and uncomfortable. Why were there two seemingly different creation stories in Genesis? Why did Old Testament prophets live so long? Why do Christians eat pork, when the Bible seems to prohibit it? And why did the stories about Jesus's miraculous birth seem to suspiciously echo the birth stories of so many other religions?

To some modern minds, the Bible's awkward contradictions served as proof of its irrelevance. Why follow rules from this particular collection of myths?

It was not only conservative creationist scholars who furiously rejected this question. Liberal scholars, too, defended the Bible's divine importance, but in a different way. Liberal theologians argued that the texts were cobbled together by human editors, pulling together an eclectic group of texts from across several centuries. They may have included mythic elements that came originally from other religions. But that didn't rob the Bible of its religious value. Perhaps the Bible was not simply God's Word unfiltered, but it did tell the story of our search for God and for godliness. Simply because modern ways of thinking punctured huge holes in a naive reading of biblical stories didn't mean those stories weren't valuable guides to becoming better Christians.

As the twentieth century approached, this liberal attitude toward the Bible became dominant at leading mainstream colleges and seminaries—the elite sorts of schools that horrified early creationists. Christianity, many scholars believed, didn't rely on a naive interpretation of Bible stories. Christians didn't need to think the world was created in six days. Christians didn't need to think that the stories of Jesus's birth were literally true. Rather, the Bible was unique and uniquely valuable because it contained the collected wisdom of religious people for so many centuries. Its pages contained invaluable spiritual truths that didn't rely on crude, literal interpretations.

Outside of elite universities, though, a very different approach to the Bible gained steam. If we want to do more than scratch the surface of creationist intellectual life, we need to understand this kind of thinking. Especially at Bible institutes and Bible-prophecy conferences, dispensational thinkers offered a different solution to the modern dilemma. If the Bible were cut into eras, or dispensations, its seeming inconsistencies could be seen for what they really are.

There are almost as many dispensational schemes as there are dispensationalists, and the give and take between them can get as heated and as abstruse as the fights at any academic conference at any mainstream school. In rough outline, though, dispensational thinkers cut human history into discrete divine eras, each with its own set of rules. More than that, physical reality itself could be different in different eras. In some dispensations, lions might not eat meat. Humans might live for hundreds of years. Water might be suspended above the earth in enough volume to flood the entire planet.

For example, the world of Eden was obviously vastly different from our own. The rules of this Dispensation of Innocence were clear and delightful. There was no need for labor; there was no death or strife. With the Fall, however, history entered the era of Conscience, which lasted through Noah's flood. Between the end of the flood and the leadership of Abraham was the Dispensation of Human Government, followed by the Dispensation of Promise. Between the Exodus and the death of Jesus was the Dispensation of Law. From Jesus's time to now has been the Dispensation of Grace.

Finally, when Jesus returns in glory he will bring the final dispensation, the Millennial Kingdom.

So, yes, for modern readers the dispensational system offered a satisfying answer to the questions that bothered them. Why could Noah drink wine and we can't? Because he lived in a different dispensation. How could a flood cover the entire earth? Because it was a unique event, in a time in which different physical and supernatural laws were in effect. Dispensationalism provided a modern solution to some of the gotcha questions posed by smug village atheists.

Dispensational reading was profoundly modern in other ways as well. As the nineteenth century turned into the twentieth, dispensational thinking claimed to take a very modern-sounding scientific approach to the Bible. Dispensationalists quantified, measured, compared, and cross-referenced. They created charts; they counted words. Dispensational scholars created vast, intimidating taxonomies, poring over biblical texts to make new discoveries, uncovering meanings that careless or untrained readers would surely miss.

Perhaps most important for our purposes, dispensationalism offered an academic system that included endless opportunities for enlightenment and mastery as well as for dispute and deliberation. Colleges, universities, seminaries, and institutes devoted to teaching dispensational thinking gave students everything they expected from modern higher education.

For instance, students could grasp the basics of dispensational thinking relatively quickly, but they could be assured there were depths to the system that took lifetimes to perceive. Dispensational experts insisted that their rigorous study had shown them ever-greater revelations. Seen as a whole, the Bible became an even more wondrous work, tying together the writing of human authors into a supernatural masterpiece surely greater than human minds could accomplish. The text was marbled with subtle patterns, codes, and typologies that only a divine editor could have envisioned and that only master readers could connect.

In astute dispensational readings, the entire Bible was connected. Once readers' eyes were opened, they could discern the ways the whole Bible supported itself throughout all its different books. There were "types" that were used from the first books to the last; there were predictions and prophecies tying together the books in a seamless pattern. If modern critics were right and the Bible was written by unconnected authors over the years, how much more wondrous and obviously supernatural did it become that those human authors managed to incorporate such patterns—patterns that could clearly only be seen when the whole book was seen at once? Like Nazca Lines that can only be appreciated from far above, the patterns and typologies described by dispensationalists seemed proof that the entire Bible was one unified supernatural work.

When it came to creationist thinking, too, the divine dispensational unity of the Bible encouraged evangelicals to think in new ways. Or, at least, it made fairly novel interpretations make sense in ways they hadn't to earlier generations of Christians. The most relevant example is the notion that the stories told in Genesis were literally true. There had been plenty of Christians throughout the ages—even fundamentalist evangelicals in the twentieth century—who had seen no reason to insist on that notion. As we've seen, for example, leading radical creationists in the 1920s such as William Jennings Bryan and William Bell Riley saw no reason for earnest Christians to insist on a young earth. If the entire Bible were read as a seamless supernatural text, however, taking Genesis as mere literature threatened to degrade the whole thing. If the story of Adam and Eve were mere allegory, in other words, how can we trust the story of Jesus's sacrifice? If Jesus was the "last Adam," both stories reinforced one another; the central Christian element of Christ's self-sacrifice vouched for the vital importance of a literal Edenic Adam.

Not incidentally, the complexities of dispensational reading also gave scholars plenty of room for academic dispute and disagreement. Were there seven dispensations? Or nine? Was a reading really tapping into a previously unnoticed prophecy, or was it merely articulating one scholar's unfounded ambition?

In short, dispensationalism offered an intellectual system that a subset of fundamentalist radical-creationist colleges taught each new generation. It was a modern science with endless opportunities for new research and dispute. It was a modern system that answered the questions naive Bible readers might come up with. And it offered a way of thinking in which radical ideas of young-earth creationism made perfect sense.

True Creationists

Many naive anti-creationists don't seem able or willing to grasp this point. The fervent missionaries for science we'll meet in chapter 6 often assume that creationists are merely plugging their intellectual ears to block out the ideas of modern America. Some creationists might do that, to be sure, but most don't.

The colleges and institutions that support the young-earth form of radical creationism don't just layer creationism on top of an otherwise mainstream college experience. From dispensationalism to political conservatism, from drinking to dancing, creationist colleges offer a world in which creationism simply makes more sense. And, most important, radical-creationist colleges tell their students their world is encircled and threatened by untrustworthy outsiders and under relentless attack from liberals and atheists who hope to crumble the foundations of a righteous society.

Yes, evolutionary theory is a danger, but it is not seen as a danger in itself. Rather, at radical-creationist colleges, the real danger comes from mainstream attitudes about the implications of evolutionary theory. It is the immorality and anti-Christian thinking that usually accompanies and promotes evolutionary theory that radical-creationist colleges are worried about.

Of course, we need to be careful: There isn't just one network of creationist colleges but several. And no one offers more savage ridicule of dispensational thinking than do the scholars at non-radical-creationist colleges.

As we saw in chapter 3, the middle of the twentieth century saw a profound fracturing among evangelical Protestants. Bernard Ramm, Russell Mixter, and the other evangelical scholars we met insisted that true Christian creationism didn't need to turn its back on mainstream science. At the same time, Henry Morris, John Whitcomb Jr., and other young-earth creationists insisted just as fervently that they did.

The split between creationists was a split also between creationist colleges. Many schools that were creationist in the broad sense embraced the essential value of modern evolutionary science. They insisted, however, that God had created it all, possibly including the wondrous mechanism of natural selection.

As with many family feuds, the dispute among creationists was often far more ferocious than the dispute between creationists and mainstream scientists. The non-radical "evangelical" camp embraced the rough outline of evolutionary theory, and they blasted their "fundamentalist" radical-creationist cousins as head-in-the-sand ignoramuses. Fundamentalists labeled evangelicals as worse than apostates.

The crux of the dispute—when it came to creationism—was about Noah's flood and the age of the earth. Fundamentalist young earthers—the most influential kind of radical creationists in America today—insisted that real

Christian belief needed to take the whole Bible at face value. If it described a six-day creation, loyal Christians had no cause to doubt it. Evangelical non-radical creationists, on the other hand, insisted that there was no need to believe such a scientifically and—to them—theologically unnecessary notion. God created, they insisted, and the Bible told us how . . . but we didn't need to resort to crude, literal interpretations.

Creationism, though, was only one part of a wider divide. As non-radical evangelical intellectual leader Carl Henry argued in 1966, "scientific obliviousness" was one of the serious problems with modern fundamentalism, but it was not the only one. Young earthers, Henry insisted, clung fearfully to their "extreme dispensationalism" and their overall "anti-intellectual inexcusableness."[25]

If students came to a college like Wheaton, evangelicals promised, they would learn real creationism, not the desperate "inexcusableness" of the radical young earthers.

For their part, the young-earth crowd warned followers that colleges could still be dangerous places, even if they were full of self-identified evangelical Christians who agreed with Professor Henry. Even if their science professors claimed to be creationists.

In 1974, for example, young-earth leader Henry Morris traveled to Wheaton College to make his case. He was shocked and dismayed to discover that none of Wheaton's faculty—at least none of the ones he talked to— thought a worldwide flood had really happened. They did not believe that evangelicals needed to embrace the idea of a literal six-day creation or of a young earth. Yet, Morris reported incredulously, they still called themselves "creationists."[26]

The so-called creationists at Wheaton, Morris warned his young-earth friends, weren't "true creationists" at all. There was no Christian reason to dispute the idea of a young earth. Rather, Wheaton's sorry false creationists had abandoned real faith in a pathetic, desperate attempt to win "acceptance in the academic world."

Beware, Morris warned his fundamentalist readers. Many colleges that claimed to be creationist—schools like Wheaton and its ilk—had really "compromised with evolution to an alarming degree." Worst of all, such false-creationist colleges readily lied about it to the creationist public, pretending to be friendly to young-earth beliefs for "promotional purposes."[27]

Just as the first generation of creationist-college founders in the 1920s had used evolution as a litmus test, so too did later creationists. By the 1970s, the world of creationist higher education was bitterly and profoundly divided. As we saw in chapter 3, radical young earthers insisted to a smaller and smaller circle of listeners that only their ideas represented real creationism. Only by teaching that a young earth was a vital tenet of real Christianity could colleges earn the trust of fundamentalist young earthers.

And as that circle of young-earth creationist-colleges grew smaller and tighter, its defenders grew more and more insistent on keeping true to their peculiar creationist beliefs. These days, Ken Ham has become America's leading young-earth pundit, and he promotes young-earth colleges with even more zeal than did his former mentor Henry Morris.

These days, people looking for trustworthy young-earth schools can consult Ham's list of "creation colleges." Schools such as Bryan College in Tennessee and Cedarville University in Ohio bend over backward to assure Ham that there is nary a whiff of non-young-earth teaching on their campuses. And no target is too small to escape Ham's prickly defensiveness. In 2014, for example, Ham responded defiantly and defensively when I publicly noticed his behind-the-scenes influence on creationist colleges.[28]

When we talk about young-earth creationist colleges, then—the alternative intellectual world of dispensational thinking, the strict student rules, and the ferocious political conservatism—we need to remember that we are only talking about a small and shrinking fragment of radical-creationist higher education.[29]

And we should remember, too, that creationist colleges are no longer the only institutions in the world of creationist education, though they remain the most influential. Just as the world of evangelical creationists split in the middle of the twentieth century, so too did the changes in the world of K–12 public schooling cause a dramatic transformation in creationist elementary and secondary education.

Schools of Our Own

There was absolutely nothing coincidental about the timing. In the middle of the twentieth century, America changed. And American creationism changed right along with it. It was those broader changes that explain how we can fight so much and so hard about creationism even though we don't really disagree all that much about actual evolutionary science.

As we saw in chapter 3, by the 1950s mainstream science had come to exert a new authority in popular culture, politics, and intellectual life. But that wasn't the only epochal change that transformed the world of American creationism. As we saw in chapter 2, mainstream attitudes about the proper relationship between religion and government had also been subtly but utterly transformed. When it came to K-12 schooling, the old rules didn't seem to apply anymore. Creationists who had liked the old rules were forced to reexamine their relationships toward public elementary and secondary schools.

Just as it had been with creationist colleges, this was a creation-evolution battle, but one that didn't really have much to do with real evolutionary theory. Creationism was only one dramatic part of a profound conservative religious dissent against the new directions of modern public education.

The evidence was everywhere creationists looked. In the early 1960s, for example, the Supreme Court made some groundbreaking decisions that challenged the traditional religiosity of American public schools. As we saw in chapter 2, in its 1962 *Engel v. Vitale* decision, the Court ruled that public schools could not impose a prayer on students, not even a profoundly bland ecumenical prayer. At issue in the case was New York's please-no-one compromise. New Yorkers thought they had solved the old questions about religion in public school by keeping their mandated prayer utterly vanilla: "Almighty God," students prayed vaguely, "we acknowledge our dependence upon Thee, and we beg Thy blessings upon us, our parents, our teachers and our country. Amen."

By 1962, even such a non-specific prayer was seen as too much religion for a public school. In the past, public schools had tended to be relatively religious places. As long as dissenters were allowed to opt out—and as long as no one complained too loudly—local schools were able to incorporate a good deal of religion into their day-to-day functions. No longer. At least, not without going against the Court's decision.

The next year, 1963, saw an even bigger Supreme Court dust-up. Many creationists had cheered the decision in *Engel v. Vitale*. They didn't want the government telling kids how to pray, either. But in 1963, the decision in *School District of Abington Township v. Schempp* left many creationists speechless. The *Schempp* decision ruled that reciting the Lord's Prayer and reading devotionally from the Bible were too much religion for public schools.[30]

The Court was careful to point out that religion was still fine in public schools, as far as the Constitution was concerned. Students could continue to pray all they wanted to on their own. Classes could study the history of religions. But schools could no longer actively promote any particular religion by leading students in prayerful Bible readings.

I don't want to overstate the case. After all, as political scientists Kenneth Dolbeare and Phillip Hammond discovered, many school districts simply ignored the Supreme Court decisions and continued with their prayers and Bible readings.[31]

Symbolically, however, the decisions had enormous implications. Many creationists wailed that the Supreme Court had kicked God out of America's classrooms. The public schools had never been churches, but they had been places where religious students had felt at home. For generations, they had been places that served as friendly public spaces for religious creationist kids and their families. They had been institutions that creationists could trust.

At least, that's how many creationists saw it. And for many of them, it only got worse. Just as the Supreme Court was kicking God out of public schools, secular reformers kept pushing a bunch of other stuff in to take his place.

By the end of the 1960s, for example, about half of American public schools had begun formal sex education classes. Many of them used a controversial curriculum inspired by the work of the Sex Information and Education Council of the United States (SIECUS). The reach of SIECUS's information about sexuality was never really as large as it was rumored to be, nor did it encourage students to have premarital sex the way it was rumored to, but for many religious conservatives, sex-ed was just another reason to be suspicious of public education.[32]

It wasn't just sex. Many creationists reacted with alarm to news about a different federally funded curriculum, too. Man: A Course of Study (MACOS) was a set of social-studies books and school materials that examined humans from a variety of social-science perspectives. By the end of 1974, about 1,700 schools in forty-seven states had purchased the materials. To many creationist activists, the curriculum taught the very worst, deadliest sort of idea: Humans were animals just like any other.[33]

As radical-creationist pundit Tim LaHaye warned, MACOS was nothing less than "an ingeniously evil technique" to warp children's minds. It came from the schemes of "atheistic humanist educators," hoping to use peer pressure to sap children of their moral values.[34]

Beyond the range of religion, too, the public image of public education experienced another dramatic change in the 1950s and 1960s. When the Supreme Court ruled in 1954 that racially segregated schools were inherently unequal, it sparked a new fight over segregation and desegregation.

Some white creationists, like many white Americans of all religious backgrounds, objected violently to the notion of racially mixed schools. Many of them were simply unreconstructed racists. They did not like the idea of white children mixing with African Americans. But even if they didn't have racist objections, or, to be more precise, even if racism was not their primary motivation, many white Americans—including creationists—reacted angrily to the notion that the government could bus their children around to create a better racial balance in schools.

By the 1970s, the fight over school segregation had become, in large part, a battle over busing and control of local schools. As one Boston protester insisted, she was not racist, but she didn't like busing. In her words, "If under a court order a child can be forcibly taken from his parents into unfamiliar, often hostile neighborhoods, then we shall have opened a pandora's box of new, unlimited government powers."[35]

Throughout the 1950s, 1960s, and 1970s, folks who wanted to keep public schools the way they always had been felt as if they were losing ground, inch by inch, battle by battle. The Bible was out. Prayer was out. Schools were teaching sex; schools were teaching bad morals; and schools were no longer racially segregated; and thus no longer under local parents' control.

The fact that some public schools had begun to embrace evolutionary theory in science classrooms, then, was only yet another log on an already-raging fundamentalist fire. We need to remember to take creationists' jeremiads with a grain of salt since the presence of real evolutionary theory in America's public schools remains woefully limited.[36] But just as the Supreme Court ruled against the Bible and prayer in public schools, and just as some schools adopted sex-ed classes and new social-science classes, the federal government poured money into a new series of science textbooks.

The Biological Sciences Curriculum Study (BSCS) was supposed to help jump-start America's faltering science-education system. Timorous politicians had always respected the political power of radical creationists, but when the Soviet Union humiliated America by putting *Sputnik* into orbit in 1957, even crusty conservatives agreed something had to be done. More American kids needed to learn more science, they agreed, even if it raised the hackles of creationist dissenters.

Instead of relying on cautious private textbook publishers, the BSCS series used federal funding to create better, more authentic science textbooks.[37] Instead of downplaying the importance of evolutionary theory, as many earlier textbooks had done, the BSCS texts incorporated the new consensus about evolution among mainstream scientists. By the end of the 1960s, nearly half of American high schools included BSCS materials to some extent.[38]

By that time—in the eyes of creationist dissenters—public schools had become schools of drug deals, sexcapades, and soul-destroying secularism. Public schools had banned traditional Protestant faith, stripping kids of their last spiritual defense. We shouldn't be surprised, then, by the explosion in numbers of a new sort of school. Beginning in the 1970s, creationists yanked their kids in huge numbers from public schools and enrolled them in a new burst of private religious schools, often calling themselves "Christian schools" or "Christian Day" schools.

To be sure, there had always been private religious schools. Catholic schools, especially, had always served large numbers of families. Some Protestants, too, especially Lutherans and Reformed groups, had always maintained their own school networks. Since the 1920s, there had even been a small but active network of interdenominational evangelical schools.

Beginning in the 1970s, however, the network of interdenominational evangelical Protestant schools experienced dizzying growth. One journalist guessed that about three new evangelical schools opened every day in the late 1970s and early 1980s.[39] By 1975, these schools enrolled about 400,000 students.[40] By the early twenty-first century, that number had more than doubled. By 2002, the category of "conservative Christian" schools rivaled Catholic schools in number and dwarfed other types of private schools in the United States.[41]

Just like the network of creationist colleges that sprang up beginning in the 1920s, this network of creationist private schools taught much more than just creationism. Like creationist colleges, they appealed to parents for a wide range of reasons. Were parents concerned about a new emphasis on teaching evolution in public schools? Yes, indeed. But they also worried about other issues, including racial integration, drugs, sexual morality, and old-fashioned academics. Evolutionary theory alone was not the main problem for radical creationists. Rather, radical creationists fretted most about what they saw as a new scheming anti-Christian attitude.

If we could ask parents why they left public schools for private creationist ones, we would expect a lot of different responses. And when scholars have done so, that's just what they found. One study surveyed parents in Philadelphia who pulled their kids out of public schools and put them in evangelical Christian schools in 1982. It found, not surprisingly, that far and away the leading cause parents gave was their vision of the negative "moral values learned in the public schools." A whopping 84.4 percent of parents picked that as their main motivation. But "drug use" (68.8 percent), "secular humanism" (68.3 percent), "discipline," (64.9 percent), and "peer companions" (60.0 percent) also ranked high on the list. Parents were also very concerned with academic quality, with 56.1 percent of respondents listing quality of teaching as "very much" the reason for their switch. Were parents concerned that students might learn evolutionary theory? Yes, but only insofar as evolution implied all the amoral baggage that creationists tended to load into it.[42]

Across the country in Northern California, parents listed a similar mix of reasons to choose a creationist school. One Stanford researcher found that a creationist school offered parents an attractive combination of conservative features. Yes, the school taught creationism. But students would learn their creationism in an atmosphere that emphasized a number of seemingly unrelated features. The school touted its back-to-basics academic program, with regular rigorous standardized tests. The school insisted on old-fashioned discipline in the classroom, including corporal punishment. Students had to dress up; students could only eat healthy snacks; students all participated in a patriotic flag-raising ceremony every Monday morning.[43]

What do healthy snacks and flag waving have to do with evolutionary theory? There's no strictly logical connection, theo-logical or otherwise. But if we want to understand the world of American creationism, we need to recognize that the radical-creationist revolt has not fundamentally been a revolt against mainstream evolutionary theory alone; as argued throughout this book, creationist schools have always been about much more than just creationism. They have offered havens from the secularizing trends of modern America. They have offered parents an easy way to send their kids to school, to get them into college, and to support them through graduate school without giving up the bundle of conservative ideas that includes creationist religion. They have created, in short, a trustworthy institutional world where creationism seems like an obvious choice, a reasonable, safe, patriotic, traditional choice.

And the logic of creationist schooling soon developed a ferocious momentum of its own. As the perfect storm of sex-ed, evolution, busing, and secularism pushed many creationist families out of public schools, it soon pushed many families out of schools altogether. If public schools weren't necessary, many religious parents asked, why was any sort of school necessary? Wouldn't it be better to shape the intellect and faith of children at home? What could be more secure than that? By 2012, the exodus of creationist families from public schools had become a flood of homeschooled students. In 2012, over 1.7 million American students were homeschooled—3.4 percent of all American students. That was up from just a decade earlier, when the number was slightly over 1,000,000, which constituted only 2.2 percent of students.[44]

It's impossible to make easy generalizations about homeschoolers, as historian Milton Gaither has shown.[45] We can say a few things about them, though. First of all, we know that a large proportion of the current crop of those who homeschool are creationists, because conservative evangelical Protestants make up a significant proportion of the new trend.

We can also say with confidence that leaving school does not mean that creationist homeschoolers are simply striking out on their own. Rather, many creationist homeschoolers become reliant on a different creationist institution. Fundamentalist publishers, including Abeka Book and Accelerated Christian Education, have provided radical-creationist homeschool families with everything they need to educate their children.

Just as with creationist schools, the message of these homeschool curricula includes some radical creationist ideas, but it wraps them in a much broader framework. They don't just insert radical ideas about science and religion into an otherwise mainstream curriculum. Instead, they provide students, teachers, parents, and preachers an intellectual world where radical creationism seems obvious, that is, the only moral, Christian option. Homeschool textbooks do not ignore evolution; they don't simply leave evolution out. To the contrary, creationist homeschool textbooks explicitly promise to teach about evolutionary theory, only in a way that does not threaten the souls of creationist students.

Rebirth of Our Nation

Curriculum companies such as Abeka Book and Accelerated Christian Education (ACE) aren't the only ones producing creationist textbooks and classroom materials, but in the world of young-earth creationism—the most prominent sort of radical creationism in America today—they are among the most influential.[46]

Both Abeka and ACE promise both a reliably young-earth perspective and a total "biblical worldview" in which that kind of radical creationist thinking makes sense. Both companies grew out of their founders' desires for more reliable textbooks.

As had an earlier generation of frustrated creationists, in 1954, Abeka founders Arlin and Beka Horton opened their own creationist college, Pensacola Christian College (PCC). They believed even resolutely radical-creationist schools such as Bob Jones University—their alma mater—had strayed too far from true religion and true schooling. PCC would be different. When other fundamentalists debated, PCC would stick to its guns. When other creationists wondered about the necessity of radical young-earth ideas, PCC would never waver.

As did other fundamentalists, the Hortons soon recognized the growing desire for more reliably conservative creationist schools. To serve the new burst of such K–12 schools, during the early 1970s the Hortons bought up expired copyrights for old, traditional textbooks. They pasted in a few Bible verses and patriotic slogans. Soon, due to the popularity of their revived traditional textbooks, they began producing books of their own.[47]

Abeka materials promised to wrap their creationism in a full fundamentalist context. What will students learn from Abeka textbooks? One creator offered a long list. Any worthwhile school, Abeka's A. A. "Buzz" Baker wrote in 1979, will teach the following vital principles:

You learn the Bible.
You learn that God created.
You learn the worth of your soul.
You master the three R's and other subjects.
You sit up straight and pay attention.
You learn that it is right not to cheat.
You learn to recite when called upon.
You learn honor and respect for your parents.
You learn respect for authority.
You learn that a man's word is his bond.
You learn that a job worth doing is worth doing well.
You learn personal initiative.
You develop pride in America.
You learn that the free enterprise system is still the best system.
You learn that competition is healthy.[48]

Yes, students that use Abeka books—whether in homeschools or private schools—are supposed to find out that "God created." But that creationist mantra is only one vital part of a much bigger package of creationist schooling. At schools that embrace Abeka's educational philosophy, creationism is part and parcel of a bundle of notions, including "pride in America" and love for "the free enterprise system." It's about sitting up straight, obeying teachers, and learning through rote recitation.

It's tempting to write off such traditionalist dogma as merely incidental. It's tempting to think that creationist schools of the Abeka variety simply happen to hold such old-fashioned ideas about obedience and patriotism. If we stop there, though, we'll never get a handle on the ways creationist schools function as an alternative educational institution, teaching children creationism in a context that insists on a much broader cultural conservatism, a broader cultural context in which creationism isn't an outlier, in which radical creationist ideas aren't radical at all, but rather mere common sense. If we dismiss the profound and many layered conservatism at the heart of Abeka books, we won't understand that our battles about creationism are not—at heart—really battles about actual evolutionary theory.

In practice, radical-creationist curriculum is not really about science or even specific theological notions. Like the Abeka list, it teaches a ferocious conservatism as the only trustworthy way to be American. At the same time, it hopes to equip students with an unshakeable distrust of outsider thinking.

Abeka is by no means alone in its efforts to wrap its creationism in a wider conservative package. Accelerated Christian Education (ACE) materials, too, promise to teach a breathtakingly conservative worldview in which creationism seems merely a sensible part of a coherent way of understanding the world. The intellectual world of ACE, like Abeka, is not built solely—or even primarily—on creationist ideas about science or the Bible. Rather, the most important building-block of the ACE curriculum is the notion of a world rigidly divided between the trustworthy and the others; between real creationists and the scheming atheists and deluded false Christians who hope to lure them into sin.

ACE was the brainchild of school founder Donald Howard. In 1970, Howard started his own private school with forty-five students. He created learning packets for each student so that they could study at their own pace. Due to the explosion in numbers of creationist private schools and homeschools, Howard soon found his homemade curriculum in high demand. By 1977, ACE claimed its curriculum was used at over 2,000 fundamentalist schools. At its peak in the early 1980s, ACE claimed to serve over 8,000 schools.[49]

Like Abeka's founders, Howard was convinced of the need for reliable textbooks that did not reflect warped mainstream values. It wasn't just the science books that Howard worried about. Howard warned in 1979 that the soul-destroying atheistic philosophy at the root of evolutionary thinking had permeated public schools. As he put it:

> Pick up a textbook used in government education today. It doesn't matter where you get the book and it doesn't matter what discipline it covers, but nine chances out of ten you are going to run into evolution somewhere in that book.[50]

For Howard, "evolution" worked as more than a scientific idea. It served as a red flag, a warning that a textbook reflected the terrible trends that had taken over mainstream schools. Clearly, if it showed up in history books, math books, and literature books, Howard was not talking about the actual science of evolution. No, for Howard, as for all radical creationists, "evolution" was not really about evolutionary science, but rather about a terrible slide toward sin in American mainstream culture.

ACE materials offered an alternative. If conservative evangelical creationists wanted, like Howard, to spark the "rebirth of our nation," they could flee perverted and soulless "government education" and open creationist schools of their own. Those schools, ACE promised, could give students a better education than the corrupted public schools, due to both their religiously superior textbooks and their pedagogically superior layout.

At ACE schools and homeschools, students work independently on workbooks. At the end of every lesson students take a test about what they read. When they have successfully completed one section, they can move on. The goal was to offer cash-strapped creationist churches and homeschoolers a way to manage a large number of students without spending a lot on teachers or supplies.

That wasn't the only goal, of course. Like other creationist institutions, ACE produced textbooks that preach conservative ideas about every subject. ACE materials rely on social issues to make their points. In one science booklet, for example, students learn that God created everything relatively recently. But that's not all that students learn. Abortion, they read, is decidedly anti-God, as are homosexuality and other sorts of sexual behaviors.

"The Bible teaches," PACE 1107 (2001 edition) workbook declares, "that homosexuality is a sin."[51]

It's impossible not to notice. Creationist materials teach creationism. But not just creationism. As have creationist institutions since the 1920s, radical-creationist schools these days teach an alternative worldview. In the textbooks produced by companies such as ACE and Abeka, radical creationism is part of a way of seeing the world in which mainstream culture has gone woefully awry. It is possible, these creationist schools teach, for fundamentalists to rebuild "their" nation, but only if they train each new generation of creationist youth in a powerfully dissenting way of viewing things.

Mainstream institutions, mainstream leaders, mainstream scientists ... all have lost their moral authority. It becomes not only possible but positively easy to believe the outlandish scientific claims of radical creationists once we stop trusting the claims of mainstream thinking. To understand creationism, we need to understand the lack of trust that lurks at the root of creationist thinking. For generations, creationist institutions have taught that mainstream institutions can no longer be trusted.

They have also provided trustworthy alternative environments. In colleges, private schools, and homeschools, radical creationist ideas aren't merely piled on top of otherwise mainstream topics. Rather, since the 1920s, the world of creationist schools has expanded to include wholly separate educational networks, providing everything a creationist family might need to earn any sort of educational credential, all without ever leaving an intellectual world where radical creationism seems obviously true.

It's worth repeating that these radical young-earth creationist schools and textbook companies are not the only creationist game in town. Non-radical creationists at non-fundamentalist evangelical schools learn lots of mainstream science. They also learn history, literature, and religion that is much closer to the mainstream.

At radical young-earth schools, however, the creationist curriculum reaches far beyond biology class to package their outlandish science in a conservative outfit that makes the science seem normal.

Kentucky Creation

Those radical-creationist schools aren't the only institutions that matter. Young-earth organizations such as the Institute for Creation Research (ICR) and Answers in Genesis (AIG) provide believers with more proof that their young-earth beliefs do not make them ridiculous. More than simply providing evidence and arguments for radical creationists, they tell radical creationists whom not to trust and why.

Radical creationists might subscribe to magazines from either organization. Or they may simply browse through their websites, finding proof and reassurance that right-thinking Christians agree on the idea of a young earth.

By far the most attention-grabbing example of these sorts of creationist institutions is the brick-and-mortar Creation Museum in Petersburg, Kentucky. This massive tourist destination features AIG's signature 75,000-square-foot science museum. Plus, forty miles away looms the huge new Ark Encounter, purportedly an authentic reproduction of Noah's ark.

To skeptics like me, the museum seems at first to be merely outrageous, like the scientific claims of young-earth creationism themselves. Once our eyes are opened a little bit to the institutional demands of creationism, though, the museum starts to make more sense. Not that the science gets any less strange, but we can see some of the same patterns of other creationist institutions at play in the Kentucky museum.

Like a lot of curious skeptics, I've made my pilgrimage. Twice. At first glance—as we'll talk about in more depth in chapter 7—the huge Creation Museum doesn't look much different than any other large museum. The exhibits look pretty much like museum exhibits anywhere.

Of course, the content is truly extraordinary. It can be shocking to see an exhibit that claims dragons are proof that humans and dinosaurs have long coexisted. It can be weird to see careful explanations of the actual size of Noah's ark, as if we have all already agreed that it was a real thing.

If we want to understand American creationism, though, especially the radical young-earth variety, we need to put aside our temptation to dismiss this museum as mere lunacy or perhaps as cynical money-grubbing on the part of AIG.

The Creation Museum can tell us a lot. First of all, the museum reassures radical creationists that their ideas have plenty of expert scientific support. Also important, though, the museum shows us that creationism is only one part of the creationist intellectual world and not the most important part. The Creation Museum assumes a young earth and a recent divine creation, of course. But like the creationist schools discussed in this chapter, the museum does other things, too. For creationists who make the trip, the Creation Museum wraps their non-mainstream scientific ideas into a much broader conservative context, one in which those scientific ideas seem to make obvious sense. Most important, the Creation Museum offers evidence that only radical young-earth creationist thinking is trustworthy.

So, yes, visitors to the Creation Museum will see explanations of young-earth science. But an unwary visitor might be surprised to see other things there, as well. For example, as visitors meander down the main walkway through the exhibits, they encounter a "Culture in Crisis" room. It looks like the outside façade of a regular American house. When creationists peep through the windows, however, they see images designed to shock and disgust them. A boy looks at porn. A girl thinks about having an abortion. Slovenly Americans drink beer and gorge themselves on pizza and immorality.

When visitors continue, they come to "Graffiti Alley." Headlines ripped from newspapers and magazines point to "Apocalypse Now. Tsunamis. Earthquakes. Nuclear Meltdowns. Revolutions. Economies on the Brink. What the #@%! Is Next?"

It might seem as if such things have little to do with a dissenting science that disputes the central tenets of mainstream modern thought. In fact, however, the two are intimately, necessarily connected. Just as creationist schools teach a group of ideas that make young-earth science seem obvious, so too does the Creation Museum preach a broad worldview in which radical creationism is a sensible and obvious choice.

For the radical creationists of the Creation Museum, the central message is not really about actual evolutionary theory. Rather, the most important takeaway for creationist visitors is that the world has been divided into two unmistakable camps. On one hand lurks the mainstream secular and liberal establishment. Since this group took control of mainstream science and mainstream culture, morality has gone, literally, to hell. Once-trustworthy public spaces have become festering sinks of unrestrained sexuality and hedonism.

Luckily, the museum preaches, there is a simple, trustworthy alternative. The foundation of all the shameful trends in modern society is evolutionary thinking. Not really evolutionary theory itself, but the dehumanizing Godlessness with which liberals and atheists promote evolution. In the face of a dangerously backslidden world, the Creation Museum offers both a promise and a prophylactic: radical young-earth creationism.

After visitors to the Creation Museum see the moral dangers lurking everywhere in mainstream modern America, they also see the creationist solution.

For creationists, there is hope. The faithful will be saved. Those who have remained true to God's Word—like Noah and his family—will be protected and shepherded by God through tough times. As scholars Susan and William Trollinger explain, the museum is about obedience to that one universal and transhistorical law—God's Word—and about the consequences that follow from disobedience. [52]

The world is a terrifying place, the museum tells visitors, but there is an obvious Christian solution. The very radical-ness of young-earth ideas doesn't seem radical within the museum's walls, but rather serves as proof of membership in a long tradition of steadfastness.

It might not seem obvious to secular or liberal folks, the museum tells us, but young-earth creationism is one of the best ways to help people remain true to the broader message of divine truth. In the context of Graffiti Alleys and Cultures in Crisis, the museum offers an obvious connecting thread. Time and again, from the Garden of Eden through Noah's flood to Sodom's sins, grumbling, fumbling humanity has turned its back on God's Word. And time and again, humans have been punished.

Yes, mainstream science tells us that humans have evolved from other animals over millions of years. That sort of knowledge, the museum shows visitors, is no different from the false and deadly "knowledge" of the rest of mainstream culture. If mainstream America embraces rights for homosexuals, abortion rights, or even left-leaning politics, it does not make those mainstream ideas correct.

Rather, in every field, mainstream understandings are merely the latest example of humanity's stubborn insistence on its own damnable wisdom. In every case, throughout history, the museum makes clear, the faithful have been mocked. In every case, too, the faithful have eventually been saved.

So why does the Creation Museum matter? Not because it convinces skeptics like me of the scientific power of radical young-earth ideas. The museum gets its power because it puts its scientific ideas into a context that celebrates their radical distance from mainstream thinking. It tells its faithful that there are only two types of people in the world: the trustworthy and the others.

When creationists hear that mainstream science thinks they are lunatics, the museum reassures them that real religion, real Christianity, has always seemed outrageous to the damned. When radical creationists hear that the evidence is overwhelming for mainstream evolutionary science, the museum gives them an easy way to dismiss those claims as just another serpent's whisper.

CreationWorld

Once we are a little more knowledgeable about the institutional world of American creationism, other things start to make more sense, too. Only when we've learned about the creationism-friendly intellectual mysteries of dispensational thinking taught at radical-creationist colleges, for example, do we see why Kentucky's Creation Museum guides visitors through seven dispensation-friendly learning zones.[53]

And only when we understand that creationist institutions do much more than layer their peculiar scientific ideas onto otherwise mainstream schools can we understand how educated people can hold such seemingly outlandish ideas.

The network of creationist institutions is far broader than the schools and museum we've visited in this chapter. Yes, a creationist middle school can plan a class trip to Kentucky. They can visit a science museum that reinforces all the ideas they've learned in their Abeka textbooks. And yes, those schoolkids can attend summer camps where the message will be the same. Their teachers, too, can troop off to Pensacola Christian College in the summer to brush up their understanding of creationist science. Families can plan special creation vacations; homeschoolers can sign up for creationist-only graduation parties.

At every stage, in every part of the country, young-earth creationist families can do all the things mainstream families do without ever leaving the trustworthy world of radical-creationist thinking. At every level, too, creationists can feel sure that there are experts all the way up the academic ladder who hold even more expertise in creationist thinking.

The institutions of radical creationism are more than just scientific dissenters. They wrap their creation science in a much more profoundly dissident worldview in which only creationism makes sense and deserves trust.

Why don't more American creationists abandon their radical ideas when they hear science pundits like Bill Nye explain real science? Because the institutional network of creationism has provided them in advance with a coherent, internally consistent explanation of both creationism and the Bill Nyes of the world.

They can rest assured that their creationist science is better than mainstream science. But that's not all, and, again, actual evolutionary science is not the main issue. Radical creationists can turn to their institutional network for proof that only their own radical beliefs can save them from a deadly morass of spiritual and moral quicksand.

5

Ignorance and Evolution

As usual, Will Rogers said it best. In 1924, Rogers was nearing the height of his popularity as a cowboy comedian. Americans loved the way he poked fun at the put-on airs of fancy folk. They loved the way he lampooned the swelling self-importance of city slickers. But when Rogers pooh-poohed the rules about eating soup politely, he pushed big-city theater critic Percy Hammond too far. There was nothing funny, Hammond sniffed, about sloppy table manners. Ignorance of basic civility, Hammond wrote, was nothing to be proud of. Fair enough, Rogers conceded, but to be brutally honest, Rogers was not the only ignorant one in the room. "Everybody is ignorant," Rogers concluded, "only on different subjects."[1]

When it comes to creationism, we need to keep Rogers's warning in mind. It is tempting to think of radical creationism—the kind of creationism that disputes mainstream science and pushes creationism into public life—as a question of simple ignorance, as just another eruption of "Idiot America."[2] It's tempting to see radical creationism mainly as a yawning intellectual emptiness, a deficiency of knowledge, a scientific void.

However, if we are sincerely interested in understanding American creationism and why we don't really disagree all that much about evolution even though we keep fighting about it, we need to recognize a different and difficult truth. Namely, most of us—whether we call ourselves radical creationists, evolutionary creationists, anti-creationists, or something else—don't really understand evolutionary theory very well. Our fights about evolution are usually not actually about evolutionary theory because very few Americans actually know what evolutionary theory truly says. Instead, creationism debates are almost always just a recap of our tired old culture-war battles dressed up awkwardly and misleadingly in the language of science.

So are radical creationists simply ignorant about evolution? Well, yes, but only because almost all of us—creationists and non-creationists alike—are pretty ignorant about evolution. Radical creationists' ignorance is not what distinguishes them from the rest of the creationists out there.

Creationism USA. Adam Laats, Oxford University Press (2021). © Oxford University Press.
DOI: 10.1093/oso/9780197516607.001.0001.

To clear some of this fog, in this chapter we'll look at the confounding real relationships among knowledge, ignorance, evolution, and creationism. It's not as simple as people like me tend to think. Will Rogers was closer to the truth, though we might need to tweak him a little bit. When it comes to evolution, it seems as if everybody is ignorant on the same subject, but in different ways. As we've seen throughout this book, the real question isn't what we know, but whom we trust.

Dinosaurs with Saddles

Let's start with the most outlandish scientific claim of radical young-earth creationists (YECs). We don't need to know much about actual evolutionary science to know that museum-friendly big dinosaurs like *T. rex* died out long, long before humans ever evolved. Yet if YECs believe that life on earth is only six-ish thousand years old, then they must think most species coexisted at some time or other. At some point, if we are to believe the scientific claims of YECs, dinosaurs and humans must have shared the planet.

Ken Ham and the Answers in Genesis folks will take it one step further. Dinosaurs must have survived the worldwide flood on Noah's ark, they insist, since the Bible says that every kind of land animal did so. How is it possible for huge dinosaurs to fit on one boat? According to Ham, young dinosaurs would only have been about the same size as large dogs. And Noah didn't need to corral every single species, just samples of each "kind" of animal.[3]

So for some creationists, at least, the idea that humans and dinosaurs lived side by side is not outlandish at all, but rather obvious. But it has become embarrassing. YECs are keenly aware that their beliefs are often attacked, not only as wrong or mistaken but also as pure garbage. All too often—from the perspective of YECs, that is—the notion that dinos and humans lived together is the first thing skeptics attack.

For example, when journalist Charles P. Pierce went out in search of "Idiot America," his first stop was at Ken Ham's Creation Museum in Kentucky. And the first thing that grabbed Pierce's attention was a statue of a dinosaur with a saddle. Clearly, to Pierce, this was a display for people who just didn't care about truth, facts, or education. This was something for people who were simply "batshit crazy." To Pierce—and this is the part that likely pierced Ken Ham's creationist heart—"anyone who believed this righteous hooey should be kept away from sharp objects and their own money."[4]

As we saw in chapters 3 and 4, a big part of the appeal of young-earth creationism has always been its promise to give believers better science along with purer religion. For creationists like Ken Ham, it has been much worse to be laughed at than to be argued with. And the notion of dinosaurs with saddles seems to be the most outlandish part of young-earth creationism out there. The idea that anyone would ride around on dinosaurs seems like the ultimate crack-brained retreat from knowledge and intelligence.

Maybe that's why Ken Ham gets so defensive about it. Does his museum really have a statue of a dinosaur with a saddle? Yes, Ham admits, but it is not meant as anything other than a plaything for children, "just a fun part for kids." That statue was not meant to teach people about real science, real creationism. The other representations of dinosaurs in the museum don't have any saddles.[5]

What about Ham's 2001 book, *Dinosaurs of Eden*? In that book, critics charged, Ham depicts dinos with saddles. Right there on page 42, we see cartoons of villagers using all sorts of pack animals: donkeys, camels, oxen, and yes, indeed, *Tsintaosauruses* and *Gallimimuses* too.[6] Pish-posh, Ham retorted. That was a children's book, meant to depict science in a kid-friendly way. In reality, Ham insisted, he never taught that people rode dinosaurs. As he put it, "I don't know where people get the idea that people rode dinosaurs. I mean, there's no evidence in the Bible that that is so." The real mystery, Answers in Genesis insisted, was the "head-scratchingly bizarre" fixation of anti-creationists on the tiniest details; the sad and sinister attempts of atheists to "discredit and malign creationist groups."[7]

In spite of Ham's prickly defensiveness about dinosaurs with saddles, among creationist crowds he continues to emphasize the idea. In a more recent book, for example, Ham included a question from a child about riding dinosaurs: "Did we use dinosaurs for transportation?" To this curious creationist ten-year-old, Ham explained:

> The Bible doesn't specifically address this question, but . . . we can use the reasoning skills God gave us and His Word to come up with an answer. We see and hear about all sorts of animals being tamed by man. . . . Why not some of the dinosaurs? Who knows what they were doing? It seems to me we should at least allow the possibility that some could have been tamed to help with transportation, maybe even farming, hauling heavy loads (the strong ones!) and other things.[8]

Yet these days, it seems, Ken Ham would never publish a picture of people riding around on dinosaurs. He doesn't like to admit that he tells children it could have happened. Not because it couldn't have happened, but rather because Ham knows that putting saddles on dinosaurs seems idiotic to the rest of us.

Ignorance and Resistance

In that, at least, Ken Ham is right. Not only by putting saddles on dinosaurs, but by disbelieving in evolution as a whole, Ken Ham and other YECs seem to be ignoring a basic truth of modern science. And ever since Darwin's *Origin* was published, there have been evolution-loving pundits and promoters who have assumed that the only reason people could disagree was due to simple ignorance. For over a hundred years, science writers have blithely assumed that creationism was due primarily to a certain sort of intellectual deficit, a lack of knowledge about evolutionary theory.

When Darwin's famous book came out in 1859, for example, one of his most aggressive supporters insisted that only ignorant people could possibly object. Back then, Thomas Henry Huxley earned the nickname "Darwin's Bulldog" for his ferocious insistence that resistance was futile. As soon as most citizens learned "the facts of the case," Huxley argued, then acceptance of the theory would naturally spread. All thinking people, Huxley assumed, all educated people, would obviously "turn to those views which profess to rest on a scientific basis only."[9]

By the 1920s, it was clear that resistance to Darwin's ideas about evolution would not evaporate as effortlessly as Huxley had hoped. Yet Darwin's fans continued to assume that the obvious truth of Darwin's explanations only needed to be heard to be believed. In the 1920s, for example, evolutionary theory had few supporters more famous than Henry Fairfield Osborn. Osborn was a geologist and a paleontologist, but he made his public mark mainly as the head of the American Museum of Natural History. In the imagination of 1920s America, Osborn came to symbolize "science" as a whole, personifying a modern, scientific view of the world. As the Neil deGrasse Tyson of his generation, Osborn remained supremely confident that evolutionary theory would win the day, as soon as it could be explained to the masses. Even an "intelligent child," Osborn argued, would quickly understand how humans evolved "if the opportunity is afforded." The only reason people might doubt evolution, Osborn assumed, was due to sheer ignorance. The only people who didn't accept evolution, Osborn believed, simply hadn't had it explained to them clearly enough.[10]

One might think that radical creationism's undeniable staying power would give pause to those who dismiss it as simple ignorance. In fact, however, in our twenty-first century we still hear from pundits who tell us that radical creationism only makes sense as a lamentable lack of knowledge. Perhaps most famously, the irascible atheist Richard Dawkins has insisted that creationists could only be those numbskulls who remained stubbornly "ignorant of science."[11] Even Bill Nye, the far friendlier face of science punditry, argues that creationists like Ken Ham are only able to maintain their fight with evolution due to stubborn ignorance. Folks at Answers in Genesis, Nye wrote recently, "just can't handle the truth." Though evolutionary theory is elegant, intuitive, and "undeniable," Ken Ham and his ilk "throw aside their common sense" and insist on remaining ignorant about evolution.[12]

As we'll see, that's just not the case. For most of us, evolutionary theory is not obviously true. It is not simply understood or intuitive. Henry Fairfield Osborn's "intelligent child" usually does not think in evolutionary terms, even if those terms have been explained clearly and convincingly to him or her.

Plus, there are plenty of creationists—both leaders and the rank and file—who know plenty about mainstream evolutionary science. Even back in the 1870s, it would have been easy enough to discover creationists who knew what Darwin was saying. Our old friend Charles Hodge, for example, famously concluded that Darwinism was atheism. It wasn't because he didn't know what Darwin had said. Like many creationists since, Hodge knew plenty about evolutionary theory. He just couldn't believe it.

To be clear, we should say it again: Yes, there are likely plenty of radical creationists who are simply and naively ignorant about evolution. There must be plenty of folks who have never heard about it or have only heard distorted creationist myths about Darwin and his theory. But people who assume that the primary cause of radical young-earth creationism is naïve ignorance don't understand the real landscape of American creationism.

And our ignorance about their ignorance matters. Because if radical creationism is a simple absence of knowledge, then the solution is clear. Like Darwin's Bulldog in 1859, we could plow forward with full confidence. All we would need to do is come up with catchy slogans and fun-filled learning activities about evolution to spread the word. We might inject evolutionary public service announcements into the halftime shows at football games. We could put Darwin's ideas in fortune cookies and on billboards.

But that's not going to work. Creationism—the real creationism, not our imagined cartoonish misrepresentation of it—is not a simple lack of knowledge about evolution. Our creation-evolution battles do not pit ignorance on one side versus knowledge on the other. The truth is much more complicated. As we'll see in the next sections, creationists seem pretty ignorant about evolution, but so do evolutionists. To put it in Will Rogers's terms, we are all ignorant about evolution, just in different ways.

What Scientists Say

Let's start with an eye-opening experiment carried out by the folks at the National Science Board (NSB). The NSB is the governing body of the National Science Foundation, the federal government's organization that funds and supports American science. Among the NSB's many missions is to estimate America's knowledge about science. It is charged with telling the president what Americans know about science and what we don't know. To find out, the NSB pores over survey data.

And, unlike science celebrities like Richard Dawkins and Bill Nye, the folks at the NSB recognized a problem when they saw one. Too often, asking people about evolution led to skewed results. It was difficult not to notice. When the NSB split its results between people who identified as not very religious and very religious, the problem became starkly clear.

On most science questions, there was not much difference between what religious people knew and nonreligious people knew. They tended to look the same, statistically, when asked if electrons are smaller than atoms. (They are.) They tended to look the same when asked what the main ingredient in our planet's atmosphere was. (It's nitrogen.) And they tended to look the same when asked about the relationship between positive results on mammograms and breast cancer. (It's complicated.) But here's the kicker: When Americans are asked if humans evolved from "earlier species of animals," we see a predictable divide. Nonreligious people tend to "know" the answer is yes. Very religious people tend not to "know" it.[13]

What does that tell us? If we are ardent anti-creationists, like Richard Dawkins, we might say that creationists have a weird kind of intellectual blind spot. They know some scientific ideas, but they refuse to know evolution.

But the more reasonable minds among us smell a rat. The problem isn't with creationists' knowledge; the problem is with this sort of test question itself. The other questions—electrons, nitrogen, mammograms—are generally seen as God-neutral. But evolution isn't. For some creationists, as we saw in chapter 3, to say they "know" that humans evolved would mean saying they don't believe in their religion. For some, to say they "know" evolution occurs means to give tacit approval to things such as abortion, homosexuality, drug abuse, and even organized crime. When they say that evolution is "false," do they mean they don't know that scientists think such things? Are they saying that scientists are wrong? Or are they saying—for whatever reason—that they just won't accept what those scientists say? It's impossible to tell from the simple true-false survey question.

What was the NSB to do? They wanted to produce a trustworthy guide to the level of Americans' knowledge about science. They understood that asking people about evolution told them more about people's religious beliefs than about their science knowledge.

In 2010, they punted. Their results were about the same as always. Just over half of Americans (55 percent) said that humans had not evolved. And a whopping two-thirds said that the universe had not begun with a "huge explosion." The NSB's leaders recognized, however, that those numbers measured religious belief more than anything else. As one reviewer said, those survey questions were faulty "blunt instruments."[14] So the NSB cut that section out of their report.

It makes sense. If the NSB wanted to tell the president how much Americans knew about evolution, those numbers seemed misleading. Nevertheless, science activists howled in protest. Leaving out questions about evolution and the big bang gave a skewed vision of Americans' science literacy. Josh Rosenau of the National Center for Science Education called it "intellectual malpractice," a way to cover up the troubling question of resistance to scientific ideas.[15]

So the NSB put them back into their data review, but they experimented with ways to make the questions more useful. In their 2012 review, they examined different answers from different groups. Question one: Do you agree with the following statement? "Human beings, as we know them today, developed from earlier species of animals." As always, a majority (52 percent) of Americans said no. No way.

But when questions were reworded, they produced dramatically different answers. When surveyors asked people if "according to the theory of evolution" humans evolved from earlier species, a much larger 72 percent of people agreed. People gave similar answers about the big bang. Only a minority (39 percent) agreed that "the universe began with a huge explosion." But a much larger group (60 percent) agreed that astronomers thought it did.[16]

What does that tell us? Seems like there are lots of Americans out there who know what mainstream scientists think, but they just don't agree. Even these questions, though, seem like blunt instruments. We can't really tell from these results what people think or what we can justifiably conclude that they know.

Known Unknowns

Happily, psychologists and science educators have conducted an inspired set of studies to dig deeper into this cognitive conundrum. Do creationists actually know evolutionary theory? Do they just choose not to believe it? Or do creationists suffer from a lack of knowledge, a simple ignorance that allows them to wallow in their own fundamentalist intellectual stupor?

Of course, individual radical creationists might be stupid or ignorant, but as a group they are not. At least—and this is important—they are not any more stupid or ignorant than the rest of us. In spite of what Richard Dawkins and Bill Nye might think, we do not see a stark divide between radical creationists who don't know evolution and other creationists or non-creationists who do. In fact, in study after study, we see the same surprising results: As far as scholars can tell, there is no clear correlation between the amount people know about evolutionary theory and the amount they accept it to be true.

It's worth repeating, since it is so difficult for people like me to believe. When we dig deeper than awkward survey questions, we find that there is no simple, solid, one-to-one connection between knowing evolution and accepting it. Radical creationists, as a group, know just as much about evolutionary theory as non-creationists and moderate creationists. And people like me—people who think that evolutionary theory is currently the best explanation for the way species came to be different from one another—we don't actually know what evolutionary theory says. At least, we don't know it any better than radical creationists do.

In other words, we believe it, but don't know it. Creationists know it, but don't believe it. At least in broad statistical terms.

It seems hard to believe, but no matter how they frame the questions, psychologists come up with the same answers. In one Harvard study, for example, researchers concluded, "participants in the present study were no more likely to endorse the statement 'natural selection is the best explanation for how a species adapts to its environment' if they understood natural selection than if they did not."[17] In a different study, just under a hundred non-majors in an undergraduate biology class were quizzed on their ideas about evolution and creation. The results? Among these students, researchers found "no relation between knowledge and acceptance of animal or human evolution."[18]

It can get even weirder. Sometimes, students who learn more about evolution actually end up more likely to embrace creationist beliefs. In one study of high school students in Arizona, for example, students were asked about both their knowledge and their beliefs before and after a three-week unit on evolutionary science. Not surprisingly, as a group they knew a lot more about evolution after studying it for three weeks.[19] But knowing more about evolution did not cause them to believe in creationism any less. We might say the opposite happened. Before their unit about evolution, for example, just under half of the students (45.9 percent) agreed or strongly agreed with the statement "Genesis is the best account of how the Earth was created and populated with life." After the unit, more students (48.5 percent) agreed or strongly agreed.[20]

We can't confuse these group results with individual changes, of course. It's possible that some students learned a lot about evolution, while others didn't. It's possible that some students refused to know more about evolution because they plugged their ears for the whole three weeks and stubbornly recited creationist mantras to themselves. As a group, however, these students learned a lot about evolution. Yet at the same time, as a group, these students grew a little more attached to their creationism.

It seems to work in the other direction as well. Among a large group of students at Louisiana State University, studying evolution tended to make them believe it. But it didn't help them to know it. Among these 192 students, at least, an intense session with evolutionary theory led many more of them to say they believed it. But among those students who said they now believed it, there was no greater knowledge of what evolutionary theory actually said.

That is, after studying evolution, these students believed it, but they didn't know it any better.[21]

How could that work? We need to be careful about leaping to conclusions based on these study results. Most of them asked questions in significantly different ways. In the Harvard study, for example, researchers identified two broad categories of thinking about the ways species changed.[22] Darwin's revolutionary evolutionary idea, the core of our modern way of thinking about evolution, was that species expressed constant variation. When a variation proved beneficial, a natural selection mechanism tended to increase the proportion of individuals who expressed that variation. Individuals with that trait tended to survive and multiply at higher rates, leading to bigger and bigger proportions of the population that showed that trait.

Before Darwin, many scientists assumed that plants and animals transformed over time, because somehow the essence of each species changed. Not through individual variation and natural selection, but rather through a cumulative process of individual changes, a sort of heroic striving by species to improve themselves. Turns out, that's the way many students still think it happens, even those students who tell you that they believe in evolutionary theory.

Consider the famous example of the peppered moth. Over time, the species changed from white to dark gray. Why? Maybe because, as more and more soot poured out of England's factories, the tree trunks in the region changed in color from white to gray.[23] Before the Industrial Revolution, white moths could count on a measure of camouflage protection by blending into the white tree trunks. After the trees changed color from white to dark sooty gray, though, white moths would stand out to predators.

According to Darwin's idea of natural selection—still the core of modern scientific thinking about evolutionary change—all moths have built-in variations. Some just happen to be born different from their parents. If they are born gray, just as trees are turning gray, they will happen to have an advantage over white moths. Predators will see the white moths more easily because they stand out starkly from the now-dark tree trunks. The white moths will get eaten more often, and the gray ones will be safe more often. The moths that expressed the variation of gray coloring, over time, will tend to become a greater and greater proportion of the total population of peppered moths. The species in this region will have changed from white to gray.

That, at least, is a broad-brush outline of mainstream evolutionary thinking. Species all have natural variation. Species all tend to produce more offspring than can possibly survive. If a variation provides any advantage and it is heritable, it tends to be preserved and may even take over.

Individual moths don't get darker as time goes on. Moths as a species don't work slowly toward a group goal of turning darker in order to survive better. Some of them express a natural genetic variation of dark coloring. Others don't. As their environment changes, the ones that show the variation tend to survive and reproduce in greater numbers. As a total population, peppered moths become dark-colored more often.

But that's not how a lot of us imagine it. In the Harvard study, researchers probed students' tendency to think about the change in moth color as a kind of transformation in the essence of the peppered moth, rather than an expression of a variation among individual moths. For a lot of students, even those who say they embrace the idea of natural selection, species transform due to different factors. For a lot of us—in our unexamined assumptions—species transform because, for one reason or another, what it meant to be a peppered moth meant darker and darker coloration. To be a "real" peppered moth, a lot of us think, individuals will transform in succeeding generations to darker and darker coloration.

The way many of us think of it, at least, moths grow darker and darker over time, as individuals get a little darker with each generation. Because what it means to be a peppered moth changes from being white to being dark gray, most of us think that the transformation will happen gradually, as individual moths grow darker.

It might sound like a nit-picky detail, a quibble. When it comes to finding out what people think about evolution, though, it's not. Understanding the relationship between variation and natural selection is the intellectual heart of evolutionary theory. In the Harvard study, and in the slew of studies like it, researchers find that the accuracy of people's ideas about key evolutionary terms such as variation, inheritance, adaptation, domestication, speciation, and extinction don't have any correlation to their beliefs about it.

It's not just moths, and it's not only the idea of natural selection that gives people trouble. In a different study, one student explained how evolution worked before he studied it. He gave the example of cheetahs. How did cheetahs evolve to be so fast? "They realized," he explained, "they had to speed up or they would starve." Well, no, not really. Cheetahs might have starved more often before they evolved their trademark speed. But they did not "realize" that they needed to evolve. Cheetahs as a species did not have a meeting and conclude that they needed to take drastic steps to improve their gazelle-catching abilities.[24]

After studying evolution, this student tweaked his understanding. After learning about evolutionary theory, his take on cheetah evolution became more nuanced: "After a while cheetahs had to learn to run fast or else be eaten by predators. So with the generations they developed the ability to run faster and faster." That is better. After studying evolution, the student included the notion that evolution took a while and that it unfolded "with the generations." But even after studying evolution and improving his grasp of it, this student still doesn't quite seem to get it. According to evolutionary theory, cheetahs didn't learn to run fast with the purpose in mind of avoiding predators. Rather, faster cheetahs tended to survive better, so the trait of high-speed running was maintained in their genetic lineage.

Most important for our purposes, this student was never really able to explain evolutionary theory, but that did not stop him from endorsing it as the best explanation of the ways cheetahs got their speed. His lack of knowledge did not have anything to do with his personal beliefs.

It is difficult to know what to make of these studies. They certainly fly in the face of easy assumptions about the nature of scientific knowledge and creationism. When it comes right down to it, there's no simple scholarly consensus about the relationship between knowledge and belief. To a surprising degree, creationists seem just as likely to be able to explain the details of evolutionary theory as non-creationists, or, at least, much more likely than some assume. And people like me who accept evolutionary theory as true do not do much better than creationists when it comes to answering basic questions about it. Even when people say they believe in evolutionary ideas, they are likely—to some degree—to think in non-evolutionary ways.

Unbelievable

For those of us who want to help more and more people understand evolutionary theory, the news gets worse. The more we find out about the ways people tend to think about evolution and creationism, the more it seems that Charles Hodge was right.

As we saw in chapter 3, Hodge had a subtle take on the dilemma of evolutionary thinking. If he were to hold onto his religion, Hodge argued in

1874, he couldn't possibly accept Darwin's version of unguided evolution. Moreover, Hodge insisted, no one could. The notion that organisms could have evolved without a plan, a purpose, without a design and designer, was simply too far-fetched for the human mind to comprehend.

It was as ridiculous as imagining that a "ship or a locomotive" could suddenly appear out of a pile of iron and wood. Complexity, Hodge thought, automatically implied design. "Every man believes it," Hodge concluded, "and no man can practically disbelieve it."[25]

As much as it might pain us to do so, we need to concede that at some level, Hodge was right. Our brains seem wired, somehow, to assume that there must be some design to living things. We seem to have a difficult time imagining that wings and flowers and blood-clotting mechanisms could have evolved without a plan in mind. Though we might understand at some level that it is not so, when pressed or stressed, our minds tend to revert to what seems obvious: complexity implies design.

Even Charles Darwin tended to talk this way. As philosopher Michael Ruse has shown, Darwin never gave up the notion that evolutionary features showed some sort of purpose, some "final cause." Darwin saw cause and purpose everywhere he looked. Why do geese have long bills? To make them "well fitted," Darwin argued, for eating grass.[26] Why did some species split into male and female sexes? To help them adapt to circumstances, to give them an advantage.[27]

At first glance, the intellectual problem might not be immediately obvious. Geese's long bills *do* give them an advantage when it comes to eating grass. And sexual reproduction *does* seem to confer an advantage when it comes to passing along genetic identities. But if we're thinking along evolutionary lines, we don't think of such things as evolving on purpose in order to confer those advantages. We don't think of a great master plan by which geese came to have longer, more efficient grass-eating bills and reproduction came to be a sexual thing.

Rather, according to evolutionary theory, longer bills and sexual reproduction happened. And they happened to work. Geese who happened to have longer bills happened to be able to eat more grass. They happened to survive better than other geese. There was no plan, though, no design, no final goal in mind.

Yet our brains seem to insist stubbornly that there was. Even those of us who understand Darwin's ideas fairly well—even Darwin himself—are inclined to talk as if Charles Hodge were right. We tend not to think that our complex world could have simply happened on its own. We think, for instance, that an eagle's wings exist in order to help it fly.

And, of course, eagles' wings do help them fly. But according to evolutionary theory, at least, wings did not evolve with the purpose of flying in mind. After all, plenty of birds have wings but don't fly. What *purpose* do wings serve? If we want to think in evolutionary terms, wings don't have a *purpose*. Wings happened.

Why does this distinction matter? It shows us how deeply addicted our brains are to an intuition of purpose and design. And it helps us understand that even those of us who say we embrace evolutionary theory tend to think in distinctly non-evolutionary ways. Indeed, our tendency to assume that there is some plan and purpose to living things might lead us to conclude that—whatever label we might pick for ourselves—most of us are creationists of one sort or another, by any reasonable definition of "creationism."

At the very least, it seems apparent that evolutionary theory is not simple or intuitive. Cognitive psychologists have examined the ways we think about the world. It turns out purpose and design are the most obvious, intuitive explanations for the ways things came to be. As Kostas Kampourakis of the University of Geneva has suggested, the real problem with accepting evolutionary theory might come from "our intuitive ways of perceiving the world around us."[28]

Among children, at least, the idea of evolution without an end goal seems developmentally out of reach. Children tend to assume that living and non-living things alike are "for" something. When asked why giraffes have long necks, for example, children will often say that God made them that way to reach the tasty leaves at the tops of trees. When asked why pointy rocks are pointy on the top, children don't say that they formed that way through erosion or volcanic eruption, but because a point kept them safe from animals that might sit on them.[29]

In study after study, cognitive psychologists have found that children are, in fact, "intuitive theists."[30] Children assume that animals were designed by God (or god or gods, for that matter) to be the way they are. Rhinos have horns to defend themselves. Peacocks have fancy feathers to look good. Woodpeckers have long beaks to catch bugs. All of them, children intuitively conclude, were designed that way by some sort of higher power to fit into the grand plan of life.

It is more than just what they learn from their parents. Indeed, when E. Margaret Evans from the University of Michigan compared kids from radical-creationist families to those from non-radical-creationist families, she found some astounding results. Kids from radical-creationist families were all creationists. No surprise there. But kids from non-radical families were also all creationists, at least between the ages of eight and ten. It was only the adults and the older children from non-radical-creationist families who started to doubt if the world and everything in it was created on purpose by some divine entity.[31]

Children between the ages of five and seven, on the other hand, tended to have ideas even further divorced from any sort of boring rationality. All the kids from radical-creationist families gave creationist explanations of the origins of life. And so did lots of the five-to-seven-year-olds from non-radical-creationist families. The non-radical-creationist kids who didn't give creationist explanations gave even stranger ones, such as the notion that things had simply spontaneously generated. No youngster, no matter how intelligent, no matter what scientists like Henry Fairfield Osborn might have hoped, endorsed anything resembling evolutionary theory.

As Evans concluded, kids come up with a million ideas about how various objects and animals came to look the way they do. As they got older, their communities tended to shape the way they thought about it. Among radical creationists, kids held onto and strengthened their youthful assumptions about purpose and design. Among non-radical-creationists, people came to believe a jumble of explanations.[32]

What about adults? Do adults—even nonreligious, non-creationist adults—also tend to assume that the universe operates with a purpose? To find out, Deborah Kelemen and Evelyn Rosset subjected a group of college students to a test. They split them into three groups and asked them questions about why things were the way they were. For example, students were asked if "the sun radiates heat because warmth nurtures life."

Of course, it doesn't. The sun radiates heat and its warmth nurtures life, but scientists wouldn't tell you that the sun had that purpose in mind. And most savvy science students, too, wouldn't think that way. But when they're put under some pressure, a lot of people are apt to default to their deeply held intuitions about purpose and design.

At least, that's what Kelemen and Rosset's study suggests. In the first group, students took their time to answer. In the second, they were given a reasonable time limit. In the third, though, they were hurried. Among the students who weren't rushed, only a minority (29 percent) thought that natural things happened for a reason. Among the rushed, however, a much larger group (47 percent) thought so.[33]

What does that mean? We don't want to be too hasty in our conclusions, but it seems that adults, too, tend to revert to some sort of magical thinking when we are stressed. Even adults who know a lot about evolutionary theory and mainstream science tend to do so. Even adults who would never call themselves creationists might be disposed to think of the world in creationist-friendly terms.

Full of Sound and Fury

No matter where we look, we can see how shallow the roots of real evolutionary thinking are. Even among those of us who accept it, the idea of evolution almost always suffers from some sort of intellectual butchery. Mainstream culture is chockfull of misrepresentations and misunderstandings of evolutionary theory.

Think of the many times you've seen the meme depicting monkeys improving themselves through cavemen on their way to *Homo sapiens*. To a lot of us, that's the perfect symbol of evolution; although, it's not what evolutionary theory actually says.

Instead of a ladder of ever-improving animals, instead of moving through a long-lasting journey from monkey to man, real evolutionary change moves in every direction at once. Evolutionary biologists would never talk about evolving up, but rather evolving out, branching into a million different species in an everlasting process.

Figure 5.1 What does evolution look like?

Nevertheless, those of us who say we accept evolutionary theory as true—or, to be more precise, as the best current explanation of the way species came to be different from one another—still hold onto very non-scientific ideas about what evolutionary theory says. We think of evolution as a straight line, a ladder of ever-improving life forms. We think of changes in species as some sort of gradual transformation in their essence, rather than as an ongoing evolutionary experiment. We assume—at least when we're under pressure—that life and the universe must have some ultimate purpose, some end goal toward which we're all evolving.

But according to evolutionary theory, they don't. Or at least, they don't need to. So, yes, I'll say it: Plenty of the creationists who troop through Ken Ham's Creation Museum in Kentucky are likely idiots. They are probably card-carrying citizens of "Idiot America." When they pose their children on Ham's saddled dinosaur, they are gleefully demonstrating their vast ignorance about life and evolution and the deep history of our planet.

But those of us who laugh up our sleeves—or in their faces—at their magical thinking must recognize that we, too, are idiots. We, too, don't know much about evolutionary theory. In some ways, our ignorance is worse since it is wrapped in smug false confidence about our obvious intellectual superiority.

The thing that separates the ignorant from the wise—at least when it comes to creationism and evolution—is not the obvious division between radical creationists and the rest of us. As far as we can tell, the connections between knowledge and acceptance are not as simple as they might seem at first. There is not a simple correlation between learning about evolution and moving away from radical creationism.

In the end, terms like knowledge and ignorance don't help us much when we try to understand why we don't really disagree about evolution. In the end, Will Rogers was right. We really are all ignorant. Most people don't really think in terms of evolutionary theory. Creationism isn't the weird outlier, but the human norm that some of us discard as we get older.

With all that in mind, it's better not to talk about knowledge and ignorance when we talk about evolution and creationism. Better to follow Dan Kahan of Yale Law School and conclude that our positions about creation and evolution tell us something about who we are, not about what we know.[34] It is entirely possible—even likely—for people like me to accept evolutionary theory as true without really understanding what evolutionary theory says.

And radical creationists can easily reject evolutionary theory whether or not they understand it.

The point of our argument about ignorance and evolution is not to make fun of people. It is not to point fingers at the hypocritical arrogance of evolutionary know-it-alls who don't actually know what we're talking about. Nor is it to expose the vast and growing fungus of idiocy lurking at the heart of American creationism. Rather, as we try to understand the reality of America's culture wars about creationism, we need to wrap our heads around the difficulties involved. We need to recognize the fact that creationism is not due to a lack of knowledge about evolution.

Yet we don't need to feel despondent about the apparent difficulties in spreading knowledge about evolutionary theory. We don't need to conclude—à la Charles Hodge—that since people can't really comprehend evolutionary theory, it can't possibly be true. But we should recognize that evolutionary thinking is not as obvious or undeniable as some science pundits have liked to assume. In practice evolutionary thinking can be difficult and counterintuitive.

And that means, in practice, that creation-evolution battles are hard to understand if we think about them as a feud between knowing and not knowing. Educating people about evolution is not a case of pouring knowledge into empty vessels, but of overcoming profoundly difficult conceptual hurdles. It means overturning intuitions, not just discovering something obvious. Creationists have not picked an outlandish explanation of life; they have rather stuck to an obvious one.

Most important for our purposes, we see that acceptance of evolutionary theory does not simply increase with increased knowledge about evolution. Creationism need not retreat as knowledge of evolutionary theory advances. We generally don't actually disagree about evolutionary theory itself because, in part at least, most of us don't really know what evolutionary theory says. No matter what we say we believe about evolution, most of us don't know much about it. And people who do know a lot about it are just as likely to be creationists as not.

Instead of thinking about creation/evolution as a question of knowledge, then, we need to think in terms of something else entirely. The main questions when it comes to evolution and creationism are not about what we know, but about whom we trust. The vital split is not between the knowledgeable and the ignorant, but between people who trust in the authority of mainstream scientists and those who do not. Instead of speaking about knowledge and ignorance, we should be talking about trust and authority.

People like me trust in the authority of mainstream scientists. Even if we don't know much about evolutionary theory, we trust in our collected experts. We have faith in the idea of evolutionary theory, not primarily because we have tried and tested it against its scientific competitors, but because we accept the credentials of those who have.

People like me tend to think it is wacky, ignorant, and maybe even a little criminal to doubt an idea that all mainstream scientists have endorsed. We think it is grossly irresponsible to teach children things that scientists tell us are false. While we may not really know much about evolutionary theory, we know that our trusted authorities have endorsed it. And that's good enough for us.

Radical creationists, in this way of viewing things, are not defined primarily by their lack of knowledge about evolution, but rather by a much more complicated commitment. Radical creationists might or might not know evolutionary theory, but they do know that their trusted authorities do not trust it.

Once we grasp this notion—the idea that the heart of our creation-evolution battles is not actually knowledge or ignorance of evolutionary theory itself, but rather the difference between trusting mainstream scientists or not—the seemingly bizarre preference of creationists for creationism makes a lot more sense. It's not that radical creationists are simply unaware of evolution. It's such a central part of our culture it would be fairly difficult to be truly unaware of it. Rather, radical creationists trust a different set of authorities about what evolution means.

Radical creationism, in the end, is not a lack of knowledge, but an inherited skepticism about a certain sort of knowledge. Being a radical creationist means trusting a competing network of authorities, authorities who skewer the claims of mainstream science and vouch for a radically different sort of knowledge.

Instead of talking about our shared ignorance of evolutionary theory, however, for generations pundits have made things worse by raising the stakes. As we'll talk about in the next chapter, instead of probing the vast areas of agreement most of us share when it comes to creationism and evolution, preachers from all sides have told us that we disagree bitterly. And instead of sharing our ignorance about both creationism and evolutionary theory, we've been told time and time again that true knowledge is easy but the other side is ignorant.

If we hope to make any progress, we have to recognize that these missionary attitudes about creationism and evolution are both unnecessary and destructive for all of us.

6

I Saw the Light

We might not have fundamental disagreements about evolutionary theory, but we are often told that we do. Time after time, both radical creationists and their anti-creationist opponents tell us we need to be afraid of the other side. Why should anyone listen?

After all, almost all Americans can be considered creationists of one sort or another, and most of us don't have a solid grasp on evolutionary theory. It would seem logical to take a careful, humble, measured stance toward both creationism and evolution. Instead, the loudest voices tell us the problem is obvious—there is only a choice between good and evil; we face an all-or-nothing battle for our very souls.

In this chapter, we look at the ways the language of conversion has played a leading—and misleading—role in our conversations about evolution and creationism. People on all sides of the debates have assumed with good reason that our ideas about evolution must represent something along the lines of a religious commitment, and changing those ideas must be akin to a religious conversion. Those expectations make some degree of sense, given the religious ideas at the heart of our creationism-evolution debates, but they can create unnecessary roadblocks when it comes to making reasonable public policy about creationism.

One thing that most creation-evolution pundits agree on—whatever their religious or scientific background—is that their arguments are so clear and compelling they will overpower any resistance among open-minded listeners. Whether they speak from the Bible or from the double helix, culture-war combatants assume that only bias and prejudice keep people from agreeing with their position. If only that unfair bias was swept away, then people would convert enthusiastically to the right side, whatever that may be.

As this chapter will explore, these sorts of missionary suppositions on all sides of America's creation-evolution controversies have not only muddied the moats around our culture-war citadels, they have also often gone in some surprising directions. For one thing, secular and anti-religious

Creationism USA. Adam Laats, Oxford University Press (2021). © Oxford University Press.
DOI: 10.1093/oso/9780197516607.001.0001.

evolution activists have often showed a stronger commitment to religious-style conversions than have conservative religious creationists. For another, the missionary drive among many radical creationists has often not targeted secular people like me but rather a different group of potential converts. The conversion debates that matter to creationists have often been within the boundaries of creationism itself.

Even for those of us outside of the world of creationism, our conversations about evolutionary theory have been wrapped and tangled in the much-bigger implications of religious conversion. We ask people—nonsensically, really—if they "believe" in evolution. Radical creationists demand continuing "faith" not only in their core religious beliefs but also in the unnecessary notion that any compromise with mainstream science is a deal with the devil. Such rhetoric has made it impossible for us to recognize the huge looming middle ground we talk about in the next chapter. In this chapter, we'll walk a few of the twisting creation-evolution Damascus Roads and come to terms with the fact that while there is no simple solution to our disagreements using different words really can help.

Cuts Both Ways

Creationist conversion stories can follow a bewildering maze of different paths. For a non-creationist like me, the life story of creationists like Russell Mixter seems like the obvious direction. However, Mixter-type experiences are not as common as we might think. In a nutshell, Mixter's deep understanding of evolutionary theory led him to question and ultimately revise his thinking about the proper relationship between mainstream science and creationist faith.

Mixter's career as the "evangelical oracle on evolution" began in the 1920s.[1] Mixter (1906–2007) attended Wheaton College in Illinois and remained there as a teacher after his graduation in 1928. While he was a student he studied under the leading academic creationists of the day, including S. J. Bole and L. Allen Higley.[2]

Like all Wheaton students, the young Mixter read many different theories of creationism, including the young-earth theories of George McCready Price. Unlike a lot of Wheaton students, Mixter liked Price's best. He appreciated the clear message of Price's flood geology. If Christians really wanted to take the Bible seriously, the young Mixter agreed, it made sense to take the book of Genesis at face value.

Once he got deeper into mainstream science, though, Mixter realized how profoundly untenable young-earth ideas were. While teaching at Wheaton, he completed graduate degrees at Michigan State University and the University of Illinois. The more he learned, the more ridiculous young-earth ideas seemed.

By the time Mixter's career as an evangelical scientist was established, he had embraced a different sort of creationism entirely. The evidence for an ancient earth, Mixter decided, was undeniable. Moreover, evolutionary theory didn't require evangelical Christians to abandon their faith. Instead, they could call themselves something else—maybe "progressive creationists" or perhaps "theistic evolutionists"—and accept the power of mainstream evolutionary science while keeping their faith intact.

To a secular person like me, Mixter's intellectual journey makes perfect sense. The evidence for evolutionary theory—if understood properly and thoroughly—would seemingly make it impossible for anyone to remain a convinced young-earth creationist (YEC). To secular people, the story can end there.

For some conservative religious people, however, profound knowledge of mainstream evolutionary thinking presents a problem. How could an all-powerful, all-creating God and an unplanned evolutionary process coexist? Moreover, how could someone who takes the Bible at face value disregard its apparent creationist message?

For Mixter, the solution was to combine many of the ideas of mainstream evolutionary thinking with a continuing evangelical faith. The mature Mixter never stopped believing that God created everything. Not just once and for all, putting evolutionary processes to work and then observing from a heavenly distance. That would not be the close personal God of Mixter's evangelical faith. Plus, it would force evangelical believers to depart fairly radically from the creation stories told in the Bible, and conservative evangelicals insisted that the Bible did not include mistakes.

How could the Bible be right, God remain actively involved, AND mainstream evolutionary theory be acceptable? Mixter offered an evangelical explanation: God used evolutionary processes but also created miraculously and continuously, intervening and participating in the unfolding evolutionary saga that was life itself. The Bible told these stories truly and without error but did so in the beautiful poetic language it used so often.

During the 1950s, as historian Ronald Numbers has recounted, Professor Mixter engaged in a careful and tentative unfolding of his increasing acceptance of mainstream evolutionary theory. Among friends, Mixter implied that he believed in a version of theistic evolution. That is, he accepted the notion that mechanisms such as natural selection and other evolutionary processes were the primary ways that different species came into existence, but those processes were created by God. To skeptical conservative creationist audiences, in contrast, Mixter claimed to embrace a more God-heavy version of creationism, which he usually called "progressive creationism." In other words, Mixter sometimes argued for a process in which species could not evolve without God's repeated, deliberate, supernatural creative acts throughout time.[3]

Whether Mixter remained a "progressive creationist" or became a "theistic evolutionist," he insisted he had never changed his religion. Into the 1960s, Mixter told nervous hard-liners that he remained a resolute fundamentalist.[4] There was simply no need, Mixter told everyone who would listen, for even the most conservative, devout evangelical Protestant to feel nervous about recognizing the overwhelming evidence for mainstream evolutionary theory—at least in part.

Mixter believed evolutionary processes were mechanisms used by an all-loving, all-powerful God to assist in his eternal creative unfolding. Accepting the evidence for those evolutionary changes did not mean that those processes could explain everything. For evolution to make sense, Mixter argued, God must have intervened repeatedly and directly, creating new species as old species went extinct. Christians could—in good faith—disagree about how repeated and how direct those interventions were. Some creationists could think that God mostly used evolutionary processes. Others could believe that God stepped in more spectacularly and miraculously.

To Mixter, those disagreements could be worked out in Christian creationist fellowship. Most importantly, they could be worked out using the best available mainstream science. There was no need for religious people to shut out the breathtaking advances that mainstream science had made in the twentieth century. No matter where Christians landed, they could accept the basic outlines of mainstream evolutionary science and still retain their traditional evangelical faith. In Mixter's view, God was absolutely the creator, and mainstream evolutionary ideas were absolutely true in some form. The details could be left in a state of healthy Christian vagueness, buoyed not by false fundamentalist certainty but rather by a thoughtful Christian questioning.

I don't share Mixter's religious faith. I don't see the need to insist on a continuing involvement for a supernatural creative God, even just a little bit. Nevertheless, Mixter's intellectual journey seems perfectly reasonable. I fully understand this sort of creationist conviction. But not all creationist conversions follow this path.

Other creationist conversion stories go in radically different directions. One thoughtful YEC I've corresponded with over the past several years— I'll call her "D"—shared her conversion story with me. As she relates, she went to a mainline Methodist church growing up. Creationism—in a very non-radical form—may have been part of her church's official doctrine, but it never played a significant role in her religious experience or in her family's dinner table conversations. Even in college, she says,

> I didn't know creation-evolution was a "thing." I probably learned about evolution in college, but with no Bible knowledge about the subject, I probably just passed it off as another thing I was learning, and I didn't make any real connection between the two. I enjoyed biology, but it was also a general ed or whatever-you-call-it class that I needed to get my degree.

It was only when she met her future husband that she became interested in creationism. He was a church pastor and an ardent YEC. He never forced her to embrace his vision of creationism, but he did encourage her to investigate it.

And she did. She invested time and money in her pursuit of satisfying explanations of the creation-evolution divide, purchasing a twelve-cassette VHS series of lectures from Ken Ham's young-earth ministry Answers in Genesis. As D tells the tale, "it was those videos that convinced me to be a YEC and got me hooked on this whole subject." Just as the overwhelming evidence from the biology lab at Michigan State convinced Russell Mixter, so did this missionary outreach from Answers in Genesis convince D. Like Mixter, D went looking for answers. Like Mixter, D changed her mind. She just changed it in a much different direction.

And although Mixter's conclusions make a lot more sense to me than D's do, I can easily understand her experience. She was curious about the issue; she wanted to see if she could embrace her husband's creationist faith. After listening to the arguments, she did.

In other cases, the stories of creation-evolution conversion are much harder for me to comprehend. Most famous, maybe, is the curious career of Kurt Wise. As we saw in chapter 1, Wise earned his PhD in paleontology in the evolutionists' lion's den. Even after studying with ardent anti-creationist Stephen Jay Gould at Harvard, Wise did not follow Mixter's path; Wise did not abandon his young-earth beliefs.[5] We have to assume that Professor Wise knows evolutionary science as well as anyone. Yet that knowledge did not compel him to revise his thinking about the origins of species and the age of the earth. As his long career as a leading young-earth scientist has demonstrated, Wise believes just as firmly in a young earth and a recently created human species after learning mainstream science.

It's not only the brilliant and the famous who react unpredictably to the ideas of creationism and evolution. As educational anthropologist David Long discovered, creationist students often learn the evidence for evolutionary theory without disturbing their creationist faiths. In 2009, Long interviewed thirty-one undergraduate biology majors at a large public university in the Midwest.[6]

Long found that learning evolution did not force creationist students into any sort of conversion experience. Of the creationist students Long interviewed, only one abandoned her faith in college. And for her, the conversion was not about science. Rather, "Cindi" had grown up in a strictly anti-evolution family. However, in high school she got pregnant. Her family and church turned against her. The whole experience soured her on her faith, and she was actively looking for alternatives. Doubting her friends' and family's loyalty made her doubt her faith in radical creationism. It wasn't the evidence for evolution that did it.

Another of Long's college creationists, "Renee," had a different college experience. Like all Long's subjects, Renee was planning a career in science. For Renee, a biology major was a prelude to graduate study in pharmacology. Unlike Cindi, Renee had grown up without any particular religion. Like her mother, Renee opposed religion on general principle, vaguely considering it to be an opiate of the masses. In college, though, Renee had some life-changing experiences. She went through an ugly divorce that shook her up. Just as she was questioning her life direction, and just as she was completing her college course in mainstream science, her father took her on a trip to Ken Ham's Creation Museum in Kentucky. Renee was convinced.

Instead of learning about evolution and turning away from her creationist faith, Renee did the opposite. Learning about evolution was incidental to her conversion to radical creationism. Just like Cindi, events in her personal life forced Renee to reevaluate her basic presuppositions. Unlike Cindi, Renee moved from atheism to radical creationism.

It might sound like a one-of-a-kind case, but other studies have found similarly complicated results. As we saw in chapter 5, high school students who study evolution sometimes come away more convinced of radical creationist ideas.[7] Like Renee and Kurt Wise, for many students learning the overwhelming evidence supporting evolution can lead to a firmer embrace of dissenting creationist notions.

We don't have to endorse creationist notions to recognize how complicated the process can be. If we simply assume that every open-minded creationist who studies evolution will be convinced, even if they're not converted, we'll be dead wrong. Sometimes they do change their mind, as in the famous case of Russell Mixter and the many others out there like him. But when it comes to evolution and creationism, convictions and conversions can go in unpredictable directions.

For most people, it seems conversion is only partially a matter of intellectual study and spiritual growth. Cindi was already mad at her home church before she abandoned her creationist ideas. Professor Wise was committed to stay true to his creationist faith no matter what Harvard threw at him. D was willing to entertain radical-creationist arguments because she had already joined a creationist family. In every case, it's impossible to separate the disparate elements that lead people to change their minds or to keep their faiths. As we look in this chapter at the ways creationists and anti-creationists have striven to convince and convert their opposition, we need to keep in mind this irreducibly complex mix of factors.

Most important, we need to recognize the fact that faith can and should be separated from knowledge. Young people can learn about evolutionary theory without abandoning their faith. Indeed, sometimes people embrace radical young-earth creationism more tightly after learning more about evolution.

These complicated truths lead to a clear conclusion: No matter what we know or believe about creationism and evolution, we shouldn't listen when radicals tell us that only their ideas can save our souls.

Missionary Lizards

And they will tell us. Radical YECs are fond of preaching the gospel of creation. It's no surprise, because conservative evangelical creationists are heirs to the great American evangelical tradition. For many creationists, spreading the Good News is the whole point of creationist ministry. Once we dig a little deeper into radical creationists' attitudes toward conversion, however, we find that creationist ideas about missionary outreach are often not as simple as outsiders might have expected.

To the rest of us, radical creationists can sometimes seem like they are out to convert us, and it's scary. Any group that hopes to impose its religious beliefs on other people can be frightening, especially if it can muster significant political support at the highest levels. For secular people like me, radical creationists can seem like they want to impose a *Handmaid's-Tale*-like theocracy on our public institutions, forcing their vision of proper morals and science down our throats.

This is not a new worry. Back in the 1920s, when anti-evolution Protestant fundamentalists mobilized to criminalize evolutionary theory, science pundit Maynard Shipley warned of the imminent dangers of creationism's "armies of ignorance." These "forces of obscurantism," Shipley warned, were massing "literally by the millions, for a combined political assault on modern science." Radical creationists would not rest, Shipley howled, until they came to "dominate our public institutions."[8]

These days, organizations such as the National Center for Science Education (NCSE) have taken up Shipley's cause. In 2013, in Shipley's honor, NCSE named its blog after Shipley's organization, the Science League of America. And like Shipley, NCSE pundits shout their warnings from the rooftops: Radical-creationist activism poses a threat to science and society.[9]

If we hope to see the true contours of the culture wars about creationism, though, we need to understand exactly what the goals of radical creationists are. By and large, radical creationists really do want to influence law and public policy. They really do excel at organizing massive "armies" of supporters. Their goal, however, at least their most important goal, isn't to force the Maynard Shipleys of the world to adopt creationist religion.

Like everything else in the world of creationism, the truth is complicated. Without a doubt, on some level radical creationists want to convert the rest of us. Their entire reason for embracing dissenting science, after all, is to shepherd souls more safely to salvation. Moreover, radical creationists' radical ideas about science, they insist, can be an asset when it comes to reaching out to benighted secular people. For instance, as young-earth activist Buddy Davis of Answers in Genesis argues, dinosaurs are a terrific missionary resource for radical YECs. Everyone loves dinosaurs, Davis writes, and a savvy creationist can use dinosaurs as "missionary lizards." There's no better way to "share the gospel with unbelievers," Davis believes, than telling the true story of their recent creation. Recently created dinosaurs living side by side with humans, Davis insists, are "powerful tools in sharing the salvation message, which should be the ultimate goal of every Christian."[10]

When secular folks are confronted with the story of dinosaurs cavorting with humans, radical YECs argue, those secular people might be forced to challenge their simplistic notions of God's role in creating life. This healthy spiritual crisis can help lead people to the true faith of conservative evangelical Protestantism. And true faith, in turn, will lead wayward souls to heaven. At least, that's the radical creationists' hope.

Outreach to secular folks like me, however, though highly valued in principle by young-earth activists, generally takes a back seat to two other goals. For one thing, YECs hope to protect the faith of the already converted, especially creationist children. For another, YECs hope to target their missionary work strategically to the one group of people it stands the best chance of success, namely, their fellow evangelical Christians.

Though radical creationists would love to see all of America embrace their beliefs, that dream has largely taken a back seat since the middle of the twentieth century. These days, young-earth activists usually focus on more limited goals. As anthropologist Christopher Toumey argued about young-earth activists, they often preach "mostly to those who are already converted . . . more to sustain the beliefs of the converted than to change other peoples' convictions."[11]

The impulse to protect their children's belief undoubtedly plays a leading role in young-earth thinking. As we saw in chapter 4, radical creationists are intensely aware that mainstream American culture no longer agrees with them. They are worried that young people might indeed follow Mixter's path or worse. Because, although Mixter argued otherwise, YECs are convinced that any compromise with mainstream science will push people away from true faith in God and in the Bible.

As Ken Ham argued, for example, his fellow radical creationists needed to wake up. Instead of teaching their children happy stories about animals on arks, creationists needed to train kids explicitly and forcefully to "defend God's Word against the attacks of this age!"[12]

In theory, Ham explained, creationists should indeed be working toward a profound "revolution" intended to "change the culture" and return America to creationist faith. However, in these dark times, Ham believes, only by "strategically" focusing on their own churches and children do radical creationists stand a chance.[13]

Why?

Because radical creationists, Ham believes, are threatened today by a "spiritual epidemic," a "tidal wave washing away the foundation" of their churches.[14] When Ham's Answers in Genesis organization sponsored a survey of roughly 1,000 people in their twenties who had grown up in radical-creationist homes and churches, Ham was deeply alarmed by the findings. Most of those twentysomethings had stopped going to church. Many of them had abandoned the young-earth beliefs that had been shoved down their throats in creationist Sunday schools.

By and large, Ham concluded, creationist kids started choosing their paths in middle school. And for a majority, that choice led them away from radical young-earth beliefs. Ham blamed radical creationists. Too many were content to tell children just-so stories about Noah and Eden. Too many pastors, parents, and Sunday-school teachers led children to believe that church wasn't a place for real facts or real science. As a result, Ham argued, radical creationists were leaving in droves.

As always for Ken Ham, the question came down to proper attitudes about the Bible. It's not that good Christians can't disagree about the age of the earth, Ham has insisted. Plenty of evangelical Protestants have true faith, Ham believes, yet believe in non-radical versions of creationism, versions that assume that the earth must be millions of years old. Such beliefs, Ham warns, do not necessarily block Christians from true salvation by themselves, but they introduce a sinister wedge that ultimately cracks open true belief.

If creationists tell children that they don't "need to take Genesis as written but can reinterpret it on the basis of the world's teaching about millions of years and evolution—we have unlocked a door." Every new generation, Ham thinks, will push that door open wider and wider "until eventually all of the Bible is rejected."[15]

To stanch the flood, Ham wants his fellow radical creationists to focus on their families. Far from dreaming of converting secular types like me, Answers in Genesis hopes instead to give parents and pastors tools to keep their children from walking Mixter's path.

And, when radical creationists do talk about missionary outreach, it is more to non-radical creationists—the heirs of Mixter—than to atheists or liberal Christians. This has been the case since the rise of the modern young-earth movement. For instance, in their blockbuster radical-creationist hit *The Genesis Flood* (1961), John Whitcomb Jr. and Henry Morris explained that they were not targeting secular or non-Christian readers with their young-earth message. Rather, they hoped to reach their fellow conservative evangelical Protestants. As they put it, they hoped to convince "those whose confidence, like ours, is centered in the revelation of God."[16] Similarly, their goal was not to convince all of heathen America, but rather to "restor[e] His people everywhere to full reliance on the truth of the Biblical doctrine of origins."[17]

In other words, the primary missionary targets of young-earth ministry were not non-creationists, like me, or vague creationists, like the enormous Catholic population, but rather straying evangelical Protestant creationists like Russell Mixter. Yes, "missionary lizards" could serve as an effective way to spread the true gospel to everyone, and yes, in the end radical creationists hope to lead America as a whole back to true Christian faith, but in practice modern YECs have tended to spend most of their missionary energy on converting only non-radical evangelical creationists to their radical young-earth beliefs.

Ostenisibly, the trend toward intra-creationist conversion has increased over the years. Back in the 1970s and 1980s, for example, Ken Ham's former mentors Henry Morris and Duane Gish avidly sought debating opportunities on secular college campuses.[18] On closer inspection, however, it is clear that young-earth activists have long preached specifically to their fellow evangelical creationists. In the mid-1970s, for example, Morris traveled to the firmly creationist-but-not-radical campus of Wheaton College, Russell Mixter's home base. Like Mixter, most of Wheaton's creationists remained firmly committed to creationism. But they had abandoned the radical notions of the young-earth crowd.

Morris hoped to convince them of their mistake. Many of Wheaton's so-called creationists, Morris believed, foolishly thought that their soft-pedaled creationism helped evangelicals remain true to their faith. The Wheaton creationists agreed with Mixter that YECs put Christians in a false dilemma between atheism and radical young-earth ideas. In the end, Wheaton scientists often concluded, only progressive creationism, theistic evolution, or one of its evolution-friendly offshoots could protect real evangelical religion.

Not so, Morris argued. As he put it in 1974, "literal creationism and flood geology . . . was receiving far more attention and winning far more converts on university campuses than the compromising positions of theistic evolution and progressive creation had ever been able to do."[19] The real "battle for creation," Morris believed, was not just between creationism and evolution, but rather between real creationists—radical YECs, in Morris's telling—and the many evangelical imposters who pretended their watered-down doctrine could still lead earnest Christians to salvation.

These days, Ken Ham continues his mentor's mission. The real missionary field is among fooled and false evangelical Christians, Ham believes. Too many creationists delude themselves into thinking that Mixter-style accommodations can give them the best of both worlds. And those soft creationists are Ham's real missionary target, not secular people. Ham realized early on that the "pagan" culture was long since lost. Instead, his family worked to be "missionaries to the American church, and our first priority was to get the church back to the authority of the Word of God."[20] Would Ham like, in theory, to convert "pagans" like me? Probably. But his primary goal is to convert evangelical creationists to his particular form of radical young-earth creationism.

Jesus Loves Me This I Know, Evolution Tells Me So

As usual, the pugnacious Ham didn't pull his punches. He called out the worst of the evangelical Christian offenders by name. When it came to the biggest dangers from evolutionary thinking, Ham doesn't warn his fellow creationists about science guys like Bill Nye. Instead, he tells them to watch out for the leading organization of today's "evolutionary creationists," BioLogos.

Like Mixter in an earlier generation, the evangelical activists of BioLogos hope to reach their fellow conservative evangelicals with a religious message about evolution. Like Mixter, BioLogos tells Christians they don't need to be frightened of mainstream science.

For their efforts, BioLogos leaders have earned the bitter enmity of Ken Ham. Ham might be able to politely debate with secular science pundits like Bill Nye, but he can't talk civilly with BioLogos. He won't even sit down to a friendly meal with them.[21] BioLogos's evolutionary outreach, Ham accuses, "is absolutely destructive to the church." BioLogos is nothing less, Ham charges, than "a part of the enemy *within* the church."[22]

That's strong language for anyone, especially from one evangelical Christian to another. Why is Ken Ham so furious about BioLogos?

Once we get our bearings in the world of American creationism, Ham's young-earth fury makes some sense. BioLogos was started early in the twenty-first century explicitly to compete with Ken Ham and other radical creationists. The organization was inspired and founded by Francis Collins. Collins, head of the National Institutes of Health and former leader of the Human Genome Project, is also an evangelical Christian and creationist, in the broad sense of the term.

Like Russell Mixter in an earlier generation or Asa Gray in an even earlier one, Dr. Collins established BioLogos to spread the word among evangelical Christians that evolutionary theory is not the enemy. Collins and his colleagues hope to convince radical creationists that they have never needed to choose between good science and good religion—there is no conflict between the two.[23]

Ken Ham threw down the gauntlet so ferociously to BioLogos because the two organizations are competing for the hearts and minds of America's—and the world's—evangelical Protestant creationists. By and large, they are not fighting to convince or convert secular people like me. Rather, this is a fight between creationists about creationism. Can a "real" creationist accept the contributions of mainstream evolutionary theory?

Ham says they can't. BioLogos says they can.

For many BioLogos leaders, it's personal. They grew up believing the explanations of their young-earth churches. When they found out what evolutionary theory really said, they experienced a spiritual and intellectual crisis. For instance, BioLogos's president, Deborah Haarsma, explained that she, like Russell Mixter, grew up naively accepting young-earth stories as both scientifically true and religiously necessary. As she put it, in her youth "everyone at church and home thought that the earth was young and evolution never happened." Like Mixter, when she did graduate work at a secular university she had to confront the mainstream scientific evidence in favor of evolution and deep time. After plenty of soul-searching, she followed Mixter and the many other evangelical scientists who turned away from radical young-earth thinking. But she never had to give up her conservative evangelical faith.[24]

President Haarsma hopes to help other Christians recognize their real options when it comes to mainstream evolutionary thinking. Not every evangelical will earn their PhD in astrophysics from MIT, as Haarsma did, but they can all recognize the false choices presented by radicals such as Ken Ham.

In Haarsma's opinion, too many evangelical Christians believe they must choose between radical young-earth creationism and atheism. After all, for generations conservative evangelical Christians have been telling themselves that evolution is a dangerous notion, sure to lead young people to reject religion entirely.

BioLogos hopes to offer people "another choice." Instead of forcing young people who discover the "compelling evidence for evolution ... to choose between science and faith," the "evolutionary creationists" of BioLogos want to spread the word of a better option.[25]

Too many Christians, they worry, still don't know about it. To make their case, BioLogos members share stories of young people facing the false dilemma and losing their faith entirely as a result. Scot McKnight, for instance, a prominent theologian at Northern Seminary in Illinois, tells about one student he worked with at his conservative evangelical school. The student had grown up in a young-earth-creationist family and church. As he grew older, the student started to notice intellectual cracks in the edifice of young-earth thinking. For example, he once asked his pastor where dinosaur bones had come from. The pastor looked him in the eye and said with a straight face, "Satan buried those bones." The student struggled to accept and understand such ideas. Why would God allow such a thing? Would he set out on purpose to fool his followers? Why would he make his true faith so absurd and difficult to believe? The student kept asking questions. He received nothing but "comparably absurd responses to questions ... about carbon dating and human archaeological evidence." In the end, Professor McKnight's student faced a difficult choice. If real faith required an embrace of absurdity, it didn't seem like real faith at all. But what other option was there?[26]

Other BioLogos-affiliated academics report similarly jarring experiences among their students. Two evangelical scholars recently related tales from their former students at Bryan College in Tennessee. For many young people raised in YEC households and churches, the only options seemed to be atheism or young-earth faith. One of their former students told the following tale of evolution-creation confusion and conversion:

> I regret that I wasn't taught better about biology and some other things. My parents saw evolution as incompatible with religion; I agree, and when I decided the evidence did not support a 6-day creation, I stopped believing in God.[27]

For this student and the many more like him, BioLogos argues, the radical message of young-earth creationism forced a false choice.

BioLogos hopes to convince conservative religious creationists that there is a different way to look at the creation-evolution dilemma. They don't agree on the details, but in general the evolutionary creationists of BioLogos want to spread the word that the exact method and timing of God's creation are not the most important issues. There is no reason why Christians have to choose between mainstream science and true religion.

As one theologian put it, "Genesis 1-2 were interested in celebrating the fact **that** God created the heavens and the earth and all that live in them, including humankind—but not in **how** he did it."[28] As Francis Collins argues, evolutionary theory doesn't diminish God's creativity. Evolution, he asserts, is merely the elegant mechanism he uses. Understanding evolutionary theory means understanding God better. It is not necessary to choose between evolution and faith since they are all part of the same divinity. In Collins's famous phrase: "The God of the Bible is also the God of the genome."[29]

Dr. Collins was not talking to me. I am not interested in the evidence for God's fingerprints in the evolutionary record. Instead, like Russell Mixter and the long legacy of religious scientists who preceded him, Collins is preaching to a specific choir. And because other creationists are trying to talk to those same audiences, their creationist preaching often turns into the most bitter shouting matches of our creation-evolution controversies.

New Atheism New Religion

Of course, competing evangelicals aren't the only ones shouting. And, surprisingly, conservative religious creationists aren't the only ones trying to convert people. These days, missionaries for mainstream science tend to fight for converts much more aggressively than creationists do.

Most prominently, a loosely connected group of thinkers known as the "New Atheists" have made their case against creationism and against religion in general. As the name implies, many of the pundits associated with the New Atheism preach atheism. But they share an assumption about evolution and creation that's anything but new. For many atheist activists, the truth of evolution is so intellectually powerful that mere exposure to it will be enough to convince and convert any open-minded reader.

These quasi-religious assumptions about the missionary power of evolutionary ideas have a long history. As we've seen, earlier generations of science pundits such as Thomas H. Huxley and Henry Fairfield Osborn assumed blithely that the merest acquaintanceship with Darwin's ideas would be enough to convince anyone. At times, they phrased their faith in conspicuously religious terms. As Osborn proclaimed to his generation of benighted creationists, "The Truth Shall Set You Free."[30] Darwin was nothing less than a "prophet" of this new dispensation, Osborn declared.[31]

Some of today's science pundits share Osborn's missionary assumptions. The New Atheists have offered scathing indictments of creationism and the religious mindset that produces it. They are too iconoclastic to be called a movement, but thinkers such as Sam Harris, Christopher Hitchens, Victor Stenger, and Jerry Coyne have blasted the intellectual foundations of American creationism.[32]

Perhaps the most well-known and irascible of these science pundits has been Richard Dawkins. Dawkins has relentlessly and ruthlessly articulated the New Atheist vision. Not only is atheism true, Dawkins argued in bestselling books such as *The God Delusion*, but its proper goal is nothing less than the conversion of all religious people to atheism. As Dawkins promised with his usual self-confidence, *The God Delusion* had enormous missionary potential. As he put it, "religious readers who open it will be atheists when they put it down."[33]

To be fair, for Dawkins the transformative potential of his book comes not from his own brilliance, but rather from the awe-inspiring power of Darwin's theory of natural selection. When and if people truly understood the idea, Dawkins argued, their eyes will be opened. If they are brave and honest, they will be compelled to become atheists. Their "conversion to radical atheism," Dawkins predicted, will be due to the "power of Darwinism as a consciousness-raiser."[34]

Like good evangelists everywhere, Dawkins told inspirational stories of the missionary effectiveness of evolutionary theory. For example, popular science-fiction writer Douglas Adams, author of the cult classic *Hitchhiker's Guide to the Galaxy*, shared his conversion story with Dawkins. The power of evolutionary science, Adams related, sparked in him an overwhelming sense of awe. As Adams put it, "The awe it inspired in me made the awe that people talk about in respect of religious experience seem, frankly, silly beside it."[35]

For Dawkins and other New Atheist writers, Adams's more-religious-than-religion experience was precisely the point. Though the goal was conversion away from religion, Dawkins left no doubt that his intention was a missionary one.

Other science pundits wrap their work in friendlier tones, but they agree on the need to convert creationists. The bow-tie-wearing Science Guy Bill Nye, for example, debuted his television show with a portentous title. Bill Nye, the show proclaimed, didn't merely want to tell you about science. He didn't merely want to wow you with some amazing experiments. No, the show promised that Bill Nye would do nothing less than "Save the World."

Nye smiles more often than Dawkins and the New Atheists, but his missionary intent is just as serious. For Nye, spreading the word about science is impregnated with moral purpose, by an apocalyptic sense of the ultimate stakes. If creationists and other scientific dissenters don't get on board, Nye frets, we are all doomed.

On episode 5, for example, Nye offered a quick and entertaining description of the long history of our planet. Where did life come from? Some creationist fools, Nye points out, think it was floated around on Noah's ark. Impossible and ridiculous. Real science, Nye explains, only knows for sure that it doesn't know for sure. It is entirely possible that the germ of life on this planet blasted in on an errant Martian meteor.[36]

The idea that can save the world, Nye implies, is not one simple scientific idea. Rather, we all need to think in scientific terms, to press relentlessly against every explanation until we hone our understandings of the universe and our place within it.

Unlike Dawkins or the New Atheists, Bill Nye won't tell creationists they need to convert to atheism. But he doesn't mind insisting that only his vision of scientific thinking can save the world. He doesn't shy away from setting up science—his vision of science without any sort of religious affiliation—as something that everyone needs to accept, whatever their religious beliefs.

It's important to be crystal clear because aggressive radical creationists have long made misleading claims along these lines. There's nothing inherently religious about mainstream evolutionary theory. True, it makes some assumptions about the nature of life, but those ideas can comport just as well with a belief in God as without one. The point here is not that evolutionary thinking is necessarily about religious conversion. Evolutionary theory itself doesn't look, feel, or function like a religion. Rather, it is the missionary assumptions of mainstream science pundits such as Bill Nye, Richard Dawkins, and Henry Fairfield Osborn that smell like religion. Like radical creationists themselves, these science pundits assume that our thinking about evolution must act like a religious conviction. Like radical creationists, these missionaries for science assume that changing our minds about evolution must be something like a religious conversion.

It doesn't have to be that way.

The Missionary Supposition

To imagine better policy options about creationism, we need to ask questions differently. We need to abandon the underlying missionary thinking we've seen in the preceding pages. We need to ask: What difference would it make if we avoided talking in terms of conversion when it came to evolutionary theory and creationism? There is significant agreement on the fringes. Both radical creationists and radical atheists agree that people need to choose between them. But what if we avoided discussing creationism and evolutionary theory as a simple either-or choice between these two radical ends of the spectrum? What if we avoided speaking in terms of religious belief and focused instead on pragmatic questions of public policy? In the end, such approaches will make for better policy—and also for better science and religion.

In the next chapter, we look in more depth and detail about the proper big-picture goals of good evolution education. We examine the ramifications of the fact that we don't really disagree about evolutionary theory itself, but about other things. In this section, we look at the nuts-and-bolts benefits of ditching our unnecessary traditions of conversion-style thinking.

It's not as easy as it might sound at first. It's not enough, for instance, to think that mainstream science and creationist dissenters can simply stay in their corners and refrain from combat. Plenty of smart observers have suggested such solutions. Maybe most famous has been the late Stephen Jay Gould's prescription of "non-overlapping magisteria." Religion and science, Gould argued at the turn of the twenty-first century, each represented different sorts of intellectual inquiry. Science—mainstream science—had better claims to investigate questions of fact. Religion, however, was alone able to ponder values and purposes.[37]

In the end, such proposals aren't tenable. When it comes to creationism, at least, all sides necessarily insist that their ideas are both religiously and scientifically superior. They have to. The entire premise of modern American creationism, after all, is that its believers have the ability to evaluate mainstream scientific claims in the light of their theological commitments. Asking creationists to simply cede knowledge about the physical world to nonreligious sorts of inquiry is the same as asking creationists to convert from their fundamental religious beliefs.

Whether we'd like to see it or not, it doesn't change anything about our creation-evolution controversies to insist on a separation of religious and scientific truth. But we are not without hope. What we can and must do is shift from talk about "believing" evolutionary theory. Doing so only perpetuates the false notion that evolution is somehow a religious notion—that thinking differently about evolution requires something akin to a religious conversion. As we've seen throughout this chapter, all sides in our long battle over creation and evolution have assumed that missionary language is the right language to use. It's not.

It might be the right language for the partisans involved—whether they are New Atheists hoping to free people from the intellectual shackles of religion, radical YECs hoping to convince other creationists to read the Bible a certain way, or Francis-Collins-style creationists hoping to convert young earthers to their appreciation for mainstream science. But it's not the right language for people who hope for sensible public policy about evolutionary theory.

Changing one's mind about evolution and creation might indeed feel like a kind of conversion for the people involved, but that doesn't mean we need to focus on converting people. Conversions, after all, even if they are attempted by radical atheists instead of radical creationists, are an inherently religious goal. And when it comes to public policy, it makes sense for us to avoid working toward a religious outcome. Instead of talking in the religiously laden language of "belief," we should instead use terms such as "knowing about" evolution.

This is the right approach for all kinds of reasons. First of all, when it comes to mainstream scientific thinking, "belief" in evolutionary theory is a misleading way of speaking. Mainstream scientists don't really want anyone to *believe* in evolutionary theory. Rather, they acknowledge it as the best current explanation of the ways species came to be different from one another. Unlike beliefs, acceptance of the current superiority of mainstream evolutionary theory is frankly an iffy and changeable notion. It's not a commitment but rather an explicitly conditional sort of thing.

If mainstream scientists and science pundits want to see evolutionary theory taught more broadly and more deeply, they need to avoid and discourage any talk about "converting" creationists to their cause. Instead, mainstream scientists and science educators must be willing to endure the slings and arrows of radical anti-creationists. They must be willing to accept the accusation of "accommodating" creationists.[38] Most of all, they must be eager to share their real goal—not converting anyone to any sort of belief system, but rather spreading knowledge about evolutionary theory.

This isn't watering down science or pandering to creationist obstructionism. Rather, it means recognizing and emphasizing the laudable goals of evolution education: Not to cram any sort of religious belief down any students' throats, especially not to present mainstream science as a set of tenets to be believed or rejected, but rather help students know about the meaning and evidence for evolutionary theory and the ways they relate to good scientific thinking.

For creationists, too, "belief" is a loaded gun. For most creationists, real belief must necessarily be limited to a strictly restricted set of religious notions. In the evangelical Christian tradition, for example, it has always been a danger to believe too loosely, to believe in false idols and golden calves. "Knowing about" things, on the other hand, is of crucial importance. As we'll explore in more depth in the next chapter, even the most radical creationists want their children to *know about* evolutionary theory.

Just because they want their children to know about evolution, though, doesn't mean they want their children to believe it. Instead of focusing on a losing battle for souls, then, religious creationists should be the first to insist that creationism and evolution are not primarily about belief. After all, it is the radical young-earth crowd that should be the most alarmed by whispers of an either-or conversion choice in the world of creationism and evolution. The evidence is clear and compelling: If YEC kids are told they must either deny the evidence for evolution and an ancient planet or convert to atheism, many of them will do just that.

Young-earth leader Ken Ham likes to compare himself to the Old Testament hero Nehemiah.[39] When Nehemiah was busy building his wall to protect Jerusalem, he refused to take a break; he refused to rest from his vital labors. Ham and Answers in Genesis may hope to build a wall around their young-earth offspring, but they can never build a wall high enough to keep out the ideas of mainstream science.

If creationists—radical young-earthers or otherwise—hope to protect the religious faith of their children and grandchildren, they will be wise to join savvy mainstream scientists in avoiding and discouraging all talk of conversion when it comes to evolutionary theory. For creationists even more than non-creationists, it makes both strategic and moral sense to emphasize the fact that evolutionary theory is not something to "believe," but it is a vital thing for everyone to "know about," regardless of our religious beliefs.

When it comes to public policy, "knowing about" evolutionary theory is the only legitimate goal of public education. In spite of the heat coming off the New Atheist polemics, public institutions should never intrude on people's religious beliefs if those beliefs don't cause direct harm to others. Anything more aggressive—even a hint that creationist students need to "believe" in evolutionary theory, or that mainstream science is the only legitimate thing one can "believe"—moves public schools into precisely the wrong sort of theocratic role.

Talking about "belief" in evolution merely tangles public institutions in an inherently religious conflict. It might seem like a tiny change, but if instead we talk about "knowing about" evolutionary theory, we can sidestep the worst excesses of the conversion tradition and instead focus on real education.

Nearly a century ago, science activist Maynard Shipley warned of the "armies of ignorance" that creationists were mustering to take over schools and government.[40] As discussed, creationists are engaged in ferocious battle—but mostly with one another. It's harder to freak out about creationists "being organized . . . by the millions" once we notice that creationists can't talk politely to one another. Instead, their ferocious contests for the soul of their creationist churches takes on the tenor of a religious crusade. And when it comes to public policy about creationism, we must scrupulously avoid wading into these sorts of religious controversies. After all, if we can insist that students in public schools know about evolutionary theory, for all our sakes, we must stop there.

No one—not atheists, not creationists, not confused bystanders—wants public schools to get involved in a fight over which type of creationism Jesus would prefer. And no one wants public schools to strip children of their religious notions. Instead, when it comes to questions of evolution and creationism, we need to ditch our assumptions about conversion. We need to stop hoping that young people will see the light, and rather focus intensely on making sure they all know about evolution.

7

Evolution USA

"Dear Dr. Laats," D wrote.

"As a young earth creationist that homeschools. . . . I am not trying to protect my sons from learning evolution. . . . I am going to teach my kids about evolution, somehow."[1]

You may remember D from our last chapter. She converted to radical young-earth creationism as part of her search for the truth and to connect better with her family. In many ways, she's not typical by any stretch of the imagination, but in this chapter we'll explore one important way in which she is.

D's attitude demonstrates the ways radical creationists often feel about both evolutionary theory and science as a whole. By and large—in spite of what you might think if you only read the work of anti-creationist pundits—creationists don't hate science. Quite the opposite. Even more than most of us, radical creationists *love* science.

Among social scientists these days, creationists' fondness for capital-S Science is well understood. Sociologists Elaine Howard Ecklund and Christopher P. Scheitle studied the ways religious people thought about science. By and large, they found religious Americans "are not nearly the scientifically ignorant, uninterested, or hostile population that they are often made out to be."[2]

As anthropologist Chris Toumey argued, America's radical creationists, like the rest of us, have deep and abiding faith in the "plenary authority of science; that is, the idea that something is more valuable and more credible when it is believed that science endorses it."[3] In other words, from Ark Encounters to toothpaste advertisements, Americans feel better if things are explained to us by people in white lab coats.

Radical young-earth creationists (YECs) share that faith in science just as deeply as the rest of us. As seen throughout this book, the young-earth

Creationism USA. Adam Laats, Oxford University Press (2021). © Oxford University Press.
DOI: 10.1093/oso/9780197516607.001.0001.

variety of radical creationism emerged in the later part of the twentieth century as one response to an evangelical Protestant crisis over science. It wasn't a crisis about whether science itself had gone bad. It was a crisis about whether mainstream scientists had abandoned good science.

It is worth repeating: Radical creationists don't hate science. They love it. We all do. We disagree on what science implies. The creationist scientists in lab coats at the Creation Museum tell different stories than do the mainstream scientists in lab coats on Bill Nye's television shows. But they all wear lab coats; they all insist they represent authentic science.

Creationists don't hate evolutionary theory. Most won't come right out and say it the way D did, but most creationists, even the most radical young earthers, want their children to learn evolutionary theory. They just want their children to learn it right.

Poll results show that D is not alone. Large majorities of Americans say they want their children to learn about evolutionary theory. In 2000, for example, a survey commissioned by the People for the American Way found that a large majority of respondents—83 percent—wanted public schools to teach their kids about evolution. True, a significant minority—about one in six—wanted schools to teach only creationism.[4] But there must have been plenty of creationists—radicals and non-radicals alike—in that large 83 percent majority who wanted schools to teach their children about evolutionary theory.

We can't know for sure, but it seems there must be plenty of people like D. They want their children to learn about evolution, but they worry that public schools will do it in a way that denigrates their creationist religion. To make progress in our endless battles about creationism, we need to separate these two things.

In the most basic terms, we can say it this way: We don't disagree about evolution, but we *do* disagree ferociously about how to teach it. Radical YECs love science. They want their children to know what evolutionary theory says. But they have learned a deep, abiding mistrust of most of the people who want to teach evolution to their children. Americans as a whole, in other words, don't disagree about what evolutionary theory says, but radical creationists and radical atheists do disagree about what they want their children to think about evolution.

Once we grasp this central truth about American creationism, it can't help but change the way we think about our ongoing creation-evolution debates. We have plenty of things we can fight about, but, by and large, we have enormous areas of agreement when it comes to evolution. Almost all of us want our children to know about it. Almost all of us want public schools to teach it.

There are big disagreements as well. Some creationists want their children to learn evolutionary theory mainly so that they can explain what's wrong with it. And others hope to wedge bad science into public school science classes alongside better science. Those are significant issues to fight about. But our fights—our discussions—will be more productive and more civil if we acknowledge that we all share two huge areas of agreement.

These basic facts about American creationism are surprisingly difficult to acknowledge, both politically and intellectually. Time and again, mainstream science pundits have assumed that our culture-war fight about evolution is not a fight about the proper way to teach evolution or a disagreement about the relative merits of competing visions of science. Rather, most mainstream science pundits have assumed that our evolution-creation battle is primarily a fight between science and religion, between creationism or evolution. In some ways, of course, it is. Radical young-earth creationism, after all, is motivated and fueled by the religious peculiarities of a certain faction of conservative evangelical Protestantism. But by framing the battle over origins as a simple fight between science and anti-science, we miss the enormous middle ground that looms between our century-old culture-war trenches.

In this last chapter, we look at the ways radical creationists feel about science. When we come to grips with the fact that radical creationists love science just as much as the rest of us do, we will have a better way to talk about our areas of disagreement. Despite those important differences, when it comes to evolution and creationism, we can all support a simple and obvious two-part plan.

Denial Is Not a River in Tennessee

There's nothing new about this fundamental misunderstanding of creationism. Creationism has always been accused of being a fight against science despite the fact that creationists have always loudly insisted that they were fighting for science. Anti-creationist pundits have never been willing to notice or concede that important point.

Back in the 1920s, for example, when William Jennings Bryan was America's leading celebrity creationist, he insisted on his status as a promoter of real science. For example, he pointedly joined the staunchly pro-evolution American Association for the Advancement of Science.[5] And he always spoke of himself as a defender of science against foolish evolution-loving "pseudo-scientists."[6]

Bryan's enemies didn't see it the same way. Edwin Conklin, a leading anti-creationist of that generation, blasted Bryan's scientific pretensions in the pages of the *New York Times*. Conklin, a prominent biologist at Princeton, lamented the need to pander to the ridiculous anti-scientific ideas of poltroons like Bryan. Passing laws against the teaching of evolution, Conklin warned, meant stopping science in its tracks. As Conklin memorably put it, it meant trying to repeal a "law of nature with a law of Kentucky." Banning evolution meant caving in, surrendering to Bryan's "medieval theology."[7] For Conklin as for later generations of anti-creationists, the two sides of the battle were stark and simple. On one side was science. On the other was a sinister, warped form of religion.

In the 1960s, George Gaylord Simpson took up the anti-creationist fight. For Simpson (like Conklin an Ivy League scientist), the power of real science was blocked by Americans who preferred to remain trapped "in the older worlds of superstition."[8]

In Simpson's view of history, evolutionary theory was more than just a mere idea. It represented an epochal shift, a move from "superstition to a rational universe." The fight was not between differing visions of science, Simpson assumed. Rather, real science—evolutionary science—was being blocked and mocked by religious zealots, the Christian scoundrels whose "higher superstitions [were] celebrated weekly in every hamlet of the United States."[9]

Too many mainstream science pundits seem to share Simpson's and Conklin's outrage. They tend, too, to share Simpson's and Conklin's misunderstanding of the nature of creationism. Thinking of creationism as "anti-science" might score some short-term political points. But this willful or ignorant misunderstanding of creationism hurts our ability to acknowledge long-term solutions.

If we hope to make better progress in our old American battles over creationism, it would be wise to point out a few obvious but complicated truths. For one thing, we need to do a better job of remembering that the radical creationism on display at the Ark Encounter does not represent creationism as a whole. There are plenty of non-radical American creationists who eagerly embrace mainstream evolutionary theory and share Bill Nye's dismay at the notions of their radical co-creationists. And even more powerfully, we need to keep in mind that even the radical creationists at the Ark Encounter love science. There may be plenty of Americans who doubt the "plenary authority" of science—people, like Walt Whitman, who feel a vague and apolitical dismay at the arrogance of mainstream scientists—but speaking generally, there is no such thing as "anti-science creationism." The radical creationists in Kentucky don't deny science itself, although they do deny some closely related ideas.

"Ramming Poison Down the Throats of our Children"

What ideas? It's not fair or accurate to say that creationists are anti-science, but they certainly are anti-something. But what? In one of his books, Bill Nye almost stumbled onto the real, complicated truth about creationism.

Almost. In general, Nye mischaracterizes American radical creationists as simple science "deniers." That's not right. Like George Simpson and Edwin Conklin, Nye misses the boat when he talks about a simple fight between science on one side and religion on another. Elsewhere, though, Nye says something closer to the complicated truth when he says radical creationists are "casting doubt on science and unbelievers."[10]

Science, no. *Unbelievers*, yes.

To an extent that might shock many non-creationists, prominent radical creationists have always wanted their children to love science and to learn evolution. But they have trembled at the notion that learning evolution the wrong way might rob children of their religious faith. In other words, radical-creationist pundits have often endorsed teaching what they saw as real science, even including evolutionary science. They have wanted children to learn science that confirms creationist fundamentals. But they have worried that scientists will cram atheism into the package. They have worried about the overwhelming influence of mainstream science foisted on unsuspecting, innocent creationist children.

As sociologists Ecklund and Scheitle found in their investigation of the ways religious people think about science, most Americans don't fear science. But among evangelical Protestants, there is a more common tendency to distrust scientists. Among the general population, just under a quarter (22 percent) of respondents said that most scientists were hostile to religion. Among evangelical Protestants, however, that answer jumped to 36.1 percent of respondents.[11] In other words, though creationists don't see science it-self as dangerous, they do worry about the work of scheming self-important scientists. As one evangelical from Houston told Ecklund and Scheitle, "Really, I thought all scientists were atheists."[12] For religious people—including creationists—the notion that aggressive atheists might misuse science to promote atheism causes profound consternation.

Even the most radical and uncompromising creationists have distinguished between good science and bad scientists. Back at the Scopes Trial in 1925, for example, one of the most eye-catching of all the eye-catching displays in the streets of Dayton, Tennessee, was the bookstand of fiery creationist preacher T. T. Martin.

Martin's rhetoric shocked and dismayed the anti-creationists of his day. He certainly seemed to take a radical stand. "Ramming poison down the throats of our children is nothing," Martin fumed, "compared with damning their souls with the teaching of Evolution."[13]

Like most anti-evolution activists throughout history, Martin insisted time and time again that his beef was not with science itself. He asserted on the first line of the first chapter of his anti-evolution manifesto *Hell and the High School*: "Let it be clearly understood and kept in mind that this is not fighting science."[14] Lest anyone still misunderstand, Martin repeated this line over and over, with feeling. "*Evolution*," he concluded with bold underlines, "*is not science*."[15] Yet, in spite of parents' concerns, Martin warned, evolution "is palmed off on your sons and daughters as *real science*."[16]

The problem for Martin and for many early creationists was not with science as a whole. Real science, he believed, would soon refute the atheistic implications of Darwin's ideas. The problem, rather, was with a troublesome class of false-science enthusiasts who deliberately schemed to use their fake science to steal children's faith. When it came to raising the alarm about such false scientists, Martin spared no rhetorical excesses. These false scientists, whom Martin called the "Evolutionists," positively cheered the deleterious spiritual effects of their false teaching. As Martin put it:

> What care the Evolutionists for all this? They laugh and jeer, as the rapist laughs and jeers at the bitter tears of the crushed father and mother over the blighted life of their child.[17]

As this sort of language shows, Martin certainly can't be called a moderate when it comes to evolution-creation culture wars. Yet even this radical-creationist firebrand wanted children to learn evolutionary theory. In quieter moments, Martin offered his preferred solution to the creation-evolution dilemma. He did not want to ban evolution from public schools. He did not even want his flock to keep their children away from it. Instead, Martin proposed that all children be exposed to evolutionary ideas, starting from elementary school and working their way all the way up to college. Martin called for a new set of textbooks to teach evolutionary science. The trick, Martin felt, was in making sure that those books would give "fairly, in each book, both sides of the Evolution issue."[18]

Certainly, plenty has changed since Martin's day. But creationists have never really disagreed that evolution should be taught, as long as it is taught correctly. Even the most radical fire-breathing creationist preachers have thought so.

In the 1940s, for example, Bob Jones promised that his creationist college would always teach its students evolution. The real goal, for Jones as much as for T. T. Martin, was for young people to "believe in the creation of man by the direct act of God." But just like Martin, Jones believed that young people needed to learn evolutionary theory. Every student at Bob Jones College, Jones bragged, would read the works of Darwin, Spencer, and Huxley. The topic was one that no educated person could avoid, one no top-notch university—even a radical-creationist one—would want to skip. Yet Jones explained to parents that his school taught evolutionary theory the right way. Yes, students would all learn about it. That was the hallmark of a modern college education. But at Bob Jones College, Jones explained, "We tell them that these men were just guessing."[19]

Certainly, learning about evolutionary theory in this way would not be satisfactory for anyone outside the world of radical creationism. Most of us don't want our kids to be taught that mainstream evolutionary theory is just a string of guesses. When it comes to public policy, however, we need to exercise a little self-restraint and notice the most important point. Namely, this is an area where non-creationists, radical creationists, and non-radical creationists can all agree: All of us agree that a good, modern education needs to include knowledge about evolutionary theory. If the Bob Joneses of the world want to teach their students that Darwin was "just guessing," so be it. The main point is that even these radical creationists agree that learning about evolutionary theory is a necessity in the modern world.

By 1985, the biggest fundamentalist competitor with Bob Jones University was Jerry Falwell's Liberty University in Virginia. The feud between these radical-creationist institutions was bitter and personal.[20] But they didn't disagree with each other about evolution. Just like Bob Jones, Jerry Falwell insisted that all his students would "learn all about evolution." Every educated person needed to understand evolutionary theory, Falwell believed.[21]

There was a difference, however, between a sophisticated collegiate understanding of evolution and the false-science embrace of atheistic ideas that too often went along with evolutionary science. In Falwell's mind, real education included real science, so every Liberty student would learn evolution. But false education, Falwell thought, pandered despicably to false science, teaching students not real evolution, but damnable "evolutionism." It was the "-ism" that took science astray.

What would Liberty do? It would teach evolution, always and to everyone. But it would also teach students "why you don't believe it." A graduate of Liberty University, Falwell promised, could never be "an evolutionist."[22]

It's not that we can all agree with Jerry Falwell or Bob Jones about the definition of science or what students should learn about evolution. Students in public schools shouldn't follow Martin's 1922 prescription of learning both evolutionary theory and the creationist contenders. Doing so doesn't necessarily replace science with religion, but it does mix better mainstream science with worse creationist science.[23] The most important point is not that radical creationists want their children to learn evolutionary science the same way I do, because they don't. Rather, the central, vital thing we need to notice is that many radical creationists agree: A good modern education must include the teaching of modern evolutionary science. In many cases, radical creationists want children to learn it in order to prove that evolutionary theory is false. Nevertheless, they still want kids to learn it. For our purposes, that is enough.

Take the Creation Museum Challenge

Creationists themselves, of course, would never want to admit that their ideas constitute "worse science." To a degree that might surprise noncreationists, today's radical creationists have upped their game when it comes to presenting their work as real science. To unwary viewers, it can be decidedly difficult to differentiate between mainstream ideas and radical-creationist contenders.

Young-earth-creationism science textbooks, for example, look and feel a lot like mainstream textbooks. The Apologia series founded by Jay Wile is widely used by radical-creationist schools and homeschools.[24] Unlike what outsiders might think, Wile never disparages science. To the contrary, his biology textbook insists that students are about to embark on a "truly rigorous science course."[25]

What does that mean? At first, it might not look too much different from any mainstream science course. As Wile explains:

> Real science must conform to a system known as the scientific method. This system provides a framework in which scientists can analyze situations, explain certain phenomena, and answer certain questions. The scientific method starts with observation. Observation allows the scientist to collect data. Once enough data have been collected, the scientist forms a hypothesis that attempts to explain some facet of the data or attempts to answer a question that the scientist is trying to answer.[26]

I don't think Bill Nye or even Richard Dawkins could find much to object to in such statements. Only when readers poke a little further do they find that Apologia books do not take a mainstream approach to science. As might any mainstream science textbook, Apologia books note that scientific thinking means weighing evidence and maintaining a skeptical attitude. Unlike mainstream textbooks, though, Apologia doesn't stop there.

Because scientific thinking recognizes its own limits, Apologia reasons, smart scientists need to look elsewhere for reliable truths. And, to no one's surprise, Wile identifies for readers the best place to find that truth:

> The only thing in the universe that is 100% reliable is the Word of God. The Bible contains truths that will never be shown to be wrong, because those truths come directly from the Creator of the universe.[27]

Most of us wouldn't consider that a scientific idea, but for radical creationists, it is. Radical creationists such as Jay Wile don't tell readers to read the Bible instead of doing science. No, Apologia tells readers to rely on the Bible to do science right.

Apologia isn't an odd outlier in the world of radical creationist textbooks. All creationist publishers similarly emphasize their status as true science, even as they insist on their own forms of supernatural thinking. Their books and materials have the same look as other school publications, with colorful sidebars, lists of questions for students to answer, and bolded vocabulary terms.

Accelerated Christian Education (ACE), for example, models its materials on mainstream publications. ACE is another leader in radical-creationist publication, marketing its self-guided PACE workbooks especially for home-school families and small evangelical schools. With enough of a budget, a creationist school or family could purchase a premade curriculum in every subject. The ACE promise is that students can work at their own speed through their graded series, learning everything they need to know in a reso-lutely biblical and radical-creationist context.

In its science publications, ACE wraps its creationist message in the lan-guage of mainstream school science. In one science PACE, for example, students read about various sorts of symmetry in the living world. At first glance, this discussion and the many others like it seem very similar to main-stream science textbooks. "An important characteristic considered in the classification of invertebrates," students read,

> is symmetry. Two common types of symmetry used when classifying invertebrates are <u>bilateral</u> symmetry and <u>radial</u> symmetry. Have you noticed that a butterfly's left wing is a mirror image of its right wing? This is an example of bilateral symmetry.[28]

We might find similar paragraphs in any mainstream textbook we choose. The PACE also explains, however, that invertebrates were created on the fifth or sixth day of God's creation, depending on whether they lived on land or sea. Students are quizzed about both the scientific vocabulary and the Genesis history.

Beyond just the content, there used to be other ways a reader could dif-ferentiate between creationist textbooks and mainstream ones. The ACE offerings, in particular, used to look hokey and old-fashioned. They had goofy graphics and cub-scout-project-level editing.

In one jilted older-edition PACE, for instance, students were meant to learn the value of dependability by reading an awkward cartoon about a girl who remembers to bring the school newsletter home to her weirdly drawn father. The father intones, "Attending a Christian school is a blessing to Christi." To which Christi robotically replies, "Yes it is. I also get many blessings working there as a monitor."[29]

These days, the publications of radical creationists—some of them, at least—have shed their old-fashioned hokiness. Print materials from Answers in Genesis (AIG), for example, look just as slick and professional as anything that might be produced by a mainstream textbook publisher.

When the new *Cosmos* television series came out in 2014, for instance, Ken Ham and his creationist crew rushed to rebut the show's claims about the long history of the universe. AIG produced a series of discussion guides for creationists to use in their church-group analyses of *Cosmos*'s mainstream science.

Unlike the long radical-creationist tradition of shabby graphics and underdog appeal, the anti-*Cosmos* materials looked good. They helped radical creationists challenge mainstream science without simultaneously forcing them to wallow in their status as low-budget outsiders.[30]

It's not only creationist textbooks and study guides that have beefed up the visual accoutrements of their distinctive ideas about science. Most notably, the Creation Museum of AIG has the look and feel of any mainstream science museum. As trenchant critics Susan Trollinger and William Trollinger noted in their analysis, Kentucky's Creation Museum looks like a "cutting-edge, state-of-the-art natural history museum."[31]

The new look of creationism is about more than just budgets. The presentation of ideas and of science at the Creation Museum encourages visitors to feel as if they are engaging in scientific skepticism, as if they are being presented with information and allowed to make up their own minds about the true nature of creationism and evolution. Visitors are encouraged to feel as if they are doing science, not abandoning science to shelter in their churches.[32]

In spite of the radical differences, then, between mainstream science and the Creation Museum sort, there is often not much difference these days in how they look to the general public. This dilemma was made starkly evident a few years back when a rich donor gave AIG a million-dollar Allosaurus fossil. Proud patriarch Ken Ham crowed about his plans to display it to best effect. He plunked down $500,000 to create a one-of-a-kind display, one that would rival the false-science pretensions of mainstream museums.[33]

Did it work? I wanted to know, so on my blog I conducted a very unscientific poll. Could people tell just by looking which museum displays were creationist science and which were mainstream? The question generated a lot of angry responses, but generally people on both sides had to admit the obvious truth. Creationism may be a very different sort of science, but it isn't quite not science. And to unwary observers, they look about the same, at least at first glance.[34]

Creationism's Galileo Moment

As soon as we recognize the way creationism actually works, we can't avoid the obvious truth. We are not dealing with a fight between religion and science. Creationists love science. They spend millions to prove it. We can't take comfort in the outdated notion that radical-creationist science looks obviously bogus. Older radical-creationist school materials and museums used to look and feel much different from mainstream ones. No longer. Rather, these days we have a much more difficult battle on our hands, a fight between mainstream science and dissenting creationist science, when the differences between the two are no longer immediately aesthetically obvious.

The dissenting science favored by YECs isn't the same, of course, as mainstream science. The differences are glaring, even when they are presented in a spate of similar-looking pamphlets, textbooks, and museum displays. Despite the vast differences, many radical creationists do not dissent from mainstream science as much as we might think. Even when it comes to the vital teaching of evolution, for instance, influential radical creationists share my non-creationist desire to teach all children about evolution.

To an astonishing degree, creationists are more than simply resigned to the fact that their children should learn evolution. These days, many radical creationists are even more fervent than the rest of us that their children need to know about evolutionary theory.

It might seem counterintuitive, so I'll repeat: I'm not saying we all agree about what children should know about evolutionary theory. We don't. But if we want to see the true middle ground, we need to acknowledge the fact—startling though it may be for some of us—that mainstream science folks are not the only ones who want their children to learn about evolution. In fact, due to their intense interest in the cultural dangers of evolutionary theory, radical creationists are often *more* eager to teach their children about evolution than moderate creationists and non-creationists are.

I admit I was confused and surprised when I first noticed this truth about radical American creationism. When D reached out to me about teaching evolution, I was shocked. I assumed that someone who called herself a "creationist mom who homeschools" would want to keep her kids safe from any whiff of evolutionary theory. After all, the dangers of evolution are usually cited by conservative religious folks as one of the primary spiritual dangers afflicting public education these days.

Instead, D wanted to teach her kids evolution, but not the way they did it in public schools. In her local public school, D thought, her children would not have felt "welcome in the classroom." They would have had to keep their mouths shut. As D saw it: "Learning can not take place, in my opinion, in that kind of environment."[35]

In her quest to learn about evolution, D ventured into the intellectual lion's den, reading Richard Dawkins' book *The Greatest Show on Earth*. She found herself agreeing with Dawkins on some points. As she put it:

> Dawkins says on page 155 "it would be so nice if those that oppose evolution would take a tiny bit of trouble to learn the merest rudiments of what it is that they are opposing." I couldn't believe that I totally agreed with Dawkins about something! I am happy to listen, minus the hostility.

D wanted to teach her children the best evolutionary science, "minus the hostility." Far from being unique or even unusual, D's attitude is widely shared among YECs as well as other sorts of creationists. The real danger from evolution, creationists have argued time and again, is that evolution's promoters have unfairly mixed evolutionary science with atheism. "Evolutionists," radical creationists charge, have insisted that the power and potency of evolutionary theory proves the obvious truth of atheism.

If and when evolutionary theory can be taught "minus the hostility," most creationists are enthusiastic supporters. Of course, creationists are just as just as likely to disagree with one another as they are to disagree with secular people. Moreover, many creationists may indeed take a simplistic "keep-out" attitude toward evolutionary theory. We can't assume too glibly, then, that we can capture a single "creationist" attitude about these questions. But we can examine how widespread D's attitudes might be.

Once D helped me see that some radical creationists actually want to teach evolution to their children, I noticed that her attitude was not new. In my research for my book about evangelical higher education, I couldn't help but see that schools—even radical-creationist schools like Bob Jones and Liberty—positively insisted that their students would learn evolutionary theory.

But that was back in the twentieth century. Did creationist school leaders still do so? To get a clue, I called the principal of a local radical-creationist high school. This school takes a back seat to no one in its young-earth rigor. The school promises that children will learn in an environment dedicated to the notion of an "inerrant Bible." Staff agrees on the importance of teaching a "special creation" of humanity.

Historically, the school had been affiliated with the General Association of Regular Baptist Churches (GARBC), a staunchly young-earth organization. As GARBC's articles of faith spell out:

> We believe the Biblical account of the creation of the physical universe, angels, and humanity; that this account is neither allegory nor myth, but a literal, historical account of the direct, immediate creative acts of God without any evolutionary process; that Adam and Eve were created by a direct work of God and not from previously existing forms of life; and that all people are descended from the historical Adam and Eve, first parents of the entire human race.[36]

At this evangelical secondary school, families enroll so that their children will be educated in a Christian environment, an uncompromisingly radical-creationist one. Would they be expected to learn evolutionary theory? I asked the principal.

At this creationist school, the principal confirmed, all students must learn about evolution. It isn't in spite of the school's ardent creationism. Rather, for the principal at least, knowing about evolution was a vital part about being an authentic creationist. As the principal explained to me:

> We teach creationism. Yet it is insufficient if students only know *what* they believe (or what we want them to believe); they should also know *why* they believe certain teaching. An answer to the why question, though, cannot simply be "because the Bible tells me so" as such an answer falls flat outside of Christian or Bible-believing circles. Instead, Christians ought to be prepared to defend their beliefs against seemingly good arguments from those who would promote anti-biblical or extra-biblical arguments. It is difficult to be prepared to do that if one does not know what others believe.[37]

In other words, if a radical creationist really wants to raise a new generation of radical creationists, he or she must insist that children learn what evolutionary theory says. Children should be able to explain why evolutionary

theory doesn't disprove their religion, so they need to know why not. They
need to know evolutionary theory well.

At least, that was the assumption of my local creationist school principal. I wanted to see if other creationists agreed, so I reached out to celebrity radical-creationist Don McLeroy. As documented so engagingly in the
film *The Revisionaries*, Dr. McLeroy was the chair of the Texas State Board
of Education in the first decade of this century, when the conservative-
dominated board pushed through a new set of guidelines for reviewing
textbooks.

McLeroy's moves earned him the enmity of the mainstream science establishment. His proposed 2009 textbook-adoption revisions, critics charged,
were "unworkable and confusing." They were intended mainly to "promote
the idea that living things were specially created in their current forms."[38]

For his part, Dr. McLeroy never denied his creationist beliefs, but he always insisted that his textbook plans were all part of improving science education. He wasn't foisting religious ideas on Texas's science classroom, he
argued, but rather simply pushing for more and better science education.

He has long since retired from the State Board of Education, but he still
feels strongly about teaching evolution. When I asked him what he thought
kids should learn about evolution, his answer was undeniably in support of
teaching evolution. As he put it, "All, and I mean all of my creationist friends
welcome the mandated teaching of evolution and always have."[39]

Of course, he has different end goals from this "mandated teaching." Like D
and my local Christian-school principal, Dr. McLeroy wants to teach evolution in a way that doesn't threaten evangelical faith. More than that, McLeroy
assumes that the scientific evidence for evolutionary theory is so weak that it
will drive students into the arms of creationism. As he explained to me:

> The number one misrepresentation of creationists is that we want to teach
> creationism in the public schools. . . . The second greatest misrepresenta-
> tion is that we do not want to teach evolution. It is commonly assumed that
> we are afraid of the facts of science. No, we welcome the teaching of evolu-
> tion because this is the only way a young person will discover that science
> doesn't support the idea of evolution.[40]

If students learn evolutionary theory, McLeroy assumes, they will learn why
it's not the best science out there. They will presumably turn to creationist
explanations about the differences between species instead.

Other radical creationists agree. The young-earth pundits at AIG positively encourage the teaching of mainstream evolutionary theory among their radical flock. As one AIG writer explained: "Some Christians avoid teaching their kids anything about evolution. We think that's a mistake."[41]

Why? The AIG writer articulated a similar rationale to D, my local Christian-school principal, and Don McLeroy. Young people—radical creationists or not—will eventually run across the ideas of mainstream evolutionary science. If they learn a lot about it in their homes, churches, and schools, they will be better prepared to handle that intellectual encounter. Plus, in order to defend young-earth creationism, the AIG pundit argued, young people need to understand the other side. In the end, like Dr. McLeroy, the radicals at AIG believe that teaching children about real evolutionary science will make them better, more committed creationists.[42]

I don't agree. I don't think learning mainstream evolutionary theory will drive students into the arms of young-earth creationism. Quite the opposite, in fact. I agree with science pundits such as Richard Dawkins and George Gaylord Simpson that the intellectual splendors of an evolutionary perspective will tend to entrance students with their elegance and evidence. But my creationist friends and I don't need to agree on that.

As we've seen, creationist educators and I all agree on a more important question. We all want our children—and all the children in public school science classes—to learn about mainstream evolutionary theory. To learn *about* evolution, to be clear, means to learn what mainstream scientists think and why. It means to learn why so many scientists agree about evolution. It means to learn about fundamental concepts such as natural selection. It does not mean to learn that all intelligent people think evolution has made the notion of a divine creator obsolete. It does not mean that science is somehow at odds with religion. It does not even mean that students can't continue to believe in a young earth, or Adam and Eve, or a flying spaghetti monster, for that matter.[43]

Public schools should teach all kids—whatever their religion or nonreligion—*about* evolution.

If we can agree on that, we don't need to worry if creationist teachers in private schools hope that learning about evolutionary theory will help their students refute atheistic arguments about the origins of life, the way my school principal friend does. We don't need to care if creationist politicians think that learning about evolutionary theory will drive students away from mainstream science, the way Dr. McLeroy does. We don't even need to care if homeschool parents like D want to keep their kids home and teach them mainstream evolutionary theory on their own.

In all these ways—and these are the only ways that really matter when it comes to public schools—we don't disagree about evolution. Creationists and non-creationists alike can agree that all children should learn about evolutionary theory, "minus the hostility."

We Can't All Just Get Along (And That's OK)

What might that look like? There are two simple and obvious goals we can agree on. Most of us, at least. Once we recognize our enormous, thriving middle ground, we can redirect our discussions about creationism and evolution. Certainly, some radicals on both sides will resist. In the end, though, such naysayers will be a small enough fringe that we can safely allow them to wail and gnash their teeth, knowing they will no longer be able to attract significant support.

As we've seen in this chapter, our areas of agreement vastly overshadow our points of contention, once we sweep aside unnecessary anxieties and culture-war histrionics. All of us love science. No one needs to be convinced that science is awesome and that children should learn about it.

What some creationists worry about is not that their children will learn science, but rather that they will be force-fed a witches' brew of science and anti-religion. Radical creationists don't hate the idea of their children learning about evolutionary theory, but they do hate—with good reason— any notion that public schools will treat their children's faith as a problem to be solved, as a deficit. Creationists hate the idea that their children's faith is looked on by public schools as a hostile and unfortunate accretion that needs to be scraped away for children to learn scientific ideas.

We non-creationists can agree on that point. Just as creationists ardently want their children to learn about evolutionary theory, if it can be done right, so non-creationists should insist that public schools must never force any religious belief on students. And just as creationists want their children to learn evolution for their own creationist reasons, so too do the rest of us need to insist that public schools must rigorously refuse to attack religious beliefs for our own non-creationist reasons.

It might sound complicated and difficult, but it boils down to two simple parts.

First, public schools will teach everyone about evolutionary theory.
Second, public schools will keep religious belief out of it.

The Pander's Thumb

Simple and obvious, with plenty of room for objections. Non-creationists like me will fret that limiting our goal to teaching students "about" evolution will allow creationists to continue their latest efforts to toss in other forms of creationism-friendly science along with mainstream evolutionary science. We will worry that this approach threatens to water down evolution education by limiting its goals.

Some of the more radical anti-creationists will insist that this proposal represents a capitulation to creationism's political power. It doesn't. Rather, clearly delimiting the goals of evolution education is just as important for atheists as for theists. It is just as vital for people of all religious faiths as it is for those of none. The notion that real evolution education must limit itself to communicating to students a profound and powerful understanding of evolutionary theory is not a concession to creationism. Instead, it represents a distinctly secular attempt to scrub theocratic assumptions out of our public school curriculum.

It is built on a few basic assumptions about the proper goals of public education. First, public schools have a right and a duty to spread the best available knowledge to students. Right now, that knowledge includes mainstream evolutionary theory, freed from radical-creationist carping.

But schools can only maintain their authority to teach real evolutionary science if they do a better job of enforcing a second basic assumption. Public schools, that is, must maintain a certain type of rigid neutrality in the face of diverse religious beliefs. Just as creationists must struggle to overcome their historic assumptions that their evangelical Protestant faith deserves a special favored place in public education, so too do we non-creationists need to overcome our tradition of assuming that certain forms of creationist religion must be denigrated in order for students to truly comprehend evolutionary thinking.

That tradition, after all, emerged from the unfortunate and unnecessary missionary suppositions examined in the last chapter. Good public education, to the contrary, must devote itself entirely to the notion that religious conversions are not part of the public school mission.

It's an important point and it's worth repeating: Public schools have too often assumed that teaching evolution properly means teaching students to appreciate what Darwin and his later fans and followers called the "grandeur in this view of life."[44] For a student to have really learned evolutionary theory, the false assumption goes, she needs to agree that evolutionary theory is beautiful, elegant, and deeply true in a scientific sense. As Richard Dawkins put it memorably, we might think that teaching evolutionary theory can only succeed when it imparts to students "a proper understanding of the magnificence of the real world," a world in which the "delusion" of supernatural thinking has taken its rightful place in the dustbin of history.[45]

We don't need to be creationists to see the problem. To see it clearly, we need to back up one step: Forcing students to abandon certain religious beliefs has problematically religious implications. Devotional religion—preaching—has no place in any public school. This is the main reason why most creationist sciences have no place in public school science classes. For decades now, those creationist alternatives have only attracted followers for religious reasons. What Dawkins, Simpson, and other well-meaning science pundits have missed is the flip side of this vital rule. If we won't allow public schools to preach any religious ideas as true, we must also insist on banning any pressure on students to abandon any religious ideas as false. We need to draw a bright line between teaching children about modern evolutionary theory—which all public schools must endeavor to do—and preaching that students embrace *or disavow* any religious ideas whatsoever about biology.

What do we do, then, when a student or parent objects that learning evolution amounts to religious indoctrination? Do we simply throw up our hands and agree that we can't force religious ideas on students? Or do we force that student to learn evolutionary theory in the face of her protest? After all, schools have a duty to teach all students the best available knowledge. These days, that knowledge includes mainstream evolutionary theory. It might seem like we are stuck. Schools must avoid religious teaching while simultaneously teaching an idea with religious implications.

How do we square this circle?

It's not as difficult as it might seem. The answer lurks in this chapter—in the fact that most creationists love science and want their children to learn about evolutionary theory. The real problem is not that creationists want their children protected from knowledge about evolutionary theory. Rather, creationists want their children protected from the religious notions that are so often and so unnecessarily attached to mainstream science. As this book has tried to make clear, the problem is not a matter of science, but a matter of trust. Some radical creationists have grown so wary of public schools' intentions that they no longer trust them to teach students evolution without adding on religious beliefs about the nature of life and of knowledge.

If public schools can persuade creationists that they are committed to teaching evolution, not preaching atheism, we can make huge strides. It might feel to some of my fellow non-creationists that this effort will be mere truckling to creationists, but it isn't. Spreading real evolution education that doesn't insist on any religious-style belief is vital to all of us, not just to creationists. It represents a fundamental tenet of American public education, not a pandering to religious minorities.

In the end, it is the flip side of the same valid reasoning that allows us to eject creationism from science classes. That is, we can logically block creationism from science classes if and only if we insist public schools leave religious belief outside the schoolhouse doors, in the hands of students, churches, and families. School must always be about teaching, never preaching. That applies to religious beliefs we agree with just as much as it does to ideas we don't.

Creating Trust

Just as non-creationists like me will worry about this two-part compromise, so too will creationists. For generations now, creationists of all varieties have been told that public schools are out to get their children. Whether they are radical YECs or more moderate believers, creationist parents have agonized about the religious implications of abandoning their children's faith to the mercies of a hostile secularized public school system. It hasn't been science or evolution that made creationist parents nervous, as we've seen throughout this book. Rather, it is the attitude with which secular schools teach such notions, the "hostility" that D worried about.

Too often, creationists have tried to guarantee their children's spiritual safety by banning or watering down evolution education. In the end, though, that's not in their children's best interest. Rather, as a religious minority, it is in radical creationists' best interests to make sure their public schools are committed to an environment that welcomes and includes students of all religious backgrounds, including their own.

It might seem like a strange conclusion, so it's worth repeating: When it comes to pushing religion into classrooms, the biggest losers will always be religious minorities. Whether they are Muslim, Christian, Jewish, Hindu, Buddhist, or any other religion, the first victims of any government-imposed religion will always be smaller groups without the political power to have their voices heard.

For radical creationists, that's a concern. If they want their children to learn in an environment that doesn't attack their religious beliefs, radical creationists should be the first to insist that all public schools do a better job of purging themselves of any sort of implied religious orthodoxy. Radical creationists should be the first to call for fair, inclusive public schools that do more than just pay lip service to secularism.

To their credit, some radical-creationist organizations have taken baby steps in this direction. AIG, for example, has adopted the idea that public school teachers should not be teaching about creationism. Most public school teachers, AIG admits, would not necessarily push AIG's preferred form of young-earth ideas. Moreover, if the teaching of creationism were forced into public schools—even the right sort of young-earth creationism— many teachers would likely teach it only in a mocking way.[46]

In the end, as AIG has come to acknowledge, it is radical creationists who have the most to fear from teachers who might imply that their beliefs about the age of the universe or the origin of our species are not legitimate. When radical creationists complain that public school teachers should not attack their children's religion, they are exactly right. But radicals can only make that complaint—at least, if they want to have any consistency—if they insist on schools that do not attack or promote any particular religious doctrine, including their own.

Just like non-creationists ought to be the first to protest against any attack on a creationist student's belief, so too should radical creationists be the first to protest any infiltration of religious thinking into public school science curricula. It's not a question of magnanimity, but rather of simple naked self-interest. If radical creationists want to have their beliefs respected, it can only happen as a broader insistence on having *all* religious beliefs respected.

Of course, a radical creationist might be tempted to pick another option. Instead of teaching evolutionary theory and leaving religious belief out of it, radicals might hope to simply cut the teaching of evolution altogether. That, too, would be cutting off evolution's nose to spite creationists' faces. As we've seen in this chapter, even radical creationists want their children to learn about evolutionary theory. It is a fundamental intellectual building block of the modern world and no one wants their children to be simply ignorant of it. We all want our children to learn the best of everything in school, including science. None of us disagree about that.

But we still have plenty of disagreements. Some radicals, for example, agree that creationism should be kept out public schools, but they hope to squeeze in a few of the "weaknesses" of mainstream evolutionary science. AIG, for example, considers at "the very least," public school students should learn "various models of the history of life on earth and teach the strengths and weaknesses of those models."[47]

And AIG has plenty of company. Since 2004, state legislators all around the country have proposed a variety of "academic freedom" bills.[48] Most of these bills promise to make the radical-creationist dreams of AIG come true. For instance, one failed Oklahoma bill hoped for "the creation of a school environment that encourages the exploration of scientific theories; allowing teachers to help students analyze certain scientific strengths and weaknesses."[49]

Are these kinds of bills a solution? After all, we can all agree that public schools should encourage the exploration of scientific theories. We can all agree that students should be analyzing the strengths and weaknesses of the ideas they are learning. In the end, however, these "academic freedom" bills fail the sniff test just as other radical-creationist school bills have.

Why? Because the goal of public education—and this is a goal that radical creationists should share with non-radicals and non-creationists—is to have an atmosphere in which no religious group is able to push religious ideas into the curriculum. If we don't, then any minority religious group—including radical creationists—faces the threat of having a majority religion crammed down their kids' throats in the public schools. The "academic freedom" bills do not aim for religious neutrality. The bills' supporters want to mix in scientific ideas that are only supported for religious reasons.

Though plenty of radical creationists won't agree on the goal of keeping creationism-inspired curriculum out of science classes, we can all agree that public school science classes should only teach the best available science. What we disagree on is the definition of the "best" science. Outside of the young-earth faction—America's most prominent type of radical creationism these days—most creationists and non-creationists alike tend to trust the mainstream scientific consensus about evolution. If so many experts agree that the modern evolutionary synthesis is important and our current best understanding of the ways species came about, most people see it as a no-brainer—schools must teach students about it.

Radical creationists also want their children to learn about the best science, but many of them don't trust the mainstream scientific consensus. More relevant to our point here, many of them don't trust that public schools won't use those mainstream evolutionary ideas to imply that smart people couldn't possibly hold religious ideas that conflict with those mainstream scientific ideas.

No one is asking creationists to put blind trust in their local public schools. Faith is for their churches, not their government institutions. Rather, creationists need only to trust that they have the absolute unalienable right to be included in their children's education. They will be given every right to monitor the teaching that goes on. Like all Americans, they have every right to insist on their rightful role in their local public schools.

What will that allow them to do? It won't give them veto power over the teaching of mainstream evolutionary science. But it will allow them to insist and to monitor the way that science is taught. Creationist parents—like *all* public school parents—have the right and the duty to insist that science classes—like all classes—remain religiously neutral.

Public schools will provide the education that almost all parents want: teaching all children about evolutionary theory. Schools will agree to maintain a strict and scrupulous neutrality about any religious implications of that teaching. If a parent agrees with my local creationist principal that the main goal of learning about evolution is so that children can believe more strongly in their dissenting religious view of science and creation, so be it. If a parent agrees with D that children must learn mainstream evolutionary theory to be truly educated, but they also must learn why they don't believe it, fair enough. And if a parent agrees with Dr. McLeroy and AIG that evolutionary theory itself will teach children why it is flawed, that's her right. By the same token, if a parent agrees with Richard Dawkins that the main goal of learning evolutionary theory is to open people's eyes about the intellectual splendors of an atheistic universe, that's OK too.

We never need to agree on the ultimate religious aim of evolution education. Like all religious ideas, religious ideas associated with evolutionary theory must be kept outside the schoolhouse door. This is not something that only creationists want. All of us need to recognize our shared interest in maintaining truly religion-neutral schools, schools that actively welcome religious diversity among students, not merely grudgingly tolerate it.

Just as public school science classes won't teach religiously inspired alternative forms of evolutionary science, so too must they insist that they will teach every student about evolutionary theory. They need to insist and guarantee that successful students gain a profound knowledge of evolutionary theory. At the same time, they will earnestly and steadfastly refuse to promote or denigrate any sort of religious thinking about that knowledge.

The Texas Two-Step

Will this ever be easy? Not at all. Schools are complicated places, and pressure from parents, administrators, curricula, and high-stakes tests push and pull students and teachers in all sorts of directions at the same time. Many teachers are doing all they can to wrangle their energetic and diverse students toward a reasonable facsimile of scientific knowledge.

It might seem ridiculous to working teachers to suggest a complicated compromise like this one. When kids and their parents seem suspicious about any kind of evolution education, it might seem pointless to encourage a teacher to think abstractly about the rights of religious dissenters and the ultimate purpose of public education. When a principal or department chair encourages teachers to avoid stirring up trouble, it might seem silly to point out that evolutionary theory—theoretically—shouldn't be considered troublesome at all. When a school board lectures teachers not to offend influential religious citizens with talk of Darwin and finches, it might seem futile to suggest that religious citizens should *want* their children to learn evolutionary theory.

In other words, for people in the trenches of our creationism culture war, it might seem absolutely absurd to suggest that our disagreements aren't really about evolutionary theory itself. When someone throws mud in your face, it rarely helps to explain calmly and clearly that they really should be aiming at a different target.

As we'll see in the conclusion, though, life in real classrooms has long been more hopeful than headlines tend to suggest. Science teachers have long practiced the most important element of reforming evolution education. Namely, they have been building trusting relationships with parents and students.

That sort of trust is the most fundamental step we can take. Acknowledging our real goals and our wide areas of mutual agreement will not end debates about creationism, but a clearer view of the roots of our disagreement will help us put into context the difference between red herrings and real controversy.

In the end, we need to think about two basic truths that we can agree on when it comes to evolutionary theory. First, we want our children to learn about it. Second, we want public schools to keep religious ideas out of the equation.

With fundamental agreement about those two hugely significant notions, we can avoid pointless accusations about whether creationism should count as science. (It should, but as a religiously inspired science it has no place in public school science classes.) We can avoid endless debate about whether evolution is a religion. (It's not, but creationists and atheists alike should be allowed to decide whether it has religious implications for them.) If we can focus on the fact that we want our children to learn evolutionary theory but we do not want public schools to preach any religious ideas, we will have a better chance of moving forward toward our shared goals.

Conclusion

Trust Falls

We don't disagree about evolution. It might have seemed hard to recognize, but once we take the time to understand the landscape of creationist America, the truth stares us in the face: Our never-ending culture wars about creationism and evolution aren't really about evolutionary science itself.

But they are about something. We might not disagree about real evolutionary theory, but it sure feels as if we do. Why? Because we tend to disagree about everything. A divided America stares itself in the face angrily and skeptically across its many divides. The real dispute when it comes to evolution and creationism—and the real issue we should be talking about—is our fundamental, divisive, enduring lack of trust. The vast majority of us want our children to learn about evolution. Only a tiny minority of people want public schools to denigrate creationist religion. But radical creationists don't trust non-radicals not to cram atheism down their children's throats. Non-creationists don't trust creationists not to wedge religious ideas into science classes.

This central problem of trust is not isolated to our creation-evolution culture wars. Social scientists have noted the central role of trust in a healthy society and the enormous cost to be paid when trust breaks down.[1] They have also noted that a "loss of familiarity" is the first step to losing the ability to trust one another.[2]

Building trust isn't simple or easy, but the first step will be to build familiarity, to create the conditions in which trust can flourish. We need to start with a hard look at the real diversity of creationism. We also need to be brutally honest about our flawed ideas and understandings about both evolution and creationism.

For outsiders like me, the most radical ideas about creation and evolution tend to hog our attention. Seeing a dinosaur in a cage on a replica Noah's ark at Kentucky's Ark Encounter is truly shocking, but exhibits like that are not

Creationism USA. Adam Laats, Oxford University Press (2021). © Oxford University Press.
DOI: 10.1093/oso/9780197516607.001.0001.

representative of all creationism. Indeed, the assumption that creationism as a whole is the same as radical creationism might be the most important misunderstanding in the history of American creationism.

To understand that Americans don't really disagree about evolution, we need to notice that most creationists are non-radical about their creationism. Indeed, if we understand creationism to mean a feeling that some divine force must be involved in the history of life, almost all Americans could be considered creationists of one sort or another. Too often, when people say "creationist," they mean the radical few who are convinced that a real worldwide flood wiped out the planet a few thousand years ago. By any reasonable definition, though, the creationist label should include all those people who think God (or gods, or spaghetti monsters) must have had some role in creating life. Once we grasp the real contours of American creationism, we can't help but notice that almost all of those creationists have absolutely no problem with mainstream evolutionary theory.

We will also notice that the young-earth creationist rump—today's most prominent sort of radical creationism, at least in the United States–is a relatively recent creation. To be fair, many religious people throughout history may have believed in a recent creation and a literal worldwide flood, but in modern American history, the young-earth creationism of the Creation Museum only gained popularity beginning in the 1960s. Before that time, even the most ardent anti-evolution Christian fundamentalists assumed that the Bible was talking about long geological ages, or perhaps a vast expanse of geologic time between creations. Only when mainstream science gained confidence in its revised version of evolutionary theory did creationists have to choose. Some went with mainstream science, modified to fit their creationist requirements. Others decided to take a more aggressive course, to throw out mainstream science entirely and build a set of independent scientific institutions and ideas of their own.

Those institutions and ideas have often ranged far beyond the narrow issue of mainstream evolutionary theory. Logically, opposition to same-sex marriage, drug abuse, and rock and roll music would seem to have nothing to do with Darwin's ideas about speciation. In practice, however, the radical creationist protest has bundled together a compelling package of conservative dissent that, at heart, doesn't have all that much to do with evolutionary science itself. As the Reverend Avis Hill noted, it was not really specific scientific ideas he abhorred, but the "attitudes of evolution and all that."[3] For many radical creationists, evolution came to serve as a potent symbol of every social trend they hate; evolution came to represent a society that they no longer trusted, a society where they no longer felt that their beliefs were respected.

Since the 1960s, as a result, radical young-earth creationists have built an entirely separate network of trustworthy radical-creationist institutions. Not only could young people attend creationist schools, read creationist textbooks, purchase creationist yearbooks, and buy creationist class rings, they could also visit creationist museums, attend creationist colleges, take creationist vacations, and vote for creationist political parties. For radical young-earth creationists, distrust of mainstream evolutionary theory was made deeper and more profoundly divisive through the creation of a coherent, convincing, completely trustworthy creationist alternative.

Radical-creationist schools certainly teach creationism, but more important, they teach creationists that only their own brand of creationism is trustworthy; only their own type of creationism can protect them from socialism, drug abuse, and same-sex marriage equality. Perhaps most important of all, radical-creationist institutions teach people not to trust the other side. They hope their listeners will be safe from the allure of mainstream science and other sorts of creationism. They hope to build a wall high enough that no evidence or argument could climb over it.

When radical creationists believe that mainstream scientists and science guys are not to be trusted, it becomes very easy for them to avoid mainstream scientific outreach. The notion that creationism is merely a lack of exposure to convincing evolutionary ideas is woefully naive. Yet for the past century and more, non-creationists like me have assumed that simply spreading the word about evolution will suffice. We have assumed that adding evolution to state science standards will convince creationists of their errors. We have found evolution to be so convincing that we haven't noticed the failure of our missionary attitudes.

In fact, though, as we saw in chapter 5, people seem to default to creationism, to being "intuitive theists."[4] The ideas of natural selection and species change are not as simple and obvious as they seem. Even those of us who say we believe in evolutionary theory don't really understand it any better than creationists who say they don't. We trust it without knowing it, while radical creationists distrust it without knowing why.

Yet it is not only people like me who say they want children to learn about evolutionary theory. A vast majority of creationists have no religious problem with evolutionary theory. Even the most radical-creationist dissenters want their children to understand what evolutionary theory says. To be sure, they often want it for different reasons than I do; they want their children to know why it isn't true. In the end, however, they desire a modern education for their children. Like me, they want their children to know what mainstream evolutionary theory is all about.

And that fact gives us a glimmer of hope. It is sobering to realize that radical creationism now includes an extensive set of alternative institutions devoted to teaching radical ideas about science as well as teaching young people not to trust either mainstream scientific ideas or competing creationist ones. How can we reach out to people who have learned not to trust any outreach?

For starters, we should abandon talk of converting people. We should stop trying to convince radical creationists to give up their religious convictions. We should actively avoid the sorts of conversion talk that have long dominated our creation-evolution discussions. Such missionary outreach will not only be ineffective, it will deepen our divides by building even more distrust of our motives.

Instead, once we better understand the real issues of trust and distrust we can focus more effectively on reasonable solutions. Once we see that creationists share our desire to teach all children about evolutionary theory, we can move away from our faulty missionary ideas about creationism and evolution and instead concentrate on what really matters.

We don't need to agree about what Jesus would want. We don't even need to agree about what Darwin would want. It is okay for us to sidestep such questions. Instead, we can begin to build trust by acknowledging our shared goals. First, we want public schools to teach our children about mainstream evolutionary theory. Second, we do not want public schools to promote or inhibit religion.

Both of those goals sound simple, but both can be devilishly tricky in practice. The key is to recognize and remind ourselves of what we want from public schools. We want schools that we can belong to. Our local schools must be open to all of us, not grudgingly, but enthusiastically. That can only happen if we agree to leave religious preaching outside the schoolhouse door.

It is radical creationists who should want secular public schools more than anyone. Simply strategically, it is the only goal that makes sense for them. As a minority, they should recognize the dangers of religious public schools. Unless schools are relentlessly secular, the rights of any religious minority are at risk of being unrecognized and disrespected.

As a religious minority, then, radical creationists should join with other creationists and non-creationists in insisting on secular public school classrooms. Only by ensuring that public school classes scrupulously avoid pushing religious ideas into students will the rights of radical-creationist students be protected. Science teachers should never try to change the religious beliefs of their students, whatever those beliefs might be.

Hard as it might be for some of my fellow secularists to agree, we need to join with our radical-creationist neighbors to insist that public schools remain agnostic about students' religions. If students want to be atheists and embrace evolutionary theory as an elegant intellectual connection that provides profound insights into the nature of reality, that's their right. If students want to insist that our species must have originated from two instantly created people in a garden, that is also their right. We can only help students know and understand evolutionary science; we can and should never try to get them to believe anything that hints at religion.

If that is the case, why do we need to include evolutionary science at all in public schools? If evolution presents a religious challenge for some people, why can't we simply leave it out of public education altogether? Both today and in the past, this has in effect been the solution public schools often settled on. But it is not adequate. Just as we all should insist on secular, inclusive public schools for everyone, so should we all insist that those schools teach our children the best of everything. In history class, English, math, and everything else, we want schools that expose students to the very best ideas.

When it comes to life sciences, evolutionary theory is the best science out there. It is not the only science. Rivals such as intelligent design purport to expose the weaknesses in mainstream evolutionary science. Advocates of those counter-sciences, though, are guilty of pushing religious ideas into public schools. So, although we can never really prove that mainstream evolutionary thinking is real science and creationist options are bogus science, we don't need to. All we need to do is look for the best science on offer. Today, that is clearly mainstream evolutionary science.

Just as it would be unfair to students to leave out the best ideas about science, it would also be an unconscionable disservice to our public school students to include anything but the best thinking in their curricula. Attempts to wedge religiously inspired scientific ideas into public school science classes dilute the quality of science education and pollutes the nonreligious ethos of good public education. We need instead to acknowledge our shared dream of giving all our children the best of everything.

How can we get there? The key challenge will not be changing science textbooks or state science standards, though those are crucial elements of good public education. The key challenge, again, will be building trust. Creationists need to trust teachers and schools to teach their children about evolutionary theory without insisting that students change their religious beliefs. Non-creationists need to trust creationist parents and pundits that they don't want to cram God back into the classroom through some sort of sneaky backdoor.

It won't be easy. As political theorist Francis Fukuyama argued, building trust between social groups is a "complicated and in many ways mysterious cultural process."[5] In the case of our hundred years' culture war over evolution and creationism, especially, we need not only to build trust, but also to tear down border walls and bridge trenches built by generations of ferocious and angry distrust.

But there is plenty of reason for hope. Science teachers have long been experts in more than biology, geology, chemistry, and physics. Good teachers have long known that the key to good teaching is building good relationships with students and families. Yes, at times teachers come into conflict with parents and students, but those stories get headlines precisely because they are unusual. Most teachers in most schools know where their students are coming from; teachers know that good teaching can begin only when students and parents trust their teachers and vice versa.

That's why polls of parent attitudes consistently show that Americans tend to trust their local schools. Since the 1980s, Gallup has asked people what they think of public schools. When it comes to the schools that their children attend, large majorities of parents—ranging from 65 percent to 77 percent—give them an A or a B. For the nation's schools as a whole, however, far fewer parents—between 18 percent and 27 percent—can say the same.[6]

What's going on? We don't want to assume too much, but it seems fair to conclude that the hard work of real teachers, real parents, and real students has paid off. When parents have some familiarity with teachers and schools, they trust them. It is only school in the abstract that makes parents nervous. As political scientist Mark E. Warren has noted, trust comes in a variety of flavors, but "the *core* trust relation is interpersonal."[7] It may be difficult to rebuild trust in a vague, generic institution of public education, but in most cases Americans never lost their trust in their local public schools and their children's hard-working teachers.

Even for those of us who aren't focused on one local public school but on public education as a whole, there are things we can do to build trust. The first step will be a better knowledge of the real issues. For non-creationists like me, that means a better understanding of the real world of American creationism. As this book has argued, creationism is never as simple as we might think. To every generalization there is an exception, to every stereotype a correction.

If we want to move forward in our endless dispute over evolution and creationism, we should start with better mutual knowledge. After all, the real problem, the festering sore buried under our generations of angry dispute over creationism is not our most obvious disagreements about religion, science, education, and knowledge. We won't agree on such things, and we don't need to.

When it comes down to it, we don't disagree about evolution. Not really. We just hate each other. We disagree about politics, about music, about sexuality, civil rights, and what it means to be a good American. We disagree about child-rearing, schooling, and proper etiquette. We disagree about hairstyles and the opening ceremonies at football games. We disagree about so many things, in fact, that we tend to throw evolutionary theory into the mix out of sheer weariness and habit.

It doesn't have to be this way, especially because the overwhelming majority of us want our children to learn real evolutionary theory. We can make it happen. We can stop accusing our opponents of ideas they don't really advocate. We can instead start with the goals and hopes that we all share. We can teach evolutionary theory in every public school without watering it down with disingenuous criticisms and religiously inspired counter-science.

If we want to make any progress in our eternal battles about creationism, we need to stop trying to prove the unprovable. We need to stop debating whose science is real or whose religion is better. We can move forward, but we need to acknowledge that we won't agree on those things, and we don't need to. Instead, we need to begin by acknowledging our shared goals.

What's in a Name?

Sometimes, radical creationists don't like being called radical. When I used the term in the past to refer to young-earth creationists (YECs) who try to push public policy in creationist directions, I heard complaints from prominent radicals. Dr. Don McLeroy, former head of Texas' state board of education and a radical creationist, told me that he didn't like the term because it implied bad associations with "today's culture of violent radicals."[1]

Dr. McLeroy asked, why call YECs "radical?" He had a few alternative suggestions. "Why not 'strict, rigid, exacting, picky, unsparing?' "[2] Or how about "recent creation-ist,"[3] "short age,"[4] "literal," "strict, or stern, or serious, or young earth!"[5] In the end, none of those options captures the meanings of the "radical" label I use in this book.

What does it mean to be a "radical" creationist? It's not a perfect label, but it is the best label available to describe a small subset of American creationists, that is, those creationists who believe that their religion dictates that they reject mainstream evolutionary science. But being a radical isn't only about rejecting evolutionary theory. To be radical, creationists also have to attempt to influence public policy somehow, to nudge (or shove) public schools in creationism-friendly directions or to add religion to other sorts of public venues. Simply calling these radicals "literal" or "strict" might help explain their view of themselves, theologically speaking, but it doesn't capture their outward-focused activism. When it comes to talking about schools, science, and society, it is only the outward focus that matters.

To be sure, Dr. McLeroy's brand of young-earth belief, based in the more conservative wing of evangelical Protestantism, certainly fits the bill for radical creationism. It is important to remember, however, that the radical label isn't limited to young-earth evangelical Protestants. In the United States, young-earth Christians tend to be the most prominent radical creationists, but in other contexts there are and have been different sorts of radicals. As we saw in chapter 2, non-young-earth kinds of creationists led the fight against evolution in the public schools in the 1920s. In recent decades, intelligent design (ID) pundits who preach skepticism of mainstream science and push for ID-friendly textbooks in public schools might also fit the bill, even though they don't preach about Jesus or mention dinosaurs.[6] And in other countries, Muslim or Jewish creationists have played the radical role.[7]

After all, when it comes to public policy, the most important distinction among American creationists is not whether they believe in a young earth or an old earth. It is not whether they insist that the six days in Genesis can represent long geologic ages or must instead be read as literal days. It is not whether they think that species evolved by progressive divine intervention or via a single mechanism instilled by God at one time in the distant past and is unfolding across long ages. No, if we care mainly about creationism's role in American society as a whole, the key distinction we need to make to understand creationism past and present is between the small group of creationists who deny the scientific truth of evolutionary theory and hope to influence public policy in creationism-friendly directions and the vast body of creationists who do not. For that reason, with apologies to Dr. McLeroy and other radicals who do not prefer the term, this book uses the label "radical" to describe anti-evolution creationists who push their beliefs into the public square somehow.

In this appendix, I make the case for using the "radical" label. There certainly are problems with the label, but it is far and away the best available option. Other labels—as we'll see in this appendix—tend to suffer from a few fundamental problems.

Angels and Pins

The first problem is a big one. It might feel satisfying to use specific labels to describe specific sorts of creationism, to create a vast catalogue of all the different types of creationist belief. But we quickly find that any such attempt runs into insuperable obstacles, both intellectual and practical. The distinctions among different versions of creationism might not be literally infinite, but given the nature of theological debate, they get pretty close.

This book defines creationism broadly to include anyone who thinks—or who simply assumes without thinking about it—that there must have been some kind of divine or supernatural spark to life. It might be the God of the Judeo-Christian-Islamic traditions, it might be a set of indigenous gods, or it might be a vaguely supernatural intelligence at work. For our purposes, it doesn't matter. Being a creationist simply means believing or assuming that life as we know it didn't just happen on its own. As we've seen, by that definition large majorities of Americans count as creationists. Anyone who thinks of themselves as religious or even spiritual can fit in this category.

Once we try to be more precise about what it means to be a creationist, the labels can pile up in intimidating ways. In chapter 1, we offered a brief survey of the broad categories of creationism common in today's America. That brief look barely touched the true diversity of creationist belief. As with any religious idea, creationism has been sliced and diced into a dizzying array of possible permutations.

Consider, as just one example of the possibilities, an argument from Russell Mixter's 1959 book about redefining creationism. As you may recall from chapter 3, Professor Mixter hoped to popularize a new vision of creationism and evolution among conservative evangelical Christians. There was no reason, Mixter believed, that evangelicals couldn't take the Bible seriously while still accepting some elements of modern evolutionary theory.

Even among those who agreed with Mixter, however, there was not one single, agreed-upon definition of creationism. One of the creationists who contributed to Mixter's book offered a brief catalogue of the different visions and versions of creationism he found theologically acceptable. Good Christians, he argued, could choose to believe in "Progressive Creative Catastrophism," "Day-Age Catastrophism," "Progressive Creationism," "Alternate Day-Age," "Eden-Only," "Concurrent (Overlapping) Ages," "Split Week," or "Revelation Day" creationism. None of these theories required belief in a young earth. None of them required Christians to disrespect the authority of the Scriptures. Yet all of them were different; all of them disagreed with one another about the real Christian message of creationism.[8]

When it comes to defining and labeling creationism, we can't hope to come up with a system that catalogues all the diversity of belief possible among creationists. We would end up with almost as many types of creationism as there are creationists. Instead, we should try to understand the types and tendencies among different sorts of creationist belief.[9] We can outline a variety of ways of being creationist—a wider description that explains the many different types of creationism without attempting the impossible task of sorting and labeling every single different type.

We should start with the biggest distinction among types of creationists: *anti-evolutionary* or *evolutionary* creationists. A large majority of creationists are evolutionary ones; they have no problem accepting the mainstream science of evolution. Their backgrounds can be diverse—someone could be a Catholic evolutionary creationist or an evangelical Protestant one or a spiritual-not-religious type.

A smaller subset of creationists, the *anti-evolutionary* ones, have objections to accepting evolutionary science as the best science out there. The most prominent sorts of anti-evolutionary creationists these days are of the young-earth variety. Like the activists at Answers in Genesis (AIG) in Kentucky, these are creationists who say that the earth experienced a worldwide flood and that dinosaurs and humans walked the earth at the same time. These creationists object to mainstream science textbooks and built a huge replica of Noah's ark in Kentucky. Most of the time, when the general public talks about creationism, they mean the anti-evolutionary kind.

But there are also plenty of anti-evolutionary creationists out there who don't attract much public attention. We may refer to these creationists as *insular* creationists, people who believe strongly that mainstream evolutionary theory is a religious danger but who don't try to influence public policy very much. As we saw in chapter 1, there are plenty of examples of this kind of insular creationism in today's United States, including Orthodox Jewish leaders who push for anti-evolutionary beliefs but only within their own religious circles.

In contrast, other creationists might be described as having a *proprietary* or *imperialist* attitude about public institutions. Unlike insular groups, these *proprietary* creationists tend to think public life should reflect—or at least not challenge—their group's religious beliefs. In the United States, these proprietary groups are usually from Protestant backgrounds, especially the evangelical wing. In other societies, of course, Catholic, Jewish, Islamic, or other sorts of creationists might feel a more proprietary interest in public life. In the United States, we hear a lot from proprietary creationists about the proper role of evolutionary theory in public schools, but we also hear from proprietary creationists about proper restrictions on abortion or LGBTQ rights, the proper role of sex education in public schools, and even the proper greetings for the end of December.

There are other distinctions in the world of creationism that help us sketch a practical typography. For instance, some creationists tend to tip more in a *science-focused* direction, while others tend to be more interested in *culture-war* justifications. Those who are more science-focused tend to discuss creationism and evolutionary theory in mainstream scientific terms; they tend to focus on evidence with which mainstream scientists could agree, even if those mainstream scientists tend not to agree with the creationist conclusions. Michael Behe of Lehigh University serves as an example of this sort of science-focused creationism. In his public writings, Dr. Behe argues that the notion of an intelligent designer is the clear conclusion of mainstream scientific evidence.[10]

Culture-war creationists, on the other hand, tend to focus more exclusively on political issues such as abortion, LGBTQ rights, gender roles, and climate change. Certainly, culture-war creationists also cherish scientific arguments, but in their rhetoric they rely primarily on the culture-war ramifications of evolutionary belief. Raising children with an evolutionary worldview, they might argue, will lead both to individual damnation for those children and social disintegration for the country as a whole.

None of these distinctions should be taken as cut-and-dried labels. Rather, they are descriptions of broad tendencies in creationist thought. Creationists might have a proprietary feeling about public schools and believe firmly that scientific evidence disproves evolutionary theory yet avoid culture-war battles and focus instead on the insular goal of protecting their children in a homeschool environment. It is entirely possible for creationists to feel at home with a variety of different labels, even within the same organization or religious group. Because of these vagaries of definition, any attempt to impose simplistic labels on specific kinds of creationist belief will fall short of the complicated reality. Trying to catalogue every single different vision of creationism is both an impossible task and an ultimately unhelpful one. Instead, using multiple types and tendencies—talking about different, overlapping ways of being a creationist—is a more useful way to describe real creationism.

And once we begin sketching the differences in types and tendencies of creationist thinking, we realize that there is one distinction that matters the most when it comes to understanding the role of creationism in American society. The distinctions that matter to public policy have nothing to do with whether a creationist comes from a Christian or Jewish or Muslim background. They have nothing to do with creationists' beliefs about the precise meaning of the words of the Bible. Rather, the only distinctions that matter to the rest of us are whether creationists reject mainstream evolutionary science and try to push those beliefs—somehow—into public life.

This is not a distinction that creationists tend to make about themselves. Unlike the labels that various sorts of creationists have used to describe themselves—theistic evolution, evolutionary creationism, progressive creationism, young-earth creationism, old-earth creationism, intelligent design, and so on—we need to focus on the distinctions that matter to all of us. Whatever they might label themselves, the most important distinction among types of creationism is between those few creationists who reject mainstream science and who try to influence public policy in creationism-friendly directions and the large body of creationists who don't.

We could use a variety of labels for this distinction. We could separate "activist" creationists from the rest. We might call the minority group the "extreme" creationists or "combative" creationists. In the end, the best term is "radical" because it captures both the scientific attitude and aggressive, outward focus of this small subset of American creationists. It emphasizes the point that these ideas about evolution and creation—namely, the notion that creationists need to reject mainstream science and that they have a right to insist on a special public recognition of their beliefs—are not generally held among creationists as a whole.

Radical Solutions

But using the "radical" label to distinguish the subset of American creationists who reject evolutionary theory and who push their religious ideas into public life has problems of its own. First of all, calling creationists "radical" might further the misconception that they are somehow opposed to science as a whole. As seen throughout this book, that's just not true. Like most Americans, radical creationists love science; they simply insist that mainstream science has gone off the rails. And, in general, radical creationists don't even oppose the idea that their children should learn mainstream evolutionary science or at least learn a lot about it.

Many radical creationists don't oppose evolutionary theory in its entirety. AIG, for example, an organization with a fair claim to being America's leading radical-creationist organization, preaches that some forms of evolution really happened. Unlike mainstream scientists, but like many of their young-earth allies, AIG distinguishes between "micro" evolution—which they think really happens—and "macro" evolution—which they think does not. The radical creationists at AIG agree that evolution takes place "within kinds," as the Bible describes. That is, dogs can descend from wolves, and one kind of cow can evolve from another kind of cow. It's only the "macro" sort of evolution that they object to—the mainstream notion that the vast diversity of species descended from common ancestors.[11]

Calling these sorts of creationists "radical" risks sending the untrue message that they absolutely oppose the notion of evolution in all its forms and they don't want their children to know anything about it. And that's not the only problem. Calling YECs like the ones at AIG "radical" might suggest that they are America's most obdurate deniers of mainstream science. They're not. Believe it or not, AIG faces criticism that they are too loose in their interpretation of the Bible, too willing to adopt modern scientific ideas, and too willing to sacrifice the obvious meaning of the book of Genesis.

Some Christians point out that a truly devout interpretation of Genesis leads us to believe in things such as a flat earth and a geocentric solar system. After all, the Bible seems to describe things that way. In response, AIG finds itself in the awkward position of defending its acceptance of some tenets of the modern scientific consensus. It's not something AIG is used to doing. As critics William and Susan Trollinger have charged, the argument made by AIG's geocentric critics "is precisely the same argument made by young Earth creationists against Christians who are old Earth creationists and Christians who are theistic evolutionists."[12] How can YECs defend themselves against their own trump card?

To deflect the even-more-radical criticism, the radical creationists at AIG have denounced their denouncers. AIG complained that

> flat-earthers who demand this hyper-literal approach to the Bible readily abandon it when it suits them. Ultimately, flat-earthers place themselves in a position of authority while simultaneously deconstructing the idea that there can't be any authority other than Scripture.[13]

These tussles between anti-evolutionary organizations leads us to some tricky questions about our use of the "radical" label. If young earthers defend modern science against even-more-radical groups like flat earthers and geocentrists, then how can we fairly call AIG "radical?" If YECs like the ones at AIG actually like science as a concept, and if they even want their children to learn about mainstream evolutionary science, how can they be radical? And, not least of all, if creationists like Don McLeroy don't like the label, why should we force it on them?

In spite of the problems, calling organizations such as AIG "radical creationists" is the best choice, or at least the least poor choice. For one thing, the fact that there are creationists out there who object to mainstream science even more radically does not imply that the YECs at AIG are not radical, too.

Plus, though other labels might promise more precision, that precision is both impractically cumbersome and ultimately illusory. Instead of calling them "radical," we could describe AIG instead as "culture-war proprietary anti-evolutionary creationists, moving toward a more insular focus." After all, in nearly every public appeal, the creationists at AIG focus on *culture-war* issues such as LGBTQ rights, climate change, and abortion rights.[14] They certainly articulate a *proprietary* feeling about public life, too, bemoaning the tendency to turn "Merry Christmas" into mere "Happy Holidays"[15] and lamenting that public libraries welcome transvestites as role models.[16] There is no doubt about AIG's *anti-evolutionary* focus, with its constant warnings that talk of "millions of years" will lead young people to damnation.[17] Yet as seen in chapter 6, AIG's Ken Ham has indicated that he is more interested in saving the souls of the already converted than of moving the whole nation to a creationist conversion, so we could say AIG is moving toward a more *insular* focus.[18]

We could do all that, but it would not be a practical solution. It would not even be as precise as we might hope. After all, the creationists at AIG also tend to focus at times on scientific-sounding arguments instead of culture-war ones. They tend to zig-zag between insular ideas and proprietary/imperialist ones. So even if we were to use an impractically long label for every major creationist organization, we would end up with both an impossibly cumbersome book and one that offered a false sense of precision.

For these reasons, instead of using long, intricate labels and trying to hash out the many doctrinal specifics of every creationist group and individual, it makes more sense to focus on the big divide among creationists that really matters: the one between the aggressive, anti-evolution rump and the evolution-accepting majority. And for those purposes, the "radical" label is the best fit.

Using the "radical" label to identify anti-evolution creationists who push their beliefs into the public square offers additional benefits as well. For example, if we focus only on young-earth beliefs, we might miss the continuities that have connected radical creationists across history. Today, young-earth organizations like AIG are the most prominent radical-creationist organization, but they haven't always been, and they won't always be. As we've seen, in the 1920s radical creationists tended to reject the idea of a young earth. Rather, like 1920s anti-evolution leader William Bell Riley, they mocked those who implied they believed in outrageous ideas like " 'a flat earth,' . . . 'an immovable world,' . . . 'a canopy of roof overhead.' "[19] At the time, Riley thought those ideas, like the ideas of a real, literal worldwide flood or a real, recent six-day creation, were laughable. Yet with his 1920s campaign against the teaching of evolution and his assumption that his religious ideas deserved special treatment in America's public schools, Riley certainly fits with our definition of radical creationism.

And in the future, who knows? Maybe new groups will gain new popularity with new kinds of creationist messages. They might be Islamic groups, old-earth creationist groups, or groups we haven't heard of yet. If we limit ourselves to labels that suit today's prominent radical creationists, we will miss the continuities with other groups in other times and places that oppose mainstream evolutionary science and push their religious beliefs into public schools.

Finally, using the "radical" label to describe creationists who oppose mainstream evolutionary science and who push their beliefs into public life helps underline the most important point of all. Namely, most creationists—and most Americans count as one kind of creationist or another—are not at all radical. Most creationists have no problem with mainstream evolutionary science, or they only disagree here and there with various elements of mainstream thinking. More important, they do not want their religious beliefs to shape public school curriculum.

If we understand the real landscape of American creationism, we see that the radicals form only a small and dwindling presence. Yes, radical creationism can still identify fellow travelers in the highest political offices. They can point to poll results that seem to indicate vast support for their ideas. As seen throughout this book, however, that sort of Make America Great Again creationism is a paper tiger.

When we understand American creationism as it really is, we can see that Americans do not and have not ever really had fundamental disagreements about the actual science of evolution, at least not in ways that matter for public policy. Very few Americans really understand evolutionary theory, whether they say they believe it or reject it. And almost all Americans want their children to learn about mainstream evolutionary theory, whether they want kids to embrace it or reject it. Our apparent disputes about evolution are actually disputes over whom we can trust. As this book has argued, the real kernel of disagreement is not about evolutionary science, but whether people can trust mainstream experts.

Our culture-war battles about evolution and creationism have long suffered from a confusion of labels, with a few radical creationists being allowed too often to speak for a much larger group of non-radicals. By separating radical creationists from the rest, we get a clearer picture of the areas of agreement and disagreement about creationism and evolution.

And with the correct labels, we can see that our areas of agreement are vastly larger than our areas of disagreement. By labeling things more clearly, we can't resolve all our fights. But at least we can get a clearer picture of what we are and aren't fighting about.

Notes

Introduction

1. See David E. Long, *Evolution and Religion in American Education: An Ethnography* (New York: Springer, 2011), 13.
2. Megan Brenan, "40% of Americans Believe in Creationism," Gallup, July 26, 2019, https://news.gallup.com/poll/261680/americans-believe-creationism.aspx.
3. See Michael D'Antonio and Peter Eisner, "Mike Pence's Problem with Science," CNN, September 2, 2018, https://www.cnn.com/2018/08/31/opinions/mike-pence-problem-with-science-dantonio-eisner/index.html. On Ben Carson's creationism, see Jeff Jacoby, "So What If Ben Carson Is a Creationist?," *The Patriot Post*, October 29, 2015, https://patriotpost.us/opinion/38544. See also Rod Dreher, "Ben Carson Is a Creationist. So?" *The American Conservative*, October 29, 2015, https://www.theamericanconservative.com/dreher/ben-carson-creationist/. For the creationism of Betsy DeVos, see Annie Waldman, "Devos' Code Words for Creationism Raise Concerns about 'Junk Science,'" *ProPublica*, January 29, 2017, https://www.propublica.org/article/devos-education-nominees-code-words-for-creationism-offshoot-raise-concerns.
4. Answers in Genesis, "Major Expansions Continue at Ark Encounter: More than 1 Million Guests Visit in Second Year," *Answers in Genesis blog*, July 7, 2018, https://answersingenesis.org/about/press/2018/07/07/major-expansions-continue-ark-encounter/. For a review of criticism, see Thomas Novelly, "Visitors Aren't Flocking to the Kentucky Ark Encounter as Expected . . . or Are They?" *Louisville Courier Journal*, August 2, 2018, https://www.kentucky.com/news/state/article215998125.html.
5. Why "radical?" In this book, "radical" is the label used to designate those creationists who do two things: dispute the validity of mainstream evolutionary theory, and try to push their views into the public square in some way. For details and a fuller explication, see the appendix, "What's in a Name."
6. See, e.g., Kostas Kampourakis, *Understanding Evolution* (New York: Cambridge University Press, 2014).
7. The list of books that attack or defend creationism is vast. A couple of good places to start to understand the mainstream critique of creationist thinking include Philip Kitcher, *Living with Darwin: Evolution, Design, and the Future of Faith* (New York: Oxford University Press, 2009); Michael Ruse and Robert Pennock, eds., *But Is It Science? The Philosophical Question in the Creation/Evolution Controversy*, exp. ed. (New York: Prometheus Press, 2009); for the intelligent-design argument, see, e.g., Michael Behe, *Darwin's Black Box: The Biochemical Challenge to Evolution*, 2nd ed. (New York: Free Press, 2006); for an explanation of theistic evolution, see, e.g., Francis Collins, *The Language of God: A Scientist Presents Evidence for Belief,*

repr. ed. (New York: Free Press, 2007); for the young-earth creation vision, see John Whitcomb Jr. and Henry Morris, *The Genesis Flood: The Biblical Record and Its Scientific Implications,* 50th anniv. ed. (Phillipsburg, NJ: P & R, 2011); for a mid-century statement of "progressive creation," see Bernard Ramm, *The Christian View of Science and Scripture,* 7th ed. (Grand Rapids, MI: Eerdmans, 1968); for a mainstream scientist's vision about creation, evolution, religion, and science, see Kenneth R. Miller, *Finding Darwin's God: A Scientist's Search for Common Ground Between God and Evolution,* repr. ed. (New York: Harper, 2007).

Chapter 1

1. Megan Brenan, "40% of Americans Believe in Creationism," Gallup, July 26, 2019, https://news.gallup.com/poll/261680/americans-believe-creationism.aspx.
2. Answers in Genesis has made a transcript of the debate available. See Bill Browning, "Transcript of Ken Ham v. Bill Nye Debate," February 10, 2014, http://www.youngearth.org/index.php/archives/rmcf-articles/item/21-transcript-of-ken-ham-vs-bill-nye-debate.
3. See my "Time for Ham on Nye!" *I Love You but You're Going to Hell,* February 4, 2014, https://iloveyoubutyouregoingtohell.org/2014/02/04/time-for-ham-on-nye/.
4. For a detailed description of Bryan v. Darrow, see my book, *The Other School Reformers: Conservative Activism in American Education* (Cambridge, MA: Harvard University Press, 2015), 25–72.
5. Karl Giberson, "Ken Ham: The Making of an American Religious Huckster," *Daily Beast,* February 9, 2014, http://www.thedailybeast.com/articles/2014/02/09/ken-ham-the-making-of-an-american-religious-huckster.html; for more on Giberson's background, see his webpage http://www.karlgiberson.com/about/.
6. Randall J. Stephens and Karl Giberson, *The Anointed: Evangelical Truth in a Secular Age* (Cambridge, MA: Harvard University Press, 2011), 11.
7. Stephens and Giberson, *The Anointed,* 261.
8. John MacArthur, "Evangelicals, Evolution, and the BioLogos Disaster," Grace To You Ministries, n.d., https://www.gty.org/resources/sermons/GTY136/Evangelicals-Evolution-and-the-BioLogos-Disaster.
9. There are many more divisions among types of creationists. For a more detailed look at some of the distinctions, see the appendix, "What's in a Name?"
10. "Our Mission: Engage & Equip," Reasons to Believe, n.d., http://www.reasons.org/about/our-mission.
11. "Dr. Hugh Ross," Reasons to Believe, n.d., http://www.reasons.org/about/who-we-are/hugh-ross.
12. Theodosius Dobzhansky, "Nothing in Biology Makes Sense Except in the Light of Evolution," *American Biology Teacher* 35 (1973): 125–129.
13. Francis Collins, "Why This Scientist Believes in God," CNN.com, April 6, 2007, http://www.cnn.com/2007/US/04/03/collins.commentary/index.html?eref=rss_tops; see also Francis Collins, *Language of God: A Scientist Presents Evidence for Belief* (New York: Free Press, 2006).

14. For more about BioLogos and "evolutionary creationism," see "Biologos Basics," n.d., http://biologos.org/resources/biologos-basics.

15. William Paley, *Natural Theology, or, Evidences of the Existence and Attributes of the Deity* (Philadelphia: John Morgan, 1802).

16. See Behe, *Darwin's Black Box: The Biochemical Challenge to Evolution* (New York: Free Press, 1996).

17. "Pope Francis' Address at Inauguration of Bronze Bust of Benedict XVI," October 27, 2014, https://zenit.org/articles/pope-francis-address-at-inauguration-of-bronze-bust-of-benedict-xvi/.

18. Rabbinical Council of America, "Creation, Evolution, and Intelligent Design: The View of the RCA," *Torah Musings*, December 27, 2005, https://www.torahmusings.com/2005/12/creation-evolution-and-intelligent/.

19. David Klinghoffer, "Genesis and the Scandal of Jewish Indifference," *Evolution News and Views*, October 16, 2009, http://www.evolutionnews.org/2009/10/genesis_and_the_scandal_of_jew026901.html.

20. David Klinghoffer, *The Lord Will Gather Me In: My Journey to Jewish Orthodoxy* (New York: Free Press, 1999), 175.

21. Jennie Rothenberg, "The Heresy of Nosson Slifkin," *Moment Magazine*, October 2005, http://zootorah.com/controversy/MomentMag.pdf.

22. Rothenberg, "The Heresy of Nosson Slifkin."

23. Cornelia Dean, "Islamic Creationist and a Book Sent Round the World," *New York Times*, July 17, 2007, http://www.nytimes.com/2007/07/17/science/17book.html?_r=1&ref=science&oref=slogin.

24. Harun Yahya, *Atlas of Creation* (self-pub., 2007), 15. Emphasis in original.

25. Yahya, *Atlas of Creation*, 15.

26. Scott Korb, *Light Without Fire: The Making of America's First Muslim College* (Boston: Beacon Press, 2015).

27. See "Shaykh Hamza's Book Recommendations," n.d., http://shaykhhamza.com/recommendations/.

28. Hamza Yusuf, "The Big Bang, Science & Islam," August 5, 2012, https://www.youtube.com/watch?v=mAEMCTMW7Ys.

29. Richard K. Nelson, *Make Prayers to the Raven: A Koyukon View of the Northern Forest* (Chicago: University of Chicago Press, 1983), 17.

30. Masakata Ogawa, "Science Education in a Multicultural Perspective," *Science Education* 79 (1995): 583–593. See also Ray Barnhardt and Angayuqaq Oscar Kawagley, "Indigenous Knowledge Systems and Education," in *Why Do We Educate?: Renewing the Conversation* (107th Yearbook of the NSSE, vol. 1), ed. David L. Coulter and John R. Wiens (Malden, MA: Blackwell, 2008), 223–241; Derek Hodson, "In Search of a Rationale for Multicultural Science Education," *Science Education* 77, no. 6 (1993): 685–711; Angayuqaq Oscar Kawagley, Delena Norris-Tull, and Roger A. Norris-Tull, "The Indigenous Worldview of Yupiaq Culture: Its Scientific Nature and Relevance to the Practice and Teaching of Science," *Journal of Research in Science Teaching* 35, no. 2 (1998): 133–144; William B. Stanley and Nancy W. Brickhouse, "Multiculturalism, Universalism, and Science Education," *Science Education* 78, no. 4

(1994): 387–398; Stanley and Brickhouse, "Teaching Sciences"; and Gloria Snively and John Corsiglia, "Rediscovering Indigenous Science: Implications for Science Education," *Science Education* 85, no. 1 (2001): 6–34.

31. Kenneth Miller, *Finding Darwin's God: A Scientist's Search for Common Ground Between God and Evolution* (New York: Harper Perennial, 1999), 219.

32. Miller, *Finding Darwin's God*, 258.

33. Fred Hoyle, *The Intelligent Universe* (London: Michael Joseph, 1983), 19.

34. See Laura Helmuth, "Virginia Heffernan's Shameful Confession," *Slate*, July 15, 2013, http://www.slate.com/articles/health_and_science/science/2013/07/virginia_heffernan_s_creationism_why_evolution_matters.html.

35. Kurt Wise, "Geology," in *In Six Days: Why 50 Scientists Choose to Believe in Creation*, ed. John Ashton (Green Forest, AR: Master Books, 2011), 351–355.

36. "Public Opinion on Religion and Science in the United States," Pew Research Center: Religion & Public Life, November 5, 2009, http://www.pewforum.org/2009/11/05/public-opinion-on-religion-and-science-in-the-united-states/.

37. Brenan, "40% of Americans Believe in Creationism."

38. George F. Bishop, Randall K. Thomas, Jason A. Wood, and Misook Gwon, "Americans' Scientific Knowledge and Beliefs about Human Evolution in the Year of Darwin," *Reports of the National Center for Science Education* 30, no. 3 (May–June 2010): 16–19, http://ncse.com/rncse/30/3/americans-scientific-knowledge-beliefs-human-evolution-year-.

39. See "Science and Nature," PollingReport.com, 2019, http://www.pollingreport.com/science.htm

40. "No Consensus, and Much Confusion, on Evolution and the Origin of Species," Harris Interactive, February 18, 2009, https://theharrispoll.com/wp-content/uploads/2017/12/Harris-Interactive-Poll-Research-BBC-Darwin-2009-02.pdf.

41. Pew Research Center, "Public Opinion on Religion and Science in the United States."

42. Michael Berkman and Eric Plutzer, *Evolution, Creationism, and the Battle to Control America's Classrooms* (New York: Cambridge University Press, 2010), 49.

43. Harris Interactive, "No Consensus, and Much Confusion."

Chapter 2

1. For a more detailed discussion of this definition of "radical" creationism, see the appendix, "What's in a Name?"

2. Quoted in Ronald L. Numbers, *The Creationists: From Scientific Creationism to Intelligent Design*, exp. ed. (Cambridge: Harvard University Press, 2006), 60.

3. Bird, "Freedom of Religion and Science Instruction in Public Schools," *The Yale Law Journal* 87 (January 1978): 561. Bird attributed the bigotry quotation incorrectly to Clarence Darrow. The legend that Clarence Darrow "thundered" against the "bigotry" of teaching only one theory of origins has played well among creationists. For example, Bird's colleagues at the Institute of Creation Research cited it widely during the 1970s. See, e.g., Richard Bliss, "A Comparison of Students Studying the Origin

of Life from a Two-Model Approach vs. Those Studying from a Single Model," *Acts & Facts* 7, no. 6 (June 1, 1978), https://www.icr.org/article/142. Nevertheless, the story has only a very tenuous basis in fact. As Tom McIver documented, Clarence Darrow almost certainly never said any such thing. Darrow's co-counsel Dudley Field Malone said something along those lines, but he, too, has been misquoted by creationists. Malone actually said, "For God's sake let the children have their minds kept open—close no doors to their knowledge; shut no door from them. Make the distinction between theology and science. Let them have both. Let them both be taught." See Tom McIver, "Creationist Misquotation of Darrow," *Creation/Evolution* 8, no. 2 (Spring 1988): 1–13. See also Ronald L. Numbers, *Darwinism Comes to America* (Cambridge, MA: Harvard University Press, 1998), 91. The legend of Darrow's quote remained strong among radical creationists for a long time. In the 1990s, ICR pundit Duane Gish still repeated the Darrow legend. See Duane T. Gish, *Teaching Creation Science in Public Schools* (El Cajon, CA: Institute for Creation Research, 1995), v.

4. George McCready Price, "Modern Scientific Discoveries," *Christian Fundamentals in School and Church* 5 (October–December 1922): 74. George McCready Price, "Modern Problems in Science and Religion," *Moody Bible Institute Monthly* 21 (February 1921): 256.

5. G. M. Price to Bryan, 7 February 1922, Bryan Papers, Library of Congress, Washington, DC. (Hereafter Bryan Papers.)

6. Ronald L. Numbers, ed., *Creation-Evolution Debates* (New York: Garland, 1995), 160–161.

7. In the run-up to the Scopes Trial, Bryan worked with increasing desperation to wrangle some expert witnesses that could poke holes in the scientific pretentions of evolution. Tellingly, only one expert agreed—Howard A. Kelly of Johns Hopkins University—and even Kelly thought that nonhuman animals and plants had evolved in ways similar to what Darwin had described. For his part, Price tried to convince Bryan that the trial was not the right forum to debate the scientific merit of evolution, and Price planned to be out of the country at time. See Bryan to G. M. Price, 7 June 1925; Bryan to C. B. McMullen, 7 June 1925; G. M. Price to Bryan, 1 July 1925; Bryan to H. A. Kelly, 10 June 1925; H. A. Kelly to Bryan, 15 June 1925; Bryan to H. A. Kelly, 22 June 1925; Alfred McCann to Bryan, n.d.; Bryan to H. A. Kelly, 17 June 1925, Bryan Papers.

8. William Jennings Bryan, "Letter to the Editor," *Forum* 70 (August 1923): 1852. Bryan was responding to a scathing attack on Bryan and fundamentalism by Newell Dwight Hillis in the July issue of ["Religion or Dogma?," *Forum* 70 (July 1923): 1681].

9. See Ronald L. Numbers and Jonathan M. Butler, eds., *The Disappointed: Millerism and Millenarianism in the Nineteenth Century* (Knoxville, TN: University of Tennessee Press, 1993).

10. See Numbers, *The Creationists*, 137–142.

11. John Whitcomb Jr. and Henry Morris, *The Genesis Flood: The Biblical Record and Its Scientific Implications*, 8th ed. (Philadelphia: Presbyterian and Reformed Publishing, 1966), xxvi.

12. *The Genesis Flood*, xxii.

13. This snippet is from the preface to the 1961 second edition, included in the 1966 eighth edition, xxiv.

14. Thanks to historian Edward Larson, the myths of the Scopes Trial are slowly being replaced by better historical fact. See Larson, *Summer for the Gods: The Scopes Trial and America's Continuing Debate over Science and Religion* (Cambridge, MA: Harvard University Press, 1997). See also Jeffrey Moran's edited collection of relevant documents: *The Scopes Trial: A Brief History with Documents* (New York: Bedford/St. Martin's, 2002).

15. From Moran, *Scopes Trial*, 49.

16. In the research for my first book, *Fundamentalism and Education in the Scopes Era: God, Darwin, and the Roots of America's Culture Wars* (New York: Palgrave Macmillan, 2010), I dug through every state legislative record to seek out relevant debates. Between 1922 and 1929, I found fifty-three anti-evolution bills or resolutions from twenty-one states, plus two proposals for federal laws for Washington, DC teachers. Five bills became laws or resolutions, in Oklahoma, Florida, Tennessee, Mississippi, and Arkansas.

17. At least, that's the story the bill's author told his ally William Jennings Bryan. See George W. Ellis to Bryan and J. W. Porter, 13 March 1922, Bryan Papers.

18. Kentucky House Bill 191, *Journal of the House of Representatives of the Commonwealth of Kentucky 1922*, 1668–1669; 35. Amendment to Kentucky Senate Bill 136, *Journal of the Kentucky Senate 1922*, 1062.

19. Willa Cather, *Not Under Forty* (New York: Knopf, 1953), v. Originally published in 1936.

20. The ranks of America's US Congress have been full of representatives from all sorts of minority groups, but the number of atheists in its membership rolls has always been small. Representative Barney Frank, for example, proudly came out as homosexual while in office but thought it prudent to wait until he retired to "come out" as an atheist. See Jennifer Michael Hecht, "The Last Taboo," Politico, December 9, 2013. https://www.politico.com/magazine/story/2013/12/the-last-taboo-atheists-politicians-100901.

21. See Charles Taylor, *A Secular Age* (Cambridge, MA: Harvard University Press, 2007), 21.

22. John W. Burgess, *Reminiscences of an American Scholar: The Beginnings of Columbia University* (New York: Columbia University Press, 1934), 147–148.

23. No doubt plenty of science mavens—of both the mainstream and creationist varieties—will find lots to quibble with in this thumbnail sketch of the history of modern evolutionary thinking. For more complete but still accessible explanations, see Edward Larson, *Evolution: The Remarkable History of a Scientific Theory* (New York: Modern Library, 2004), or Peter J. Bowler, *Evolution: The History of an Idea*, 25th anniv. ed. (Chapel Hill: University of North Carolina Press, 2009). For some I-was-there perspectives, see Ernst Mayr and William B. Provine, eds., *The Evolutionary Synthesis: Perspectives on the Unification of Biology* (Cambridge, MA: Harvard University Press, 1998).

24. Philip J. Hirschkop, "Brief of the National Education Association of the United States and the National Science Teachers Association as Amici Curiae," *Epperson v. Arkansas*, 393 US 97 (1968), 4.

25. *Epperson v. Arkansas*, 393 US 97 (1968).

26. Bird, "Freedom of Religion," 515–570.

27. Richard M. Bliss, *Origins: Two Models, Evolution Creation* (San Diego: Creation-Life, n.d. [1978]), 31. Emphasis in original.

28. *Edwards v. Aguillard*, 482 US 578 (1987).

29. See Michael J. Behe, *Darwin's Black Box* (New York: Free Press, 1996). See also the ID textbook that became the cause of the Dover trial: Percival Davis and Dean H. Kenyon, *Of Pandas and People: The Central Question of Biological Origins,* 2nd ed. (Dallas: Haughton, 1993).

30. It was difficult for some ID types to hide their religious enthusiasm. As Ron Numbers has pointed out, the ID textbook at issue in the Dover case was cowritten by Percival Davis, who had long claimed that his motives were religious, not scientific. See Numbers, *The Creationists*, 375.

31. Bird, "Freedom of Religion," 518.

32. Louisiana's "Balanced Treatment for Creation-Science and Evolution-Science Act," (1981); Louisiana Revised Statutes 17:286.1–7.

33. Duane T. Gish, "The Scientific Case for Creation," in *Evolutionists Confront Creationists: Proceedings of the 63rd Annual Meeting of the Pacific Division, American Association for the Advancement of Science*, ed. Frank Awbrey and William Thwaites, vol. 1, part 3 (San Francisco: Pacific Division, American Association for the Advancement of Science, 1984), 26.

34. The science watchdogs at the National Center for Science Education have been keeping tabs on these efforts. See their "Chronology of 'Academic Freedom' Bills," *NCSE Blog*, February 7, 2013, https://ncse.com/creationism/general/chronology-academic-freedom-bills. See also Nicholas J. Matzke, "The Evolution of Antievolution Policies after *Kitzmiller v. Dover*," *Science* 351, no. 6268 (2016): 28–30.

35. *The Genesis Flood*, xxi.

Chapter 3

1. Del Ratzsch, *The Battle of Beginnings: Why Neither Side Is Winning the Creation-Evolution Debate* (Downers Grove, IL: InterVarsity Press, 1996), 9.

2. Francis Fukuyama, *Trust: The Social Virtues and the Creation of Prosperity* (New York: Simon & Schuster, 1995), 26.

3. Fukuyama, *Trust*, 270.

4. This was one of the episodes I studied in my 2015 book, *The Other School Reformers: Conservative Activism in American Education* (Cambridge, MA: Harvard University Press, 2015).

5. Rev. Avis L. Hill interviewed by James Deeter, March 12, 1985. Transcript. Oral History of Appalachia collection No. OH 64-236, Special Collections, Marshall University, Huntington, West Virginia.

6. Jon H. Roberts, *Darwinism and the Divine in America: Protestant Intellectuals and Organic Evolution, 1859–1900* (Madison: University of Wisconsin Press, 1988).

7. Ronald L. Numbers, *Darwinism Comes to America* (Cambridge, MA: Harvard University Press), 24–48.

8. Gray's articles about Darwin and Darwinism from 1860 to 1876 were collected and published in a single volume: Asa Gray, *Darwiniana: Essays and Reviews Pertaining to Darwinism* (New York: Appleton, 1876), 103.

9. Gray, *Darwiniana*, 176.

10. Gray, *Darwiniana*, 87.

11. Gray, *Darwiniana*, 54.

12. Gray, *Darwiniana*, 93. And like an earnest suitor who still had his pride, Darwin himself encouraged Gray to explain away the accusations of atheism, yet he refused to water down his ideas to pander to America's religious anxieties. He was happy that Gray took to the pages of the widely read *Atlantic Monthly* to tackle the issue, and Darwin even suggested the title for the series, "Natural Selection Not Inconsistent with Natural Theology." (See Roberts, *Darwinism and the Divine*, pg. 253, footnote 45.) However, just as Professor Gray insisted that Darwin's hypothesis was not a gateway idea to atheism, Darwin insisted that he himself would insist on no such thing. He could not share Gray's Christian confidence, Darwin wrote in 1868, but rather only concluded that the notion of an "omnipotent and omniscient Creator" presented "a difficulty as insoluble as is that of free will and predestination." From Charles Darwin, *Variation of Animals and Plans under Domestication,* vol. 2 (London: John Murray, 1905), 526; originally published 1868.

13. Gray, *Darwiniana*, 85.

14. Gray, *Darwiniana*, 103.

15. For more on these revolutions in American higher education, see George M. Marsden, *The Soul of the American University: From Protestant Establishment to Established Nonbelief* (New York: Oxford University Press, 1994); Roger L. Geiger, *The History of American Higher Education: Learning and Culture from the Founding to World War II* (Princeton, NJ: Princeton University Press, 2015); Jon H. Roberts and James Turner, *The Sacred and the Secular University* (Princeton, NJ: Princeton University Press, 2000). See also my recent book, *Fundamentalist U: Keeping the Faith in American Higher Education* (New York: Oxford University Press, 2018).

16. See Bradley J. Gundlach, *Process and Providence: The Evolution Question at Princeton, 1845–1929* (Grand Rapids, MI: Eerdman's, 2014), 6–7.

17. See, as just one example, Harold Lindsell's controversial 1976 book, *The Battle for the Bible* (Grand Rapids, MI: Zondervan Publishing). Lindsell celebrates Hodge and Warfield as "stalwarts" (150) and "giants" (197).

18. Gundlach, *Process and Providence*, 3.

19. Charles Hodge, *What Is Darwinism?* (New York: Scribner, Armstrong, 1874), 177.

20. Hodge, *What Is Darwinism*, 4.

21. Hodge, *What Is Darwinism*, 5.

22. Hodge, *What Is Darwinism*, 46.

23. Hodge, *What Is Darwinism*, 52.

24. Hodge, *What Is Darwinism*, 104.
25. See the most famous recent example, Stephen Jay Gould, "Nonoverlapping Magisteria," *Natural History* 106, no. 2 (March 1997): 16–26.
26. Hodge, *What Is Darwinism*, 142.
27. Hodge, *What Is Darwinism*, 77.
28. Edward J. Larson, *Trial and Error: The American Controversy over Creation and Evolution*, 3rd. ed. (New York: Oxford University Press, 2003), 237.
29. George Gaylord Simpson, *This View of Life: The World of an Evolutionist* (New York: Harcourt, Brace and World, 1964), vii.
30. George G. Simpson, "One Hundred Years Without Darwin Are Enough," *Teachers College Record* 60 (1961): 617–626.
31. Bernard Ramm, *The Christian View of Science and Scripture* (Grand Rapids, MI: Eerdmans, 1954), 25.
32. Ramm, *The Christian View of Science and Scripture*, 23.
33. Ramm, *The Christian View of Science and Scripture*, 27.
34. Ramm, *The Christian View of Science and Scripture*, 32.
35. Ramm, *The Christian View of Science and Scripture*, 50.
36. Ramm, *The Christian View of Science and Scripture*, 26.
37. Ramm, *The Christian View of Science and Scripture*, 35.
38. Ramm, *The Christian View of Science and Scripture*, 117.
39. Michael S. Hamilton, *The Fundamentalist Harvard: Wheaton College and the Continuing Vitality of American Evangelicalism, 1919–1965* (PhD diss., University of Notre Dame, 1994).
40. Russell L. Mixter, ed., *Evolution and Christian Thought Today* (Grand Rapids, MI: Eerdmans, 1959).
41. Thomas D. S. Key, "The Influence of Darwin on Biology," in Mixter, *Evolution and Christian Thought Today*, 30–31.
42. James O. Buswell III, "A Creationist Interpretation of Prehistoric Man," in Mixter, *Evolution and Christian Thought Today*, 169 footnote 8.
43. John C. Whitcomb Jr. and Henry M. Morris, *The Genesis Flood: The Biblical Record and Its Scientific Implications*, 8th ed. (Philadelphia: Presbyterian and Reformed Publishing, 1966), 448.
44. Whitcomb and Morris, *The Genesis Flood*, 447.
45. Whitcomb and Morris, *The Genesis Flood*, 439.
46. Whitcomb and Morris, *The Genesis Flood*, 454–468.
47. Whitcomb and Morris, *The Genesis Flood*, 439.
48. Whitcomb and Morris, *The Genesis Flood*, 20–21.
49. Whitcomb and Morris, *The Genesis Flood*, 443.
50. Whitcomb and Morris, *The Genesis Flood*, 440.
51. Whitcomb and Morris, *The Genesis Flood*, 447.
52. Dan Kahan, "What Does 'Disbelief' in Evolution Mean? What Does 'Belief' in It Measure? Evolution & Science Literacy Part 1," *Cultural Cognition blog*, June 19, 2013, http://www.culturalcognition.net/blog/2013/6/19/what-does-disbelief-in-evolution-mean-what-does-belief-in-it.html.

53. David E. Long, *Evolution and Religion in American Education: An Ethnography* (New York: Springer, 2011), 15.

54. Long, *Evolution and Religion in American Education*, 19.

55. William Jennings Bryan, *The Menace of Darwinism* (Louisville, KY: Pentecostal Publishing, n.d.), 19–26.

56. Bob Jones Jr., *Fundamentals of Faith: A Series of Chapel Messages on the Bob Jones University Creed* (Greenville, SC: Bob Jones University Press, 1964), 21.

57. Jerry Falwell, *Listen, America!* (New York: Bantam Books, 1981, orig. 1980), 179.

58. Henry M. Morris, *The Long War Against God: The History and Impact of the Creation/Evolution Conflict* (Green Forest, AR: Master Books, 2008), 132.

59. Morris, *Long War Against God*, 137.

60. Morris, *Long War Against God*, 140–141.

61. Morris, *Long War Against God*, 142.

62. Morris, *Long War Against God*, 146.

63. Ken Ham, *Evolution, Creation and the Culture Wars* (Cincinnati, OH: Answers in Genesis, 2005), 1.

64. Ham, *Evolution, Creation and the Culture Wars*, 2.

65. Ham, *Evolution, Creation and the Culture Wars*, 14.

66. James Moffett, *Storm in the Mountains: A Case Study of Censorship, Conflict, and Consciousness* (Carbondale: Southern Illinois University Press, 1988), 82. Moffett was one of the editors of the book series that led to widespread boycotts of the public schools. He journeyed to the heart of the storm to try to understand why so many people found his books so reprehensible. He conducted interviews with several of the protest leaders, including the Reverend Hill.

67. Moffett, *Storm in the Mountains*, 90.

68. Moffett, *Storm in the Mountains*, 90.

69. Moffett, *Storm in the Mountains*, 91.

70. Moffett, *Storm in the Mountains*, 88.

71. Moffett, *Storm in the Mountains*, 84.

72. Sociologists Elaine Howard Ecklund and her colleagues have documented what they call the "Al Gore effect." When it comes to climate change science, some conservative religious people refuse to accept scientific consensus because they distrust the politics of former Vice President Al Gore, thinking environmentalism has become a "tool of the political left to gain power." See Elaine Howard Ecklund and Christopher P. Scheitle, *Religion vs. Science: What Religious People Really Think* (New York: Oxford University Press, 2018), 103. See also Jared Peifer, Elaine Howard Ecklund, and Cara Fullerton, "How Evangelicals from Two Churches in the American Southwest Frame Their Relationship with the Environment," *Review of Religious Research* 56, no. 1 (2014): 373–397. The same sort of complicated denialism plays a role in radical creationism.

73. See Katie Reilly, "Read Hillary Clinton's 'Basket of Deplorables' Remarks about Donald Trump Supporters," Time.com, September 10, 2016, http://time.com/4486502/hillary-clinton-basket-of-deplorables-transcript/.

Chapter 4

1. "Editorial: Stop and Think," *Louisville Courier-Journal*, February 3, 1922.
2. In the Bob Jones University archives, for example, I found an article about an "Academy of Home Education" conference, 1990. It had been started as a one-stop shop for fundamentalist homeschool parents. The organization offered things such as class rings and class trips as well as traditional graduation ceremonies for homeschoolers. See Dave McQuaid, "University Hosts H.E.L.P. Conference," *The Collegian*, June 1990, 1.
3. Or how about planning a special "creation vacation?" Thanks to the young-earth activists at Answers in Genesis, young-earth creationist families can adopt a prescreened itinerary: See Answers in Genesis, "Creation Vacations," n.d., https://answersingenesis.org/creation-vacations/
4. Bob Jones Sr., *Bob Jones Magazine* 1 (June 1928): 3.
5. At least, these were the school statistics publicized in the student paper. See Taylor Anderson, "BJU Welcomes New Students to Campus," *BJU Collegian*, September 17, 2010, 1, http://www.collegianonline.com/files/2012/11/col_24_01.pdf. Thanks to historian Daniel K. Williams for this reference.
6. Jon H. Roberts and James Turner, *The Sacred and the Secular University* (Princeton, NJ: Princeton University Press, 2000), 28. See also George M. Marsden, *The Soul of the American University: From Protestant Establishment to Established Nonbelief* (New York: Oxford University Press, 1994); Roger L. Geiger, *The History of American Higher Education: Learning and Culture from the Founding to World War II* (Princeton, NJ: Princeton University Press, 2015); Julie A. Reuben, *The Making of the Modern University: Intellectual Transformation and the Marginalization of Morality* (Chicago: University of Chicago Press, 1996); Andrew Jewett, *Science, Democracy, and the American University* (New York: Cambridge University Press, 2012).
7. For details, see my first book, *Fundamentalism and Education in the Scopes Era: God, Darwin, and the Roots of America's Culture Wars* (New York: Palgrave Macmillan, 2010).
8. Lowell H. Coate, "Further Suggestions about the New Scholarship," *Moody Bible Institute Monthly* 34 (August 1923): 563.
9. In 1919, a group of conservative evangelical scholars and activists met in Philadelphia to debate and discuss the dramatic changes going on in their churches and colleges. One result of this meeting was a new group of fundamentalists, the World (or World's) Christian Fundamentals Association. Another product was a short book of conference papers, including Charles A. Blanchard's "Report of Committee on Correlation of Colleges, Seminaries and Academies," in *God Hath Spoken*, ed. W. H. Griffith Thomas, (Philadelphia: Bible Conference Committee, 1919), 19–20.
10. W. H. Griffith Thomas, "Report of Committee on Resolutions," in his *God Hath Spoken*, 11.
11. For details, see my book *Fundamentalist U: Keeping the Faith in American Higher Education* (New York: Oxford University Press, 2018), 48–50.

12. Michael S. Hamilton, "The Fundamentalist Harvard: Wheaton College and the Continuing Vitality of American Evangelicalism, 1919–1965" (PhD diss., Notre Dame University, 1994), 32.

13. See my book *Fundamentalism and Education in the Scopes Era*, 135–138; see also Mark Taylor Dalhouse, *An Island in the Lake of Fire: Bob Jones University, Fundamentalism, and the Separatist Movement* (Athens, GA: University of Georgia Press, 1996), 46–48.

14. Bob Jones Sr., *The Perils of America, or, Where Are We Headed?* (n.p., n.d.), 35. This was from a sermon delivered at the Chicago Gospel Tabernacle, March 5, 1934.

15. J. Frank Norris, "A Mother's Son," *Searchlight* 3 (May 12, 1921): 2. This spooky quotation proved popular among creationist activists throughout the 1920s. It was picked up, for instance, by anti-evolution leader T. T. Martin in his book *Hell and the High School: Christ or Evolution, Which?* (Kansas City, MO: Western Baptist Publishing, 1923), 155.

16. See correspondence between James W. Davis and John Roy, April 1932. Student records collection, box 2, folder 8, Moody Bible Institute archives, Chicago, Illinois.

17. These examples are also from the Student Records Collection, box 2, folder 8.

18. The school's name derives from its origin as the Bible Institute of Los Angeles.

19. Sarah Pulliam Bailey, "'Their Dream President:' Trump Just Gave White Evangelicals a Big Boost," *Washington Post*, May 4, 2017, https://www.washingtonpost.com/news/acts-of-faith/wp/2017/05/04/their-dream-president-trump-just-gave-white-evangelicals-a-big-boost/?utm_term=.f55a84dc798d.

20. The archives at Wheaton College show President Buswell's patriotic pride. He collected a large folder of clippings about Wheaton's role as an America-first kind of school. This quotation comes from one of those clippings: N. E. Merritt, "An Unafraid College," *The Advisor*, June 12, 1935, 4 in J. Oliver Buswell Papers, box 21, folder 18, Wheaton College archives, Wheaton, Illinois.

21. William Culbertson to C. F. Harris, 28 July 1947, folder: Questions answered, C. Culbertson Papers, Moody Bible Institute archives, Chicago, Illinois.

22. Jones was quoted by Mark Taylor Dalhouse, *An Island in the Lake of Fire: Bob Jones University, Fundamentalism, and the Separatist Movement* (Athens, GA: University of Georgia Press, 1996), 105.

23. Jessica Martinez and Gregory A. Smith, "How the Faithful Voted: A Preliminary 2016 Analysis," Fact Tank: Pew Research Center, November 9, 2016, https://www.pewresearch.org/fact-tank/2016/11/09/how-the-faithful-voted-a-preliminary-2016-analysis/.

24. B. M. Pietsch, *Dispensational Modernism* (New York: Oxford University Press, 2015). Much of the following section on dispensationalism follows Pietsch's argument.

25. Carl Henry, "What Is Fundamentalism?," *United Evangelical Action*, July 16, 1966, 303.

26. Henry M. Morris and Duane T. Gish, eds., *The Battle for Creation: Acts/Facts/Impacts*, vol. 2 (San Diego: Creation-Life Publishers, 1976), 18.

27. Henry M. Morris, "Evolution in Christian Colleges," in Morris and Gish, *Battle for Creation*, 80–81.

28. Ham's list of reliable young-earth colleges can be found on Answers in Genesis's website: "Creation Colleges," https://answersingenesis.org/colleges/. I covered the

pressure on schools such as Cedarville University and Bryan College at my blog *I Love You but You're Going to Hell* and elsewhere. See, e.g., "Desperate Times at Bryan College," May 12, 2017, https://iloveyoubutyouregoingtohell.org/2017/05/12/desperate-times-at-bryan-college/; and "Safety Schools: Part II," *Righting America at the Creation Museum*, May 11, 2017, https://rightingamerica.net/safety-schools-part-2/. For Ham's response to my arguments, see "Why I Care Where Your Children Attend College," *Ken Ham Blog*, May 10, 2014, https://answersingenesis.org/blogs/ken-ham/2014/05/10/why-i-care-where-your-children-attend-college/.

29. For more on the enrollment pressures plaguing radical-creationist higher education, see Liam Adams, "At a Time of Change, These Baptist Colleges Are Staying the Course," *Chronicle of Higher Education*, December 21, 2017, https://www.chronicle.com/article/At-a-Time-of-Change-These/242111; see also Adam Laats, "The Handwriting on the Wall for Christian Colleges," *I Love You but You're Going to Hell*, October 1, 2015, https://iloveyoubutyouregoingtohell.org/2015/10/01/the-handwriting-on-the-wall-for-christian-colleges/.

30. For more detail on creationist reaction to *Engel* and *Schempp*, see my article, "Our Schools, Our Country: American Evangelicals, Public Schools, and the Supreme Court Decisions of 1962 and 1963," *Journal of Religious History* 36, no. 3 (September 2012): 319–334.

31. Kenneth M. Dolbeare and Phillip E. Hammond, *The School Prayer Decisions: From Court Policy to Local Practice* (Chicago: University of Chicago Press, 1971).

32. Jeffrey P. Moran, *Teaching Sex: The Shaping of Adolescence in the 20th Century* (Cambridge, MA: Harvard University Press, 2000), 170, 181.

33. See Dorothy Nelkin, *Science Textbook Controversies and the Politics of Equal Time* (Cambridge, MA: MIT Press, 1977), 30–35.

34. Tim LaHaye, *The Battle for the Public Schools* (Old Tappan, NJ: Fleming H. Revell, 1983), 196.

35. Activist Louise Hicks quoted by Ronald Formisano, *Boston Against Busing: Race, Class, and Ethnicity in the 1960s and 1970s* (Chapel Hill: University of North Carolina Press, 1991), 192.

36. See Michael Berkman and Eric Plutzer, *Evolution, Creationism, and the Battle to Control America's Classrooms* (New York: Cambridge University Press, 2010). They found that only about 28 percent of high school biology teachers teach only evolutionary science in their classes. Most teachers (about 60 percent) teach evolution but mix in a variety of creationist-friendly ideas.

37. The process of textbook publishing can tell us a lot about the politics of creationism and evolution. Historian Adam Shapiro has written a brilliant analysis of the history of evolution textbooks: Adam R. Shapiro, *Trying Biology: The Scopes Trial, Textbooks, and the Antievolution Movement in American Schools* (Chicago: University of Chicago Press, 2013).

38. Gerald Skoog, "The Coverage of Human Evolution in High School Biology Textbooks in the 20th Century and in Current State Science Standards," *Science and Education* (2005): 14; Dorothy Nelkin, *Science Textbook Controversies and the Politics of Equal Time* (Cambridge, MA: MIT Press, 1977), 27–30.

39. Paul F. Parsons, *Inside America's Christian Schools* (Macon, GA: Mercer University Press, 1987), x.

40. Alan Peshkin, *God's Choice: The Total World of a Fundamentalist Christian School* (Chicago: University of Chicago Press, 1986), 26.

41. U. S. Department of Education, *Characteristics of Private Schools in the United States: Results from the 2001–2002 Private School Universe Survey* (NCES 2005-305). Washington, DC: National Center for Education Statistics, 9. By 2002, 5,527 schools called themselves "conservative Christian." By way of comparison, there were 4,347 parochial Catholic schools in 2002, plus 2,933 diocesan Catholic schools, and 2,939 "regular" nonsectarian private schools.

42. Martha E. MacCullough, "Factors Which Led Christian School Parents to Leave Public School" (PhD diss., Temple University, 1984), 114, 149, 212.

43. Peter Stephen Lewis, "Private Education and the Subcultures of Dissent: Alternative/Free Schools (1965–1975) and Christian Fundamentalist Schools (1965–1990)," (PhD diss., Stanford University, 1991), 137.

44. See Table 206.10, "Number and Percentage of Homeschooled Students Ages 5 through 17," Digest of Education Statistics, National Center for Education Statistics, https://nces.ed.gov/programs/digest/d15/tables/dt15_206.10.asp?current=yes.

45. See Milton Gaither, *Homeschool: An American History*, 2nd ed. (New York: Palgrave Macmillan, 2017); also see his revived blog about homeschooling: *Homeschooling Research Notes*, https://gaither.wordpress.com/.

46. Janice Guthrie, "Christian-Published Textbooks and the Preparation of Teens for the Rigors of College Science Courses," *Journal of Research on Christian Education* 20, no. 1 (2011): 46–72.

47. For the full story about Abeka, ACE, and the BJU publishing companies, see my article, "Forging a Fundamentalist 'One Best System': Struggles over Curriculum and Educational Philosophy for Christian Day Schools, 1970–1989," *History of Education Quarterly*, 50 (February 2010): 55–83.

48. A. A. Baker, *The Successful Christian School: Foundational Principles for Starting and Operating a Successful Christian School* (Pensacola, FL: Abeka Book, 1979), 36.

49. Gary Coombs, "ACE, An Individualized Approach to Christian Education," *Interest*, September 1978, 9–10; "History and Development of ACE," *CLA Defender* 1, no. 5 (1978): 6, 25–26; "Facts about Accelerated Christian Education," Accelerated Christian Education, Lewisville, Texas, n.d. [1982]; Walter Fremont, "The Christian School Movement Today," audiotape of lecture given July 31, 1989, in Bob Jones University archives.

50. Donald R. Howard, *Rebirth of Our Nation: The Decline of the West 1970s: The Christian Educational Reform 1980s* (Lewisville, TX: Accelerated Christian Education, 1979), 123.

51. PACE 1107, *Biology* (Accelerated Christian Education, 2001), 10. Old PACEs are relatively hard to come by. As ACE-school survivor and education scholar Jonny Scaramanga has noted, ACE refuses to release old editions, so researchers like him have to search flea markets to find old versions like this one. My thanks to him for sharing his collection. As we'll see in chapter 7, though, even the newer editions don't

change or challenge the deep cultural conservatism that pervades these workbooks. See Jonathan Theodore Scaramanga, "Systems of Indoctrination: Accelerated Christian Education in England" (PhD diss., University College London Institute of Education, 2017), 49.

52. Susan L. Trollinger and William Vance Trollinger Jr., *Righting America at the Creation Museum* (Baltimore: Johns Hopkins University Press, 2016), 59.

53. *Righting America at the Creation Museum*, 44–45. As the Trollingers point out, the Creation Museum tweaks dispensational tradition a little bit. The divine history of the universe, the museum explains, are cut into the "seven Cs": Creation, Corruption, Catastrophe, Confusion, Christ, Cross, and Consummation. As they also point out, the parallel between this scheme and dispensational thinking is not at all merely coincidental.

Chapter 5

1. Will Rogers, "Defending My Soup Plate Position," *The Illiterate Digest* (New York: Albert & Charles Boni, 1924), 64.
2. See Charles P. Pierce, *Idiot America: How Stupidity Became a Virtue in the Land of the Free* (New York: Penguin Random House, 2010).
3. The dinosaur theme is a big part of Answers in Genesis's ministry. See, e.g., "Were Dinosaurs on Noah's Ark?" Answers in Genesis, April 3, 2000, https://answersingenesis.org/dinosaurs/were-dinosaurs-on-noahs-ark/.
4. Pierce, *Idiot America*, 5.
5. Ken Ham, "Dinosaurs and Saddles," *Ken Ham Blog*, June 24, 2009, https://answersingenesis.org/blogs/ken-ham/2009/06/24/dinosaurs-and-saddles/.
6. Ken Ham, *Dinosaurs of Eden* (Green Forest, AR: Master Books, 2001), 42.
7. Elizabeth Mitchell, "News to Note," *News to Know*, February 2, 2013, https://answersingenesis.org/answers/news-to-know/news-to-note-february-2-2013/.
8. See Ken Ham and Cindy Malott, *The Answers Book for Kids*, Volume 2: *22 Questions from Kids on Dinosaurs and the Flood of Noah* (Green Forest, AR: Master Books, 2016), 24–25.
9. Thomas H. Huxley, "The Darwinian Hypothesis," *Darwiniana* (New York: Appleton, 1896,), 10; originally published in 1859.
10. Henry Fairfield Osborn, *The Earth Speaks to Bryan* (New York: Scribners, 1925), 50.
11. Alex Stevenson, "Dawkins: Creationists Science Teachers 'Ignorant,'" *Politics.co.uk*, January 7, 2009, http://www.politics.co.uk/news/2009/01/07/dawkins-creationist-science-teachers-ignorant.
12. Bill Nye, *Undeniable: Evolution and the Science of Creation* (New York: St. Martin's Griffin, 2014), 18.
13. Science-communication scholar Dan Kahan of Yale Law School has composed helpful graphs of these knowledge differentials. See Dan Kahan, "Weekend Updates: 'Knowing Disbelief in Evolution'—a Fragment," *Cultural Cognition Blog*, August 24, 2014, http://www.culturalcognition.net/blog/2014/8/24/weekend-update-knowing-disbelief-in-evolution-a-fragment.html.

14. Yudhijit Bhattacharjee, "NSF Board Draws Flak for Dropping Evolution From *Indicators*," *Science* 328 (April 9, 2010): 150–151.

15. Rosenau quoted in Bhattacharjee, "NSF Board Draws Flak."

16. Glenn Branch, "Evolution in Science and Engineering Indicators 2014," National Center for Science Education, February 18, 2014, https://ncse.com/news/2014/02/evolution-science-engineering-indicators-2014-0015408.

17. Andrew Shtulman, "Qualitative Differences Between Naïve and Scientific Theories of Evolution," *Cognitive Psychology* 52 (2006): 186.

18. Gale M. Sinatra, Sherry A. Southerland, Frances McConaughy, and James W. Demastes, "Intentions and Beliefs in Students' Understanding and Acceptance of Biological Evolution," *Journal of Research in Science Teaching* 40 (2003): 510.

19. Anton E. Lawson and William A. Worsnop, "Learning about Evolution and Rejecting a Belief in Special Creation: Effects of Reflective Reasoning Skill, Prior Knowledge, Prior Belief and Religious Commitment," *Journal of Research in Science Teaching* 29, no. 2 (February 1992): 149.

20. Lawson and Worsnop, "Learning about Evolution," 152.

21. Sherry S. Demastes, John Settlage Jr., and Ron Good, "Students' Conceptions of Natural Selection and Its Role in Evolution: Cases of Replication and Comparison," *Journal of Research in Science Teaching* 32 (1995): 541.

22. See Shtulman, "Qualitative Differences between Naïve and Scientific Theories of Evolution," 170–194.

23. See Michael E. N. Majerus, "Industrial Melanism in the Peppered Moth, *Biston betularia*: An Excellent Teaching Example of Darwinian Evolution in Action," *Evolution: Education and Outreach* 2, no. 1 (March 2009): 63–74.

24. Demastes et al., "Students' Conceptions of Natural Selection and Its Role in Evolution," 541.

25. Charles Hodge, *What Is Darwinism?* (New York: Scribner, Armstrong, 1874), 71.

26. Michael Ruse, *Darwin and Design: Does Evolution Have a Purpose?* (Cambridge, MA: Harvard University Press, 2003), 120.

27. Ruse, *Darwin and Design*, 111.

28. Kostas Kampourakis, *Understanding Evolution* (New York: Cambridge University Press, 2014), 63.

29. Deborah Kelemen, "Why Are Rocks Pointy? Children's Preference for Teleological Explanations of the Natural World," *Developmental Psychology* 35 (1999): 1440–1452.

30. Deborah Kelemen, "Are Children 'Intuitive Theists'? Reasoning about Purpose and Design in Nature," *Psychological Science* 15, no. 5 (May 2004): 295–301.

31. E. Margaret Evans, "Cognitive and Contextual Factors in the Emergence of Diverse Belief Systems: Creation versus Evolution," *Cognitive Psychology* 52 (2001): 217–266.

32. Evans, "Cognitive and Contextual Factors," 217.

33. Deborah Kelemen and Evelyn Rosset, "The Human Function Compunction: Teleological Explanation in Adults," *Cognition* 111 (2009): 140.

34. Dan Kahan, "What Does 'Disbelief' in Evolution Mean? What Does 'Belief' in It Measure? Evolution & Science Literacy Part 1," *Cultural Cognition Blog*, June 19, 2013, http://www.culturalcognition.net/blog/2013/6/19/what-does-disbelief-in-evolution-mean-what-does-belief-in-it.html.

Chapter 6

1. The label comes from Mark A. Kalthoff, "The New Evangelical Engagement with Science: The American Scientific Affiliation, Origin to 1963" (PhD diss., Indiana University, 1998), 635.

2. For more detail, see my book, *Fundamentalist U: Keeping the Faith in American Higher Education* (New York: Oxford University Press, 2018). See also Michael S. Hamilton, "The Fundamentalist Harvard: Wheaton College and the Continuing Vitality of American Evangelicalism, 1919–1965" (PhD diss., Notre Dame University, 1994), 228.

3. Ronald L. Numbers, *The Creationists: From Scientific Creationism to Intelligent Design*, exp. ed. (Cambridge, MA: Harvard University Press, 2006), 194–207.

4. Mixter spent lots of time in the 1960s trying to reach across the growing chasm between creationists like himself and skeptical YECs. For example, in a long correspondence in early 1963 with fundamentalist stalwart Robert T. Ketcham, Mixter made his case that his vision of evolution and creation did not make him part of the "new-evangelical" reform movement. Rather, Mixter insisted on his continuing fundamentalism as part and parcel of his continuing devotion to creationism. His "progressive creationism," Mixter wrote, was true to "the great fundamentals of the faith." See Russell Mixter to Robert T. Ketcham, 18 February 1963, folder: Creation: Ketcham—Carnell—Buswell—Mixter Correspondence, Gilbert Stenholm Papers, Bob Jones University archives, Greenville, South Carolina. For more on the divide between "new-evangelical" creationists and "fundamentalist" creationists, see my book *Fundamentalist U*, especially chapter 9.

5. See John Ashton, ed., *In Six Days: Why 50 Scientists Choose to Believe in Creation* (Green Forest, AR: Master Books, 2011), 355.

6. See David E. Long, *Evolution and Religion in American Education: An Ethnography* (New York: Springer, 2011).

7. Anton E. Lawson and William A. Worsnop, "Learning about Evolution and Rejecting a Belief in Special Creation: Effects of Reflective Reasoning Skill, Prior Knowledge, Prior Belief and Religious Commitment," *Journal of Research in Science Teaching* 29, no. 2 (February 1992): 149.

8. Maynard Shipley, *The War on Modern Science: A Short History of the Fundamentalist Attacks on Evolution and Modernism* (New York: Alfred A. Knopf, 1927), 3–4.

9. See Josh Rosenau, "Welcome to the Science League of America," *NCSE Blog*, August 19, 2013, https://ncse.com/blog/welcome-to-science-league-america.

10. Buddy Davis, "How Can We Use Dinosaurs to Spread the Creation Gospel Message?" *The New Answers Book 1*, February 14, 2008, https://answersingenesis.org/gospel/evangelism/how-can-we-use-dinosaurs-to-spread-the-creation-gospel-message/.

11. Christopher P. Toumey, *God's Own Scientists: Creationists in a Secular World* (New Brunswick, NJ: Rutgers University Press, 1994), 118.

12. Ken Ham and Britt Beemer with Todd Hillard, *Already Gone: Why Your Kids Will Quit Church and What You Can Do to Stop It* (Green Forest, AR: Master Books, 2009), 114.

13. Ham and Beemer, *Already Gone*, 165.

14. Ham and Beemer, *Already Gone*, 17, 22.

15. Ham and Beemer, *Already Gone*, 103–104.

16. John C. Whitcomb Jr. and Henry M. Morris, *The Genesis Flood: The Biblical Record and Its Scientific Implications*, 8th ed. (Philadelphia: Presbyterian and Reformed Publishing, 1966), xxii.

17. Whitcomb and Morris, xxiv.

18. See Frederick Edwords, "Creation-Evolution Debates: Who's Winning Them Now?," *Creation/Evolution Journal* 8 (Spring 1982): 30–42.

19. See Henry Morris and Duane T. Gish, *The Battle for Creation: Acts/Facts/Impacts*, vol. 2 (San Diego: Creation-Life Publishers, 1976), 17.

20. Ken Ham, "Missionaries to a Pagan Culture," *Letter from Ken*, March 25, 2013, https://answersingenesis.org/culture/america/missionaries-to-a-pagan-culture/.

21. Ken Ham, "Should I Have Dinner with BioLogos?," *Ken Ham's Blog*, October 14, 2014, https://answersingenesis.org/blogs/ken-ham/2014/10/14/should-i-have-dinner-with-biologos/. On this occasion, Ham was reacting to an invitation from BioLogos President Deborah Haarsma to come to a friendly cross-creationist meeting to talk out their agreements and differences. Did Ham go? No. Like the Old Testament hero Nehemiah, Ham explained, he was too busy "building a wall" to talk with the enemy.

22. Ham, "Missionaries to a Pagan Culture."

23. "Our History," BioLogos, n.d., http://biologos.org/about-us/our-history/.

24. See Deborah Haarsma, "Learning to Praise God for His Work in Evolution," in *How I Changed My Mind about Evolution: Evangelicals Reflect on Faith and Science*, ed. Kathryn Applegate and J. B. Stump (Downers Grove, IL: IVP Academic, 2016), 40.

25. Kathryn Applegate and J. B. Stump, "Introduction," in Applegate and Stump, *How I Changed My Mind*, 16.

26. Scot McKnight, "Who's Afraid of Science?," in Applegate and Stump, *How I Changed My Mind*, 31.

27. Brian Eisenback and Ken Turner, "Christian Education and Its Shortcomings: Why We Need a Fair and Balanced Approach to Origins Part 1," BioLogos, December 9, 2013, https://biologos.org/articles/christian-education-and-its-shortcomings-why-we-need-a-fair-and-balanced-approach-to-origins.

28. Tremper Longman III, "An Old Testament Professor Celebrates Creation," in Applegate and Stump, *How I Changed My Mind*, 50. Emphasis in original.

29. Francis Collins, *The Language of God: A Scientist Presents Evidence for Belief* (New York: Simon and Schuster, 2006), 211.

30. Henry Fairfield Osborn, *The Earth Speaks to Bryan* (New York: Scribners, 1925), dedication. For those like me unfamiliar with the Christian Bible, the line is a reference to John 8:32.

31. Osborn, *The Earth Speaks to Bryan*, 7.

32. See, e.g., Victor Stenger's *The New Atheism: Taking a Stand for Science and Reason* (New York: Prometheus, 2009); Sam Harris, *The End of Faith: Religion, Terror, and the Future of Reason,* 2nd ed. (New York: W. W. Norton, 2005); Christopher Hitchens, *God Is Not Great: How Religion Poisons Everything* (New York: Twelve, 2009); and

Jerry Coyne, *Faith vs. Fact: Why Science and Religion Are Incompatible*, 2nd ed. (New York: Penguin, 2016).

33. Richard Dawkins, *The God Delusion* (London: Bantam Press, 2006), 5.

34. Dawkins, *The God Delusion*, 116.

35. Dawkins, *The God Delusion*, 116.

36. See *Bill Nye Saves the World*, season 1, episode 5, "The Original Martian Invasion." First aired April 21, 2017.

37. Stephen Jay Gould, "Nonoverlapping Magisteria," *Natural History* 106 (March 1997): 16–25.

38. Among anti-creationists, radical atheists such as Jerry Coyne have criticized groups, such as the NCSE, for seeking pragmatic accommodations with religious creationists. Such tactics, Coyne argues, are both intellectually empty and strategically faulty. As Coyne once put it, the NCSE needs to stop its "constant coddling of religion." See Jerry Coyne, "The National Center for Science Education Becomes BioLogos," *Why Evolution Is True*, March 25, 2014, https://whyevolutionistrue.wordpress.com/2014/03/25/the-national-center-for-science-education-becomes-biologos/.

39. Ham, "Should I Have Dinner with BioLogos?"

40. Maynard Shipley, *The War on Modern Science: A Short History of the Fundamentalist Attacks on Evolution and Modernism* (New York: Alfred A. Knopf, 1927), 3.

Chapter 7

1. For the full email exchange, see Adam Laats, "Creationist Mom Reaches Out to Evolution," *I Love You but You're Going to Hell*, March 19, 2013, https://iloveyoubutyouregoingtohell.org/2013/03/19/creationist-mom-reaches-out-to-evolution/.

2. Elaine Howard Ecklund and Christopher P. Scheitle, *Religion vs. Science: What Religious People Really Think* (New York: Oxford University Press, 2018), 2.

3. Christopher P. Toumey, *God's Own Scientists: Creationists in a Secular World* (New Brunswick, NJ: Rutgers University Press, 1994), 11.

4. See People for the American Way, "Public Wants Evolution, Not Creationism, in Science Class, New National Poll Shows," Press release, March 10, 2000, http://www.pfaw.org/press-releases/public-wants-evolution-not-creationsim-in-science-class-new-national-poll-shows/

5. Bryan steadfastly maintained his American Association for the Advancement of Science membership in spite of the distaste his views caused among most other American Association for the Advancement of Science leaders. See, for example, Burton Livingston to William Jennings Bryan, 29 September 1924, Bryan Papers, Library of Congress, Washington, DC.

6. William Jennings Bryan, *In His Image* (New York: Fleming H. Revell, 1922), 69.

7. Edwin Grant Conklin, "Bryan and Evolution," *New York Times*, March 5, 1922, 1.

8. George Gaylord Simpson, *This View of Life: The World of an Evolutionist* (New York: Harcourt, Brace and World, 1964), 25.

9. Simpson, *This View of Life*, 4.

10. Bill Nye, *Undeniable: Evolution and the Science of Creation* (New York: St. Martin's Press, 2014), 4.

11. Ecklund and Scheitle, *Religion vs. Science*, 41.

12. Ecklund and Scheitle, *Religion vs. Science*, 45.

13. T. T. [Thomas Theodore] Martin, *Hell and the High School: Christ or Evolution Which?* (Kansas City, MO: Western Baptist Publishing, 1923), 10.

14. Martin, *Hell and the High School*, 17.

15. Martin, *Hell and the High School*, 72. Emphasis in original.

16. Martin, *Hell and the High School*, 60. Emphasis in original.

17. Martin, *Hell and the High School*, 150.

18. T. T. [Thomas Theodore] Martin, *The Evolution Issue* (Los Angeles, CA: n.d., n.p. [1923?]), 47.

19. See Daniel L. Turner, *Standing Without Apology: The History of Bob Jones University* (Greenville, SC: Bob Jones University Press, 1997), 334, footnote 43.

20. For details, see my book, *Fundamentalist U: Keeping the Faith in American Higher Education* (New York: Oxford University Press, 2018), 257–260, 267.

21. Anthropologist Chris Toumey watched Falwell make these evolutionary promises to a group of prospective students on April 13, 1985. See Toumey, *God's Own Scientists*, 59.

22. Toumey, *God's Own Scientists*, 59.

23. For a longer explication of this argument, see Harvey Siegel and Adam Laats, *Teaching Evolution in a Creation Nation* (Chicago: University of Chicago Press, 2016), 58–59.

24. For a first-hand account of growing up with Wile's books, see "Anna" [pseudonym], "Faith & Physics, Part II," *I Love You but You're Going to Hell*, November 3, 2013, https://iloveyoubutyouregoingtohell.org/2013/11/03/faith-physics-part-ii/.

25. Jay L. Wile and Marilyn F. Durnell, *Exploring Creation with Biology*, 2nd ed. (Anderson, IN: Apologia Educational Ministries, 2011), iv.

26. Wile and Durnell, *Exploring Creation with Biology*, 9. As John Rudolph argued, this definition of the "scientific method" has a problematic history of its own. However, it has been widely used by mainstream science textbooks as well as this radical-creationist one. See John Rudolph, *How We Teach Science: What's Changed and Why It Matters* (Cambridge, MA: Harvard University Press, 2019), 80–96.

27. Wile and Durnell, *Exploring Creation with Biology*, 15.

28. Accelerated Christian Education, *Science: 1076*, 4th ed. (Hendersonville, TN: Accelerated Christian Education, 2013), 9–10.

29. Accelerated Christian Education, *Science: 1045*, 4th ed. (Hendersonville, TN: Accelerated Christian Education, 2010), 1.

30. See "Cosmos: A SpaceTime Odyssey," Answers in Genesis, March 11, 2014, https://answersingenesis.org/countering-the-culture/cosmos-a-spacetime-odyssey/.

31. Susan L. Trollinger and William Vance Trollinger Jr., *Righting America at the Creation Museum* (Baltimore: Johns Hopkins University Press, 2016), 37.

32. Trollinger and Trollinger, *Righting America at the Creation Museum*, 37.

33. Mark Looy, "$1.5 Million Dinosaur Exhibit Dedicated Today at the Creation Museum," Answers in Genesis, May 23, 2014, https://answersingenesis.org/about/press/million-dinosaur-exhibit-dedicated-today/.

34. See Adam Laats, "Take the Creation Museum Challenge," *I Love You but You're Going to Hell*, May 26, 2014, https://iloveyoubutyouregoingtohell.org/2014/05/26/take-the-creation-museum-challenge/.

35. Laats, "Creationist Mom Reaches Out to Evolution,"

36. See GARBC's "Articles of Faith," n.d., http://www.garbc.org/about-us/beliefs-constitution/articles-of-faith/.

37. Christian school principal, email communication, October 17, 2017. Emphasis in original.

38. Glenn Branch, "Creationist Board Chair Profiled," National Center for Science Education, March 11, 2009, https://ncse.com/news/2009/03/creationist-board-chair-profiled-004643.

39. Don McLeroy, email communication, November 11, 2017.

40. McLeroy, email communication.

41. Avery Foley, "Should Christian Schools Teach Evolution?," Answers in Genesis, January 12, 2017, https://answersingenesis.org/public-school/teaching-evolution/should-christian-schools-teach-evolution/.

42. Foley, "Should Christian Schools Teach Evolution?"

43. For more about Pastafarianism, the satirical Church of the Flying Spaghetti Monster, see Church of the Flying Spaghetti Monster, https://www.venganza.org/.

44. Charles Darwin, *On the Origin of Species,* ed. Gillian Beer, rev. ed. (New York: Oxford University Press, 2008), 360. This phrase of Darwin's has a long and turbulent history of its own. As Gillian Beer notes, Darwin himself watered it down in the second edition of his book. The phrase originally said, "There is grandeur in this view of life, with its several powers, having been originally breathed into a few forms or into one." In subsequent editions, Darwin added that the powers had been breathed "by the Creator." See Beer, "Introduction," *On the Origin of Species*, xxi.

45. Richard Dawkins, *The God Delusion* (London: Bantam Press, 2006), 3.

46. See Ken Ham and Roger Patterson, "Should Christians Be Pushing to Have Creation Taught in Government Schools?," Answers in Genesis, September 17, 2013, https://answersingenesis.org/creationism/in-schools/should-christians-be-pushing-to-have-creation-taught-in-government-schools/. See also Foley, "Should Christian Schools Teach Evolution?"

47. Ham and Patterson, "Should Christians Be Pushing to Have Creation Taught in Government Schools?"

48. See National Center for Science Education, "Chronology of 'Academic Freedom' Bills," *NCSE Blog*, February 7, 2013, https://ncse.com/creationism/general/chronology-academic-freedom-bills.

49. "Oklahoma 2014 SB1765," National Center for Science Education, https://ncse.ngo/library-resource/oklahoma-2014-sb1765.

Conclusion

1. See, e.g., Francis Fukuyama, *Trust: The Social Virtues and the Creation of Prosperity* (New York: Simon & Schuster, 1995); Adam B. Seligman, *The Problem of Trust* (Princeton, NJ: Princeton University Press, 1997); Mark E. Warren, ed., *Democracy and Trust* (New York: Cambridge University Press, 1999).

2. Seligman, *The Problem of Trust*, 173. Professor Seligman would likely prefer to call creationists' mistrust of mainstream expert knowledge more precisely a "lack of confidence." See *The Problem of Trust*, 26.

3. Rev. Avis L. Hill interviewed by James Deeter, March 12, 1985. Transcript. Oral History of Appalachia collection No. OH 64-236, Special Collections, Marshall University, Huntington, West Virginia.

4. Deborah Kelemen, "Are Children 'Intuitive Theists'? Reasoning about Purpose and Design in Nature," *Psychological Science* 15, no. 5 (May 2004): 295–301.

5. Fukuyama, *Trust,* 11.

6. Shane J. Lopez, "Parents Rate Own Child's School Far Better than Americans Rate U.S. Public Schools," *Gallup*, August 25, 2010, https://news.gallup.com/poll/142658/ americans-views-public-schools-far-worse-parents.aspx.

7. Warren, *Democracy and Trust*, 348. Emphasis in original.

Appendix

1. Don McLeroy, Comment, "I Love You but You Didn't Do the Reading," *I Love You but You're Going to Hell*, February 12, 2018, https://iloveyoubutyouregoingtohell.org/ 2018/02/12/i-love-you-but-you-didnt-do-the-reading-56/.

2. McLeroy, Comment.

3. Don McLeroy, email communication, February 13, 2018.

4. McLeroy, email communication, February 16, 2018.

5. McLeroy, email communication, February 17, 2018.

6. See "*Kitzmiller v. Dover*: Intelligent Design on Trial," *National Center for Science Education*, December 15, 2015, https://ncse.com/library-resource/ kitzmiller-v-dover-intelligent-design-trial.

7. Patrick Kingsley, "Turkey Drops Evolution from Curriculum, Angering Secularists," *New York Times*, June 23, 2017, https://www.nytimes.com/2017/06/23/world/europe/ turkey-evolution-high-school-curriculum.html?emc=edit_tnt_20170623&nlid=5 3963895&tntemail0=y. Josh Rosenau, "In Israel, Will Creationists Reign?," *National Center for Science Education Blog*, March 24, 2015, https://ncse.com/blog/2015/03/ israel-will-creationists-reign-0016237.

8. Thomas D. S. Key, "The Influence of Darwin on Biology," in *Evolution and Christian Thought Today*, ed. Russell L. Mixter (Grand Rapids, MI: Eerdmans, 1959), 30–31.

9. I am indebted to Glenn Branch of the National Center for Science Education for his conversations and suggestions about understanding creationism in these terms.

10. See Michael Behe, *Darwin's Black Box: The Biochemical Challenge to Evolution* (New York: Free Press, 1996).

11. See, e.g., Gary Parker, "2.7 Speciation, Yes; Evolution, No," Answers in Genesis, March 28, 2016, https://answersingenesis.org/natural-selection/speciation/speciation-yes-evolution-no/.

12. Susan L. Trollinger and William Vance Trollinger Jr., *Righting America at the Creation Museum* (Baltimore: Johns Hopkins University Press, 2016), 147.

13. Danny Faulkner, "Reflections on the Flat-Earth Movement," Answers in Genesis, June 22, 2019, https://answersingenesis.org/astronomy/earth/reflections-flat-earth-movement/.

14. See, e.g., Dan Lietha, "One Generation Away," Answers in Genesis, August 28, 2015, https://answersingenesis.org/media/cartoons/after-eden/one-generation-away/. In this cartoon, an innocent child is portrayed as getting on board a yellow school bus. The bus displays a set of bumper stickers, including one for Darwin, one for Planned Parenthood, one for LBGTQ equality, a couple for environmentalism, and a few against the Bible, prayer, and Christianity.

15. Bodie Hodge, "The Attack on Christmas," Answers in Genesis, December 17, 2013, https://answersingenesis.org/holidays/christmas/the-attack-on-christmas/.

16. Ken Ham, "New York Public Library to Host 'Drag Queen Story Hour,'" Answers in Genesis, July 24, 2018, https://answersingenesis.org/culture/new-york-public-library-to-host-drag-queen-story-hour/.

17. Terry Mortenson, "Seven Reasons Why We Should Not Accept Millions of Years," Answers in Genesis, July 17, 2006, https://answersingenesis.org/theory-of-evolution/millions-of-years/seven-reasons-why-we-should-not-accept-millions-of-years/.

18. Ken Ham and Britt Beemer with Todd Hillard, *Already Gone: Why Your Kids Will Quit Church and What You Can Do to Stop It* (Green Forest, AR: Master Books, 2009), 165.

19. William Bell Riley, "The Fundamentalist Credo," in *Controversy in the Twenties: Fundamentalism, Modernism, and Evolution*, ed. Willard B. Gatewood Jr. (Nashville, TN: Vanderbilt University Press, 1969), 75.

Index

For the benefit of digital users, indexed terms that span two pages (e.g., 52–53) may, on occasion, appear on only one of those pages.